CRISIS CULTURES

ILLUMINATIONS

Cultural

Formations

of

the

Americas

Series

John Beverley and Sara Castro-Klarén, Editors

CRISIS CULTURES

Brian Whitener

the rise of finance in mexico and brazil

UNIVERSITY OF PITTSBURGH PRESS

Published by the University of Pittsburgh Press, Pittsburgh, Pa., 15260

Manufactured in the United States of America
Printed on acid-free paper
10 9 8 7 6 5 4 3 2 1

Cataloging-in-Publication data is available from the Library of Congress

ISBN 13: 978-0-8229-6586-2
ISBN 10: 0-8229-6586-0

Cover photo: Vera Sayão
Cover design: Joel W. Coggins

CONTENTS

ACKNOWLEDGMENTS

This project represents the culmination of many years of work, years influenced by too many people and supported by too many friends to name. However, I would like to take advantage of this space to express my deepest appreciation to everyone who has sustained me during this process. First and foremost, thanks to my friends, comrades, and families (biological and otherwise) for their companionship and for making the world in which this book was possible to write. As you all know me well, you know that I would rather thank you individually and in person.

At the University of Michigan my dissertation committee—Gareth Williams, Kate Jenckes, Jaime Rodríguez Matos, and Elizabeth Wingrove—modeled a belief in the importance of ideas and the resiliency needed to get them right. Many of the sensibilities in this project have been profoundly shaped by noninstitutional settings, and I would like to acknowledge the poets and comrades in the Bay Area and the members of La Lleca and other collectives in Mexico City for years of small reading groups, projects, and ongoing exchanges. Over the last few years at the University of South Alabama, my coworkers—Kristy Britt, Mirella Chávez, Jenny Faile, Nicholas Gossett, Katrina Kennedy, Zoya Khan, Mihaela Marin, Susan McCready, Matthew Pettway, Federico Pérez-Pineda, Terri Rice, Christine Rinne, Roberto Robles-Valencia, Harry Roddy, Kevin Tsai, and our chair Eleanor ter Horst—have shared invaluable intellectual and moral support. Moreover, this project could not have been finished without the help of the librarians in the Marx Library ILL office and without two university grants: a Seed Grant to Support the Arts and Humanities and an Arts and Sciences Summer Professional Development

Grant. Annie McClanahan and Lenora Hanson generously organized talks at UC Irvine and NYU, respectively, where I was able to present some of these ideas.

I am grateful as well to Alessandro Fornazzari and an anonymous reader for their incisive comments on the manuscript and to Josh Shanholtzer, Alex Wolfe, and the staff at the University of Pittsburgh Press for all their assistance. I am excited to have this project appear in John Beverley and Sara Castro-Klarén's Illumination's series. Extra special thanks go to Vera Sayão for allowing the use of her amazing photograph of the aftermath of a 1987 transportation and inflation uprising in Rio de Janeiro for the book cover and to Laurie Prendergast for her wonderful index.

Finally, I would like to express my sincere appreciation to the following individuals who answered email queries (even with just a few lines), discussed in person, or read pieces of this project and offered criticisms, suggestions, and advice—there is no way this project could have been written without your assistance: Paulina Alberto, Erika Almenara, Paul Amar, Paige Andersson, Jasper Bernes, Daniel Bin, Sergio Cámara Izquierdo, Mariana Cavalcanti, Maria Elisa Cevasco, Joshua Clover, Giuseppe Cocco, Eugenia Correa, Shane Dillingham, Lenora Hanson, Laura Herbert, Rosana Heringer, Lena Lavinas, Luiz Antonio Machado da Silva, FTC Manning, Annie McClanahan, Lúcia Müller, Daniel Nemser, Juan Pablo Painceira, Dawn Paley, Leda Paulani, Federico Pous, Cassandra Troyan, Ignacio Sánchez Prado, Luiz Cesar Ribeiro, Alejo Stark, Alberto Toscano, Zhivka Valiavicharska, and Ivonne del Valle.

Parts of Chapter 1 originally appeared as "Ontology and Crises of State and Finance in Jorge Volpi's *En busca de Klingsor*," *Journal of Latin American Cultural Studies* 24, no. 1 (2015): 47–64 (https://doi.org/10.1080/13569325.2014.1002457); reprinted by permission of the publisher. Parts of Chapter 3 were published in "From Racial Democracy to Credit Democracy: Finance and Public Security in Brazil," *Brasiliana* 4, no. 2 (2016), and in "Anti-sujeitos de crédito: Para-corporativismo financeiro e possibilidade política," *e-metropolis* 33 (July 2018).

CRISIS CULTURES

"¡El valiente!" *Proceso* 1 no. 3 (Nov. 20, 1976)

INTRODUCTION

The Long Downturn and the Rise of Finance in Mexico and Brazil

This book starts with an image—a book not particularly about images, but one which I tried to find a way to write about but never could. It is an image by Naranjo, the well-known Mexican political cartoonist, and it is one of many of those he produced in the late 1970s that deal with finance, declining production, and violence. Others include a Superman figure, whose "S" has been replaced by a symbol for the Mexican peso, trapped upside down in power lines like an Icarus of underdevelopment, and one of a portly banker who wears the mask of a famished peasant and who speaks from behind it a single word: "Austeridad" ("Austerity"). As soon as I found them in a dark basement corner where issues of the journal *Proceso* were stored, these images, along with the one above, have felt like the north star of this book and, in their representations of violence (of state and capital), finance and failing production, and the socialization of crisis onto the poor, a critical bridge between an almost forgotten past and a terrible present. *Proceso* was one of the first independent journals in Mexico, published without state support or intervention, and the image above appeared in its first year of publication, in the third issue, and registers the Mexican government's 1976 devaluation of the peso, the first devaluation of the postwar period, the first clear signal of an economic emergency that would wind throughout the coming decades, and the first contemporary crisis in Mexico of attempted accumulation impelled by finance.[1]

It is a scene whose cruelty is apparent: the businessman-bureaucrat stoops to examine the worker's state of being, sizing up whether after the knives of "devaluación" he can survive the axe of "energéticos" (i.e., the petroleum sector where the real debt lies). His face registers not compassion but rather calculation as to how much more the worker's body can take, a recognition that capital and the state need labor to survive but are not willing to share in the sacrifice of the devaluation's economic pain. The worker's affect can be described in one word: shock. And perhaps resiliency—even cartoonishly large knives are not enough to finish him off. Resiliency was what was needed, for in a currency devaluation, money overnight becomes worth less. From April 19, 1954 to August 31, 1976, the Mexican peso was pegged at 12.50 pesos per 1 U.S. dollar. On September 1, 1976, the currency was devalued for the first time in twenty-two years to 22.50 pesos per dollar—raising the price overnight of critical industrial inputs and other imported goods.[2] In the following months hundreds of thousands were thrown out of work and those who remained employed saw their checks buy less and less. The devaluation, brought on by extensive government borrowing to support national and foreign capitalists' accumulation, was a way of socializing the failure of finance-primed accumulation onto workers and the poor.

This is an image that today speaks of a fundamental historical continuity between our time and that of Mexico in 1976: crisis. The crisis that appeared in Mexico in 1976, and more broadly in Latin America as a whole in the 1970s, is our own: it is a crisis of production and failed financial accumulation, a product of the slow decline of the postwar boom, which has yet to be resolved and which manifests in similar and yet distinctive ways in the rise of narco-violence in Mexico and the collapse of the Partido dos Trabalhadores (PT) governments in Brazil. This book is an attempt to make this continuity of crisis and finance visible; to center it in cultural criticism and, in so doing, situate its resonances alongside and against what since have been considered the epoch-defining events of contemporary Latin American history: "neoliberalism, "democratic transition," and "the left turn." It is a continuity that perhaps we are able to see only today; one registered in Naranjo's work which calls to us from the end of the 1970s, not from the prehistory of our present, but rather if the present is that of ongoing crisis, from its beginning.

I affect this centering of finance by focusing on Mexico and Brazil, which I have chosen for the rich set of comparative possibilities they offer. Both countries, one with and one without a (formal) dictatorship, took on massive amounts of debt in the 1970s. Both passed through the 1982 financial crisis, but with different paths: Mexico was ground zero of the crisis, while Brazil struggled to keep its creditors at bay, before finally agreeing to a credit bailout in 1983.[3] Similarly, both had major crises in the 1990s, but their shape and temporality were distinct. In the post-2001 period, their paths diverge, with Brazil massively expanding consumer credit as a form of financial para-corporatism and Mexico making a turn to circulation that brought along with it mass destruction and death. In this book I follow these histories, interweaving two narrative threads. The first concerns Mexican and Brazilian cultural production across these historical moments and how they have mediated, disputed, and been touched by the rise of finance. The second tracks the cultural figures and discursive and social forms—such as ontology and *delincuencia* (delinquency), real abstraction and the favela, credit democracy and anti-subjects, immaterial cadavers and voided collectivities—that have emerged in the complicated and indeterminate aftermath of the turns to finance and circulation. This book does not claim to say everything that is possible about the consequences of finance, finance capital, and crisis in these two countries, nor even to begin to do more than scratch the surface; rather my aim is to follow the north star of Naranjo's bitter, trenchant images on whatever course they have set.

A Brief History of Finance (and Crisis) in Mexico and Brazil

To center finance as a social force and be able to trace its cultural manifestations and contestations, it is necessary to have some sense of these forms of attempted accumulation, new financial architectures, and histories of finance in the region. The historical argument that frames this book is that the rise of finance is at the center, in Mexico and Brazil and across many other sites in Latin America, of a response to failing capital accumulation, the end of the postwar cycle of expansion, and the beginning of the long downturn that occurred in the late 1960s and early 1970s. While this book's substrate is cultural production, I begin by conjuring and recalling the deeply transformative force of finance, which I do in the following section by tracing three stages of finance—dwelling mostly on the period after 1973—to develop a comparative framework for Mexico and Brazil, placing them into the context of a longer historical frame of Latin American capitalism. As will become clear later in this introduction, these "stages" are themselves marked by recurrent and discordant temporalities (what Giovanni Arrighi called "cycles"), but for clarity of presentation I will initially move through them in a sequential fashion.

Since the independence of Latin American nations, there have been three major forms or periods of their integration into the world market: resource extraction (running from Independence to the Great Depression), developmentalism (post–Second World War to 1973), and the subsequent long downturn. Each form of integration has implied a specific financial architecture and a means for controlling commodity chains and flows. The reinforcement of resource extraction economies in the middle of the nineteenth century brought with it the construction of pieces of what we would now recognize as a modern financial architecture: banks, forms of credit, consolidation of national (as opposed to regional) currencies, and, more importantly for our narrative, foreign debt.[4] While the stock market crash of 1929 and subsequent Great Depression wiped out lending to Latin American countries, after the Second World War Latin America resumed its role as a sink for flows of surplus capital.[5]

Within the post–Second World War international architecture, many Latin American countries opted for some form of developmentalism, often in the form of import-substitution strategies. By the early 1970s the import-substitution model was encountering limits, and rates of profit in Latin America began to decline.[6] In Brazil the slowing of the postwar boom was registered in the early 1960s—this accounts, in part, for the military takeover of 1964, a coup that installed a new national development plan and significantly reconstituted the country's financial structure in an attempt to attract foreign investment flows.[7] In Mexico the slowdown registers as a factor in the uprising of 1968, although Mexico had already begun to seriously court international capital flows in the 1950s.[8] What both countries have in common is that during the late 1960s and throughout the 1970s they turned to foreign debt and finance-primed accumulation as a stay against the end of the postwar boom.

A turning point in the crisis of the postwar boom in Latin America was the 1973 oil shock. Toward the end of 1973 and into 1974, in response to the United States pulling out of the Bretton Woods agreement and the 1973 Arab–Israeli War, OPEC countries increased the price of a barrel of crude from US$3 to almost $12. While the effects of the increase in price of this key industrial input and consumer good were felt throughout the world, its most important outcome in Latin America was financial. The dramatic increase in oil prices meant enormous sums of dollars accumulated in Middle Eastern countries, and in the midst of the general worldwide economic downturn, there was no profitable place to invest them.[9] This excess capital was in part recycled through the Euro-dollar market into loans to Latin American countries and Latin American debt became a partial solution to the declining rate of profit in the United States: by 1976, for example, interest payments from Brazil on foreign debt represented 20 percent of Citibank's bottom line.[10] As the financial sector and flows of surplus capital began to find their way into Latin America—even before petrodollar recycling reached its peak—the first failures of finance-primed accumulation manifested: Brazil had a major stock market crash in 1971–1972 and Mexico in 1976 declared what would be the first of many currency devaluations.[11]

During this same time, also as a response to the end of the postwar boom, a new international financial architecture was being built to prime and expedite financial forms of accumulation in both the global North and parts of the global South. The centerpiece of this new architecture was the effective end of the Bretton Woods agreement or the switch from national currencies being tied to the gold standard to a system of floating exchange rates, where national currencies were directly convertible into one another via currency markets. This had two important results. First, it allowed for the proliferation of fiat and credit money, as money creation was no longer fractionally tied to the amount of gold held by a country. Second, the U.S. dollar became what Marxist economists term "world money"; that is, as the largest economy, the dollar is the safest currency to hold, meaning it became the de facto currency for international transactions and imposed a U.S.-based financial hegemony on the rest of the world.[12] This had numerous negative consequences for economies in the global South, including creating a new link between U.S. interest rates and foreign debt.[13]

From 1973 to 1982 the Latin American external debt grew from US$42.8 billion to $260.7 billion, doubling and doubling, and then almost doubling yet again.[14] Much of this debt was short-term debt (turned over every several months) and contracted directly by governments from commercial banks. In the 1970s the United States slowly started to raise its interest rates to try to control inflation and to maintain the hegemony of the U.S. dollar as world money, and consequently this increased the interest rates Mexico and Brazil (as well as many other countries) were paying on their foreign debt. The situation came to a head in 1979 when Paul Volcker took over the Federal Reserve. In the face of the appreciation of the mark and the yen, he allowed the federal intra-bank rate to rise from 10 percent in 1979 to almost 20 percent in 1981, which dramatically increased the interest rates Mexico and Brazil were paying on their short-term debt.[15] By 1982 Mexico was no longer able to roll over its debt; Brazil was unable to find lenders willing to lend; and the first major, catastrophic financial crisis of the postwar period swept through Latin America.

The 1982 debt crisis gave rise to a new set of instruments and institutions for attempted financial accumulation and new forms of integration into the international financial system. The debt crisis dragged on inconclusively throughout most of the 1980s, and inflation especially in Brazil where it hit 223.8 percent in 1983,[16] returned as a critical problem until a plan was hatched to convert the outstanding debt into sovereign debt in the form of bonds issued on the international market. Until this time most state debt in Latin America was contracted directly from foreign banks (as lines of credit, etc.); however, after the implementation of the Brady Plans (named after then–U.S. treasury secretary Nicholas Brady) throughout the region, states began to once again issue their own debt.[17] The Brady Plans were debt restructuring plans in which Latin American countries ceded control over their economies for a small measure of debt relief, while having their debt restructured into new forms of sovereign debt, allowing U.S. and European banks and financial institutions to continue extracting financial rent and Latin American financial and nonfinancial corporations and elites to continue their rent-seeking endeavors.[18] As a part of this new orientation, both capital accounts and trade were liberalized, in Mexico starting in the mid-1980s and in Brazil more slowly throughout the 1990s.[19] The conversion of the outstanding debt was also accompanied, and in some cases preceded, by the creation of a new set of financial institutions and instruments in Latin American countries, including national stock markets, pension funds, universal banks, and new derivative and securitization instruments, all of which served as channels of attempted financial accumulation and which played key roles in the next round of crises.[20]

This new architecture of sovereign debt, personal credit flows, and stock markets set the stage for the second series of financial crises that hit Mexico in 1994–1995 and Brazil in 1998–1999. Trade and financial liberalization meant that national markets were flooded with consumer goods and industrial inputs and economies began to absorb financial inflows through the stock market and other channels. It did not take long before imports and borrowing greatly outran exports, liberalized capital accounts led to rampant inflows, and central banks began to cover up imbalances, in part, by releasing government bonds and/or reserves into international markets.[21] Eventually imbalances became so great and speculative pressures so intense that the governments of Mexico and Brazil were forced into IMF bailouts. The "Tequila" crisis hit in Mexico in 1994–1995, and Brazil experienced a similar crisis in 1998–1999 in the wake of currency crises in East Asia and Russia.

If the liberalization of capital accounts and the creation of new forms of sovereign debt were two keys to the rise of finance in both Mexico and Brazil (both forming part of a much more complicated process in each country), since the crashes of the 1990s both countries have intensified the turn to finance but in different ways (which I discuss in more detail in the opening to Chapters 3 and 4). Here we can point to at least four important similarities and differences in their internal financial architectures and their world-economy integrations. In Mexico banks became foreign-owned in the wake of the 1994–1995 crisis—from 1994 to 2002 the percentage of foreign ownership rose from 1 percent to 80 percent[22]—while Brazil maintained state control over some financial institutions, such as Caixa Econômica Federal, Banco do Brasil, and Banco Nacional de Desenvolvimento Econômico e Social (BNDES).[23] In both Mexico and Brazil, new financial instruments (such as derivatives and securitization) are now regularly used by both businesses and governments,[24] but Brazil depended more heavily on an expansion of consumer credit. Mexico turned to mortgages to finance construction, but the market was unstable and hit hard by the 2008 financial crash and an additional crisis in 2013. In both Mexico and Brazil starting in the late 1990s, large nonfinancial corporations became increasingly involved in financial means of accumulation. Having sought financing in international capital markets instead of through domestic or international banks since the 1980s, these large nonfinancial corporations entered into intensive processes of borrowing in order, in some cases, to internationalize themselves through mergers and acquisitions but also to invest in financial instruments (instead of, or at the expense of, investing in production).[25]

In 1957, at the height of the postwar boom, Sartre famously stated that Marxism was the insuperable horizon of his historical moment; today in the Latin American and global present that horizon is finance, and perhaps a Marxist and antistate critique of it.[26] It is difficult to find an aspect of social life that has not been touched by finance's rise, from the subject, to social relations, to the shape of exploitation and domination. To understand the consequences finance has had for cultural production and its ramifications for social theory, we need to move from a historical plane to a theoretical one. Beginning to frame the cultural and social effects of finance means taking positions regarding some of the key debates surrounding finance, such as: Has finance overtaken, escaped from, or entirely merged with the productive economy? Does the rise of finance represent a continuation of capitalist exploitation or its obsolescence? Has finance changed the process of subject formation by providing a new rationality to be followed, a new power relation expressed in debt, or a proliferation of state violence as a necessary supplement for credit economies? In the next section I give an account of some of the most important, ongoing debates concerning finance and how this book positions itself in relation to them.

The Conceptual Vocabularies of Finance

As is probably apparent, this book is marked by a deeper engagement with political economy than is perhaps common in many current works of cultural critique. This is due to several reasons. First, while the North

Atlantic has seen an explosion of interest in finance after the 2008 financial crisis, work on the political economy of finance in Latin America operates within a different set of temporalities. In some places like Brazil, which has a long tradition of thought on finance capital but which was less affected by the 2008 crisis, work on finance was an important but somewhat marginal critical strain when I started this project in the years after that crisis.[27] Part of the work then has been to reconnect and uncover these occasionally obscured histories of finance and their subterranean channels of crisis.

Even when there is a sustained literature with respect to finance, whether in Latin America or the North Atlantic, there is a great deal of debate and very little consensus. For example to just stick with the critical Left, there are enormous differences—which tend to be fairly consistent internationally—between post-Keynesian, post-workerist, and heterodox Marxist understandings of finance (not to mention debates internal to each of these approaches).[28] As a result, it is not possible—and this is a good thing—when thinking about finance to pull a term off the shelf and apply to it a cultural object or social matrix. Thinking about the social and cultural effects of finance means first defining what "finance" means in any given moment, and this requires drilling down into, and occasionally pulling apart, a given political economic configuration.

Finally, part of the attentiveness to political economy evidenced in this book is due to a conviction that after years in which a focus on the state tended to prevail (for obvious historical reasons), one of the tasks of cultural theory in the present is to test the question of how to bring capital back into our work as observers of and participants in cultural and social transformation. As the overcoding of the economic by the political characteristic of developmentalist and welfare states recedes, this book tracks aspects of an emergent social formation and its political horizons.

Attending to the political economy of finance has meant taking a position on three questions: how to name or designate the processes around finance, how or why they emerged, and how new they are. Instead of using a term like financialization or focusing on a single metric like the increasing share of financial profits in a national economy—two common approaches across a variety of literatures—in this book I discuss the "rise of finance" institutionally and systemically, meaning I focus on the emergence and effects of new financial institutions, relations, and events in a given historical moment. One event which will be discussed at length in the first two chapters is the 1982 debt crisis and its aftermath; another is the expansion of personal credit in Brazil in the period after 2003 (which is discussed in Chapter 3). Financialization is a word that, like globalization, perhaps tends to obscure more than clarify, and metrics like financial participation in a national economy, while important, don't allow for thinking about the effects of finance on social life and cultural production in a capacious sense. Because I am interested in finding ways to talk about, trace, and make visible these effects, I'm interested in the systemic, in the expansion, composition, and changes of the financial system as a whole. My generic term for this throughout this book will be "rise of finance"—wherein I will always try to specify for a given historical moment what the key processes, institutions, and relations are that compose "finance" in that moment.[29]

In the world of the North Atlantic where I am institutionally located, the importance of finance became undeniable after 2007–2008. The aftermath of this crisis also witnessed an important expansion of work on finance in Latin America, in particular in Mexico, while Brazil has had a fairly strong tradition of attention to finance capital in the context of development stretching back to the work of Maria da Conceição Tavares. Concerning the how and why of the rise of finance and the return of financial crisis, there is, as is to be expected, little consensus.[30] The popular press tends to see the problem as one of individuals or behavior, namely of greedy, speculative Gordon Gekkos wrecking an imperfect, but generally raising-all-boats capitalism. Post-Keynesians tend to see the problem as one of deregulation or rentier forms of capitalism which can be solved by state intervention. Post-workerists emphasize the breakdown of any separation between the real and financial economies. Among heterodox Marxists there is a debate between two positions: the majority who explain the recent period of financial crisis as a result of underconsumption, overaccumulation, or neoliberalism as a class project; while the minor position argues that the rise of financial forms of accumulation was fueled by a secular declining rate of profit or ongoing, underlying problems in the sphere of production.[31]

I cast my lot with this latter position because it appears to me to be the most accurate account, particularly in Latin America, but also because it enables us, in the terms of Robert Brenner, to speak of the period roughly between the end of the 1960s—with the first appearance of complications in the postwar model of capitalism—and the present day as the "long downturn."[32] The long downturn is defined by the exhaustion of a certain configuration of productive forces and the inability of capitalists to start a new sustained cycle of accumulation. This approach I find helpful as it allows us to see many of the phenomena which have appeared in the intervening years—most notably the spatialization of production, internationalization of labor markets, and the rise of finance—as attempts to weather this storm of the long downturn by attacking labor, increasing the speed of the circulation of money and goods, and producing fictitious value. This perspective can be useful as well because it demonstrates that these phenomena, especially those connected to finance, cannot be "solved" by regulation or moral bromides. The financial crises that have lashed Latin America over the last forty years have their roots in a crisis in production, in a limit internal to capital. As such, they will not end until either a new cycle of accumulation is started or capitalism has ceased to exist.

However, it is important to locate this long downturn in a more capacious historical frame, which can be done by drawing on the work of Giovanni Arrighi. A longer historical perspective is critical because frequently commentaries on recent financial crises, "financialization," and "speculative" or "finance capitalism," conceive of the present moment of finance's expansion as unique or singular, and as a result are infected with a nostalgia for the moment of the welfare or developmentalist state (as a kind of Edenic moment before the emergence of bad finance). Arrighi's pathbreaking work in *The Long Twentieth Century* demonstrates how the rise of finance in the late twentieth century was not a new phenomenon. Rather, he argues that "systemic cycles of accumulation" are split into two moments: a productive moment in which capitalists invest some of their profits in the expansion of the means of production and a second stage wherein capitalists in a geographical center are able to realize higher profits by pulling their capital out of the productive apparatus and placing it into finance, which then expands. For Arrighi there have been four such waves, the first dominated by Italian city-states, the second by the Dutch, the third by the British empire, and the last defined by U.S. hegemony in the postwar period. The present expansion of the financial sector and proliferation of new financial institutions, instruments, and relations is for Arrighi a consequence of a "switching crisis" or the decline of the U.S.-led systemic cycle of accumulation.

Throughout this book, when I use the phrase "rise of finance," I never mean it in the sense of "for the first time," but rather in the sense of the most recent rise or return of finance. We can think of the history of capitalism in Latin America from the late nineteenth century to the present as defined by three expansionary waves, each accompanied by a set of financial flows: A first wave starting in the 1870s during a global depression as British and U.S. capital invested in railroads and mining and as European capital flowed into early manufacturing industries. The second wave is that of the postwar boom as U.S. capital, multinational foreign direct investment, and then U.S. government aid flooded Mexico and other large countries. The third wave extends from 1973 to the present, that of financial expansion without an accompanying sustained expansion of production, leading to bubbles, crashes, and devaluations: 1976, 1982, 1987, 1994, 1998–1999, and 2007–2008. Thus, the failed forms of financial and finance-primed accumulation of the present are the partial result of a secular declining rate of profit or, in plainer English, the lack of a new sustained expansion of production.

So far perhaps all these debates and position-taking seem disconnected and far from the stated objective of investigating how the rise of finance has impacted social and cultural life. However, arguments over the why and how of finance's emergence underpin the various approaches that have been taken to understand finance's impact. One way of dividing up the social and cultural theory works on finance is to see them as structured around a divide between approaches that privilege the "newness" of finance and those that look first to its continuities with prior forms of capital or credit. An example of the first approach would be work that examines either how finance imposes new behaviors, rationalities, or "scripts" which subjects are required or invited to take up, or how a specific financial innovation, like derivatives, comprises a new "social logic" which comes to shape social relations.[33] These approaches, while not always directly basing themselves in historical arguments about political economy, tend to emphasize the newness of finance. An example of the second approach which emphasizes continuities would be David Graeber's widely read *Debt: The First 5,000 Years*, which explains the financialized present by rethinking our understanding of the history and social form of debt, or Maurizio Lazzarato's work on credit and debt, which similarly attempts to define our subjection to debt by scaffolding a genealogy for this form of subjection that stretches back into the nineteenth century.

In this book I draw heavily on a position which shades into the second camp, based in the work of the heterodox Marxist cultural critics of finance Annie McClanahan and Joshua Clover, but which proposes a different kind of continuity.[34] McClanahan and Clover have articulated a position—in concert with other heterodox Marxists—which sees finance as a form of temporal arbitrage or as a means of attempting to realize future surplus value in the present and, as such, intimately connected (rather than opposed) to production.[35] In this approach, attempted forms of financial accumulation under capitalism consist in the proliferation of claims on future value production, but the specific forms these claims take (securities, credit, derivatives) can change historically. I understand finance, whatever the instrument or institution, as producing a claim on future value production and track the way this form of accumulation presses upon and shapes social relations, cultural production, and state form. I also track how finance produces the conditions for crisis, as there is always a moment where some of these claims on or promises to deliver value do not materialize. The subprime crisis of 2008 is one such moment, as is the 1982 debt crisis. I primarily deploy this approach to finance in Chapter 1, where I track how a crisis of claims on future value impacts cultural production, and in Chapter 3, where I examine the proliferation of personal credit and its consequences for subject formation and social relations. However, this fundamental way of reading or thinking about finance structures this book as a whole and reappears in different guises in each of the chapters.

Finance in the Practice of Latin Americanist Thought

Within a broadly conceived field of writing about and from Latin America, my book dialogues with and draws on two traditions in particular: dependency theory and the contemporary authors who maintain its legacy of critique, and Latin American subaltern studies and current formations of critical Latin Americanist thinking. I want to specify in each case what my engagement looks like and what a perspective that focuses on finance may or may not have to contribute to each.

There have been a number of recent returns to and reconsiderations of dependency theory, but following Cristóbal Kay, I would distinguish between two primary currents within its textual corpus: the reform and the revolutionary.[36] The reform current would be composed of authors like Fernando Henrique Cardoso and Enzo Faletto or those whose primary focus was how "development" (or "dependent development") could be possible in Latin America under a given set of international conditions. The revolutionary current, comprised of writers like Theotonio dos Santos and Vânia Bambirra, was attentive to the contradictions of the development process and argued that they could only be overcome by a political solution or event (e.g., a socialist revolution). I take three elements from this tradition, in particular the revolutionary strand: a gesture toward systemic thinking; an attempt—perhaps not always successful—to examine how forces internal and external to national spaces interact, contradict, and reinforce; and an expansive political imaginary that moves both within and beyond the state.[37]

The dependency tradition, as was the structuralist tradition of Raúl Prebisch, is best known for making visible forms of exploitation between global regions or between individual countries. Prebisch accomplished this through his famous "declining terms of trade," an explanation of how agricultural producers in the nonindustrialized periphery would receive less for their products over time. Marini focused on the overexploitation of the peripheral proletariat, which made growth and higher living standards possible in the capitalist core.[38] This project draws inspiration from a strain of early, dependency-influenced Brazilian work involving finance, which focused on not only the international importance of finance, but also its centrality in projects of state and nation.[39] For example, Maria da Conceição Tavares's classic 1972 book, *Da substituição de importações ao capitalismo financeiro* (From import substitution to finance capitalism), highlighted the critical role and expansion of finance capital in the import substitution industrialization (ISI) period, while Ruy Marini's argument for Brazil as a subimperial power (that is, as subjugating other Latin America countries) was derived from the way the dictatorship both had strengthened and come to depend on finance capital.[40]

After the 1982 debt crisis it became common in both Mexico and Brazil, and across Latin America, to think about the effects of finance as a new form of domination or as a reassertion of U.S. hegemony. While the rise of finance has certainly been a project of reimposing domination, it is equally important to chart the participation of Latin American states and elites in and the cultural and social manifestations of finance's rise. As a result, my book centers its attention on how the rise of finance has transformed the social and cultural spaces of Mexico and Brazil. In order to grasp how deeply finance and circulation have altered everyday life, I think it necessary to push beyond primarily exogenous accounts and down into the cultural and social substrate. In so doing I follow in the footsteps of the best parts of the dependency tradition, which tracked the shifting of internal-external boundaries and the compositions of force across them, and I acknowledge both the existence of gradients or differentials of power internationally and that Latin American countries have become key sites for the valorization of international finance capital.[41]

The inheritors of dependency theory who have carried on its critical tradition in order to make sense of the financial crises of the 1980s and 1990s and the transition to neoliberalism are mainly located in economics and the social sciences. A formation that consistently grappled with the political and cultural consequences of these years of transition was the Latin American Subaltern Studies group, which is the other critical tradition on which my work draws. Though the work and legacy of the group remains contested to this day, I want to bring out several characteristics of the formation which have been important for my own work.

The Latin American Subaltern Studies group was, as the name implies, inspired by the work of the original Subaltern Studies Collective which had used Gramsci's notion of the subaltern as a means for rewriting colonial Indian and South Asian history and Gramsci's notion of hegemony for explaining the peculiar forms of domination of the British occupation (Guha's "dominance without hegemony"). The Latin American group that formed in the early 1990s (disbanding toward the end of the decade) emerged from within a slightly different historical context, namely that of the fall of the Berlin Wall in 1989 and the defeat of the Sandinistas in the 1990 elections. As much of the global and Latin American intellectual and political scene transitioned to a "there is no alternative" position, the Latin American Subaltern Studies group—though a contested set of experiences—was an attempt to keep open a space for critical thinking in the post-Soviet, possibly postrevolutionary era.[42]

Much, but far from all, of the work emerging from the group used one of the various definitions of subaltern then in circulation (Gramsci's, Guha's, and Spivak's being the most common), often in tandem with a notion of hegemony. In the more deconstructive wing of the group, the subaltern was thought as that which undoes, breaks from, or marks the constitutive limit of the hegemony of the national-popular state's cultural politics. The subaltern-hegemony tandem was frequently deployed to describe a socio-historical matrix formed by the developmentalist state, U.S. empire, and/or university discourse as characterized by a high level of administration, consensus, and/or banal empiricism. At the same time work from within the group attempted to grapple with the recent transformations in global capitalism and their effects on Latin American nation-states and political formations—transformations which were frequently described with terms such as finance capitalism, late or global capitalism, or neoliberalism.

The work in this book is broadly in line with the goal of maintaining a space for theoretical reflection within critical Latin Americanist thought which has one of its roots in the Latin American Subaltern Studies group. This book does two things differently. First, it places more pressure on the political economic terms and formulations that we have used to describe the transition from the national popular or developmentalist state into the present. Its wager is that there is something to be gained by examining in more detail this transition, which my work does by narrowing its focus onto finance. Second, instead of a conception of state, international, or university order which is rooted in or framed by hegemony, or even post-hegemony, this book reflects on and centers the role of direct and indirect state violence in the imposition and maintenance of order across this historical period.

The Political of Political Economy

As much as this project re-centers capital in cultural critique, it is not enough to merely point to the rise of finance as an economic condition;

to grasp it as a cultural and social force, an accounting of transformations in the state is necessary as well. Rather than a full account of state transformation, I focus here on one specific vector and view the post-1973 period as one in which the corporatist infrastructures of the developmental state entered into crisis and reformulation, resulting in a rearticulation of racialized modalities of control and an expansion of state interventions connected to finance and violence.

What I am interested in thinking through, on the level of state and society and alongside the problematic of finance, is how the corporatist, collectivizing, and representational infrastructures of the developmentalist state, after the beginning of the long downturn, are no longer able to do the work they once did. I believe there are two linked reasons why this is so. The first is that the long downturn has meant, in part, that the productivist system which scaffolded the corporatist measures of social integration during the developmental state has contracted in scope and capacity.[43] The second is that, again as a result of the dismantling and decline of a certain system of capitalist production, there has been since the end of the 1970s an expansion of surplus populations, or individuals who are either marginally integrated into or excluded from the apparatus of capitalist production.[44] In Mexico in 2009, for example, 53.89 percent of active nonagricultural workers were informally employed, meaning that they lacked basic social and legal protections.[45] Data from the International Labor Organization for 2009 estimate that 42.2 percent of nonagricultural workers in Brazil had a position that was classified as "informal employment."[46] These surplus populations—who have been a focal point of cultural production in this period—are frequently crowded into informal settlements and into the informal economy where they are subjected to precarious, highly exploitative labor regimes; as such, they exist outside most traditional forms of capitalist and state integration, in particular the corporatist bodies used in Mexico and Brazil to secure social stability during the boom years of the developmentalist state.[47] While I believe it has use as a technical term, surplus population can also conjure imaginaries of expendability, so it is important to foreclose any Malthusian overtones in its register and to remind ourselves that these living and persevering individuals are surplus in name only.

The fact that these populations can no longer be reached, or only marginally so, through corporatist, governmental, and representational measures has had three consequences, which I trace in the chapters of this book as consequences of and alongside the rise of finance. First, as the developmentalist project has sputtered, the ideologies which had grown up alongside it have been transformed: most importantly mestizaje or racialized theories of the nation, have been reworked under the twin pressures of financial crisis and surplus population. Second, the spread of individuals outside of traditional mechanisms of ordering has meant that states have turned to policing, public security, and state violence as a means of controlling these surplus populations. Finally, unable to control surplus populations through traditional corporatist machinery, states have attempted to construct new para-corporatist infrastructures, which they have frequently done through finance. While these para-corporatist structures lack the representational component (i.e., noncompeting, state-approved interest associations) found in classical corporatism, through different means they fulfill the aim of corporatism and other logics of govermentality of producing weakly bonded groups. They do so by connecting, incorporating, and subordinating, in this case indirectly, individuals to the state; targeting marginal groups whose potential politicization is a concern; and more generally organizing state-society relations.[48]

This book is deeply influenced by the observation that as surplus populations increase, states turn to violence and policing to subordinate them.[49] However, I trace as well a set of more complicated and subtle relations between state violence, finance, and surplus populations and discern a set of relations between finance and increasing state violence which directs state and structural violence toward surplus populations in previously unnoticed ways. In Chapter 2 this takes the form of a need to socialize the payment of debt onto marginal populations. In Chapter 3 I argue that there exists a connection between the changing regimes of private property necessary to support illusory financial accumulation and the threat or exposure to state violence. In Chapter 4, where the connection between surplus population and state violence is most directly investigated, violence is not seen as merely repressive, but rather as productive, through interruption and terror, of new kinds of (voided) subjects and collectivities.

This book takes common approaches in Latin American cultural studies to the state and nation and gives them a slightly different theoretical inflection. Instead of focusing primarily on the conceptual nodes of nation, ethnicity, and suture or hegemony and subalternity, I adopt an approach—taking a cue from Daniel Nemser's recent *Infrastructures of Race*—that is attentive to the infrastructures states use to organize bodies and produce them as individuals and weak collectivities.[50] I read infrastructure expansively, as an ensemble of techniques that "enable, shape, and regulate the practices of modern social existence," that tend to fade from view except in moments of crisis, and that serve "as a condition of possibility for the emergence of groupness as such, engendering social relations and structures of feeling."[51] As will become clear in subsequent chapters, I argue that race, finance, and state violence are some of the critical infrastructures of the post-1982 period. When I do draw on discourses of national belonging, it will be from a perspective of thinking about how these discourses (be they racial, repressive, or financial) and the infrastructures that accompany them organize bodies and expose some to what Ruth Wilson Gilmore has called "group-differentiated vulnerability to premature death."[52]

These arguments about finance and the state imply a different understanding of neoliberalism than the now overly familiar, and widely critiqued, trope of the shrinking state. This book focuses instead on the new ways states begin to act in the moment of surplus capital and surplus population: they actively participate in the production of financial architectures, markets, and devices; they shift resources from programs of welfare into the military, incarceration, and security and devise and envision new repressive infrastructure-imaginary nexuses that are directed at surplus and other populations; and in moments of financial crisis, once a decision has been made to bail out corporations and banks and not to default on debt owed internationally, they develop means, discourses, and justifications for socializing this debt onto determined sectors of the population.

Throughout this book, I will have recourse to a term, namely "state violence," which might strike some as overly reductive and out of step with some current research on states.[53] I acknowledge that states are complicated, multiply functional entities and that there is a vast realm of state-linked violence and trauma, most importantly incarceration, which my work does not discuss. I have decided to center death-dealing violence either inflicted or permitted by states due to its importance across the period I study. My use of the term "state violence" is located within the traditions of antiracist thought, studies of Latin American dictatorships, and antistate anarchism, which have not shied away from the difficult task of naming those violences which are most traumatic and sometimes, in public discourse, dangerous to name. Whether direct violence or what Kristine Kilanski and Javier Auyero call "lateral" forms,[54] I think it is important, in a cultural or any other register, to not lose sight of who stands behind the killing of black youth in Brazilian megalopolises or in places like Ayotzinapa or Tlatlaya in Mexico; and so my use of "state violence" is a rhetorical gesture as well, perhaps sacrificing complexity for denouncement in an attempt to not forget and to not look away.

Cultures of Finance and Critique

With respect to tracking and affecting its own complicated conduction between political economy and cultural critique, this book takes an approach that is both pragmatic and rooted in the traditions of Latin American cultural studies and *estudios culturales*. Its pragmatism is to recognize that after forty years of financial crises the import of finance or the economic cannot be ignored—and if one is interested in taking finance as an object of study, then a deeper engagement with political economy will be necessary. As a result this book locates itself in the interdisciplinary cultural studies tradition and takes as a key interlocutor political economic writing on finance.[55] It does so at the same time as it turns away from the debates and literature on base-superstructure,[56] in order to draw on a longer tradition of heterodox Marxist cultural theory, which includes figures such as Lukács, Mariátegui, and Jameson and which has always positioned itself as a counter to vulgar determinisms of all kinds.

I see this tradition as defined by three principles. First, nonorthodox examinations of the connection between political economy and culture—because they are nonorthodox—imply the necessity of specifying what one means by political economy. For example, in Jameson's *Postmodernism*, this takes the form of starting from "late capitalism" and pushing definitions of this term in new directions. In Lukács's *History and Class Consciousness*, this process of specifying places the "commodity-structure" and Taylorist rationalization at the center of capitalist social formations. Second, much of the heterodox tradition (and here both Mariátegui and Lukács are exemplary figures), in tracing the linkages between economics and culture, do not limit their investigations to just cultural or aesthetic objects, but take a perspective which we might describe as social theoretic. For example, for Lukács reification was not just a process that affected cultural production but social relations more generally; while for Mariátegui the split between indigenous and mestizo worlds created by colonization deeply impacted not only literary modes but also Peruvian society at large. Finally, heterodox cultural theory, having specified its understanding of political economy, always sees the relation between said political economy and cultural and social life as potentially indeterminate, meaning that theory neither collapses the indeterminacy of any connection into a vulgar determinism nor exaggerates this indeterminancy into an eternal feature of social structure.

In the following pages finance and culture intertwine across multiple sites of contact and contestation which have emerged, slowly and accretively, in the many years of writing this book. I approach finance throughout as a social force whose particular structure of temporal arbitrage comes to shape and color social and cultural experience. At the same time, however, I track how cultural objects register, work over and against, and give intelligible shape to elements and events in the financial economy and how expansive zones of discursive production create, occasionally fleeting, imaginaries through a complicated, indeterminate osmosis with the social world produced by finance. At particular moments in this book I approach cultural production as a privileged site from which societal transformations can be analyzed and as a privileged site for the production, in conversation and consonance with material political struggles, of new concepts and ways of being. As this book's Marxism is heterodox, anti-positivistic, and anti-economistic, its version of cultural and social criticism aims at not "abstract relations, but constitutive processes" wherein its concepts and frames are always "provisional, active, and subject to change."[57]

It feels important to say as well that this book in some ways resembles a prism, which, when spun, reveals five shades of light: finance, culture, surplus populations, racialization, and state violence. As one turns the prism, different spectrums come into focus and different sets of relations emerge, and there are many possible paths, all with their own revelations and openings, through the materials and histories that this book considers. Because I focus here primarily on finance and culture, other equally important sets of relations and ones deserving of their own detailed treatment, such as between racialization and surplus populations or culture and state violence, are necessarily pushed into the background. Deciding to discuss in detail the political economy of finance's rise and culture has meant these other elements have been forced to exist at a certain level of generality, and so hopefully readers will see in these limits not an inattention but rather an opening to the establishment of further lines of conversation and collective labor.

This book divides the rise of finance in Mexico and Brazil into two parts, each covering a different historical moment: the first, the period of multiple financial crises, roughly 1982–2001, and the second, the moment of recomposition around export, finance, and circulation, roughly 2001–2015. Each part has a chapter on Mexico and one on Brazil, and all of the chapters start by unfolding a figure or instrument of financial political economy (crisis, hyperinflation, credit, and circulation, respectively) which is crucial to the particular historical moment and national space under discussion. The chapters then trace the complicated, nondeterministic relations that exist among finance, cultural production, and racial formations (primarily Chapters 1 and 2) and among finance, state violence and/or para-corporatism, and subjects and collectivities (primarily Chapters 3 and 4).

The first two chapters of this book are dedicated to examining how cultural production reacted in the aftermath of the 1982 debt crisis and the period of ongoing financial crisis which followed. I turn to this task in the first chapter where I trace how Jorge Volpi's *En busca de Klingsor*, in the face of financial indeterminacy, participates in the reconstitution of a racialized imaginary of the national popular through a turn to ontology. This ontological turn is accompanied by a shift away from a biological or cultural racial project to a form of mobile, ontological division, which has become generalized under the name of the "delincuente." In the second half of the chapter, I develop how Volpi's work elaborates a theory of history as catastrophe which also bears the impress of finance. The chapter concludes by using this reading of Volpi to mount a discussion of the ontological turns of contemporary left political theory and to argue for the need for a turn to political economy to grasp the ways that financial indeterminacy has conditioned the field of contemporary thought.

In the second chapter I argue through readings of cultural and popular texts on peripheral areas, such as Zuenir Ventura's *Cidade partida* and Paulo Lins's *Cidade de Deus*, that the production of the favela as part of a polarized urban space or "divided city" comes, in the Brazilian post-debt crisis moment, to supplement fraying discourses of racial democracy and the real abstraction of exchange. Much like the category of delincuente, the rearticulation of an absolute division between formal and informal urban spaces serves as a means of human division in the face of expanding surplus populations and financial crisis. Drawing on heterodox Marxist work on forms of impersonal domination, the later portion of the chapter examines, in a discussion of the 2013 film *A cidade é uma só?* (Is the city just one?), how it might be possible for cultural products to work against this re-spectralization of the favela. I conclude by arguing that moments of financial crisis, like the 1980s and 1990s in Brazil, are defined by the political poles of seizure and socialization and that to protect against seizure and to enforce the socialization of crisis, states turn to racialized state violence and new discursive practices of division.

While the first two chapters of the book focus on how the infrastructures of racialized ordering inherited from national popular states were transformed by a turn to ontology and a re-inscription of the favela as part of a divided city, the chapters in the second half of the book argue that the post-2001 moment is marked by, in Brazil, failed forms of financial para-corporatism and, in Mexico, a turn to circulation and an inability of the state and capital to provide inhabitable lifeworlds. Chapters 1 and 2 examine the rearticulation of national popular infrastructures of social control in the period of ongoing financial crisis and Chapters 3 and 4 survey how in the post-2001 moment states either reformulate or abandon this machinery for the production of linked sets of individuals and collectives.

In Chapter 3 I trace three transformations occasioned by the re-entry of finance into Brazil after 2003: a form of financial para-corporatism, a projective structure of feeling, and the production of anti-subjects. In each case my aim is to be attentive to finance's fragility or instability, as finance-led booms last only as long as the financial flows do. In the opening section, I chart the expansion of personal credit as a form of financial para-corporatism during the Partido dos Trabalhadores (PT) governments and one of the principle cultural mediations of credit, or what I term "credit democracy." In the second part of the chapter, drawing on the work of Raymond Williams, I turn my attention to finance's structure of feeling and the everyday ways finance presses upon and shapes social relations and social life and the political consequences of the fragility of finance. The chapter's final section examines how the personal credit expansion has produced what I term "anti-subjects" or subjects who serve as a pass-through or gateway to an asset or income. This chapter concludes by examining some of the possible political outcomes of the expansion of mass credit in Brazil.

In Chapter 4 I argue that Mexico after 2001 has been marked by not just an expansion of finance, but rather a turn to circulation, which has meant a significant abandonment of infrastructures for the production of subjects and collectivities in favor of state violence. First, by focusing on the "drug war" film *El infierno* and the poetry of Dolores Dorantes, I trace the transformation of two key sites for producing collectivity during the developmentalist period: labor and death. I then turn to the films *Norteado* (2009), *La jaula de oro* (2013), and *Heli* (2013), which directly address the conditions of surplus population in a moment of circulation to demonstrate how they hinge on the production of new forms of relation between the individual and the collective. In the conclusion I argue that many recent political experiences in Mexico (from Zapatismo to Cherán) are marked by a similar production of nonstate forms of collectivity, and I consider how these discourses of circulation can be aligned with those of necropolitics.

Unfortunately expansions of and dependence on failed financial accumulation show no signs of slowing in the present. In the coda I return to Marx's work to build an explanation of the present as defined by a confrontation between surplus capital and surplus population and discuss why the most commonly called-for solutions (investing excess capital in production or "putting people back to work") are, in fact, more difficult to implement than might first appear. As a storm of the far right builds across the globe, the coda opens onto a different political option, one predicated not on waiting for the state and capital to solve the paradoxes of surplus capital and population for us, but rather one which sees autonomy as an alternative to the formations of state and capital which have produced the terrible present.

CHAPTER 1

The *Saltos* of Finance

CRISIS AND ONTOLOGY IN POST-1982 MEXICO

> This plethora of capital arises from the same causes that produce a relative surplus population and is therefore a phenomenon that complements this latter, even though the two things stand at opposite poles—unoccupied capital on the one hand and an unemployed working population on the other.
>
> **Karl Marx, *Capital*, vol. 3, p. 359**

In the course of a ten-year span, before the passage of NAFTA and before the currency crisis of 1994, Mexico passed through a series of three important finance-related crises: the currency devaluation of 1976, the debt crisis of 1982, and the fallout associated with the U.S. stock market crash in 1987. While 1976 was dismissed by many as a bump in the road of ever-expanding growth, the debt crisis of 1982 signaled the definitive end of a form of the national popular state and that the financial restructuring that had engulfed Mexico was not one more storm to be weathered by counter-cyclical policies, but in fact marked the implementation of a new global financial architecture and a turn in Mexico to attempted financial accumulation. The massive indebtedness of the state in the Echeverría era (which had been growing since the 1950s) signaled the end of the long postwar boom and the proliferation of new means of attempted finance-led accumulation driven by a global falling rate of profit coupled with global surpluses of capital with fewer outlets for investment. On the one hand, the national popular state was deterritorialized and its system of fixed or pegged exchange rates flowing into sectoral production incentives was rendered a brittle hold on the new fluxes of capital seeking investment, the exposure of floating exchange rates, and loss of internal control over monetary policy. On the other, the Mexican state was driven to deploy and participate in finance-led forms of accumulation—contracting debt, chasing foreign investment, and propping up corporations and banks—and the failure of finance-led accumulation put an end to the strategies, tactics, and geopolitics of development that had called forth and held in position a Mexican national popular formation before and after the Second World War.

Accounts of the last thirty years of Mexican cultural production that focus on neoliberalism tend to both overlook this long prehistory of financial crisis and to an extent de-emphasize the new financial architectonics and integrations of Mexico into the world economy. Neoliberal cultural critique has tended to focus on the clearly pivotal transformations in the state (i.e., privatization, liberalization of trade and capital movements, etc.), but that has had the effect of downplaying the centrality of certain economic transformations across this period, of which the rise of finance is one. Certainly neoliberalism marked a definitive change in the state, but the state, even a developmentalist one, is not isomorphic with the economy—and what I will argue is that our analysis needs to make space for accounting for both changes in the state and capital.[1]

In this chapter I take a different tack into the post-1982 historical period in Mexico: as one of decades of financial crisis and instability. This approach does not overlook the profound changes in the Mexican state and its attendant cultural imaginaries, but rather reads these changes alongside and as conditioned by the rise of finance in Mexico. I grapple, then, with the newness of finance and how cultural production in Mexico has responded to it, been influenced by it, and has produced meaning for it and its effects on the Mexican state form. As finance begins to rival production in importance in the 1980s and 1990s in Latin America, new events (financial crises, for example) and figures (hyperinflation, which is examined in Chapter 2) appear on the social scene. However, finance does not become legible or an object of cultural discussion through the same events or figures in all countries. As I argue in the first part of this chapter, in Mexico finance, or the results of its rise, became condensed into the figure of crisis or instability. At the same time the events and figures through which finance's rise becomes legible, because of their newness, come into the world almost without meaning; that is, meaning has to be produced around them. Cultural works, as well as other discursive productions, play an important role in making sense of finance's consequences—which, in the case of Mexico, include the spread of instability and the breakdown of the national popular formation.

I chart this process of creating meaning for the consequences of finance through detailed discussions of a single text, Jorge Volpi's *En busca de Klingsor* (*In Search of Klingsor*, 1999). I approach the problem in this way because a close, careful reading of Volpi's novel is a means to track the production of new figures and categories—which are frequently more ephemeral in other forms of popular discourse and therefore more difficult to pin down—for interpreting Mexican social and cultural life in the aftermath of finance. My readings attempt to establish lines of response to the twin crises of state and finance in Volpi and then open out from there onto the larger sphere of Mexican popular discourse.

In particular I examine how Volpi's work responds to new forms of indeterminacy and instability put into circulation by the widening gap between the real and the fictitious of finance with a turn to "first principles" or an investigation into the "fundamental" nature of the social world. Throughout this chapter, I will describe Volpi's novelistic investigations into the nature of the natural and social worlds as musings on "ontology." In contemporary philosophical and theoretical usage, as Stephen White, Carsten Strathausen, and others have noted, the once central distinction between metaphysics (the philosophy of first principles) and ontology (the science of beings) has broken down, such that it is now common to see discussions of "Badiou's set theoretic ontology" or "Deleuze's univocal ontology," which in each case refers to topics, such as the question of whether being is multiple or One, that escape the traditional purview of "ontology" but which are nonetheless named by this term now. It has also become common in social and political theory to use "ontology" to name a set of assumptions about the nature of the natural and social worlds (see, for example, Arturo Escobar's use of "flat ontologies" and the citation of an "ontological turn" in his recent work).[2] I will employ this expanded, contemporary sense of ontology as a theory of the natural and social worlds throughout this chapter in order to argue that Volpi's novel, marked by a crisis in the structures of the national popular, rearticulates a system for the racialized division of groups by means of a theory of the natural world, which is opposed to the play of representation that founds the imaginary of the national popular moment.

In the second half of the chapter I argue that in Volpi's work we can also see the elaboration of a new theory of history, not as the famously debated "an end of history," but rather a theorization of history as an ongoing catastrophe and disaster and as marked by the form of financial crisis that has unfolded in Mexico. History as catastrophe forms a second site of transmission between finance's form and the literary that also, as we will see, opens onto a wider set of popular and literary discourses. By way of conclusion, I move from Volpi to left academic social theory more generally to argue that Volpi's turn to ontology or natural philosophy is convergent with a generalized turn in social theory since the 1980s to ontology and indeterminacy and that in each case the role played by the rise of finance in producing these new indeterminacies has tended to be unrecognized.

Instability, or What Finance Makes Possible

Within U.S. and Latin American theoretical circles today, the two most common explanatory frameworks for the turn to finance, post-Keynsianism and post-workerism, both read finance as predatory or speculative with respect to the "real" or productive economy. Instead of seeing this turn to finance as merely speculative, I see finance, following the work of Annie McClanahan, Joshua Clover, and other heterodox Marxist theorists, as a form of temporal arbitrage or as a means of attempting to realize future surplus value in the present and as such intimately connected (rather than opposed) to production. Reading finance and production together, as opposed to seeing finance as parasitical on the "real" economy, is necessary if our goal is to grasp the turn to finance materially, that is as a specific form of attempted accumulation, as opposed to explaining it away as a kind of mania, lack of regulation, or set of bad behaviors engaged in by irresponsible actors. To grasp how finance has changed the landscape of cultural and social life, we have to see finance not as merely corrupting good forms of production, but rather as emerging from within production itself to solve problems of declining profitability and as part of a quest for new forms of attempted accumulation.

This approach of reading finance and production together remits back to Marx's fragmentary work on credit and finance capital in the three volumes of *Capital.* Generally speaking, for Marx finance and credit are important in simple production processes because they enable the immediate or precipitous realization of a commodity's value. To take a basic example imagine a factory producing blue jeans where a capitalist sinks several million dollars into materials and labor for production. Instead of waiting to have to sell each and every pair of jeans to then reinvest that money in the business, the capitalist is able to borrow money against the eventual sale of his commodities to continue the production of jeans without having to wait for their actual sale. Thus, credit or finance are not, by nature, supplementary to or predatory upon processes of production but rather, at a certain level of capitalist development, *essential*, necessary to keep production flowing smoothly.

What the presence of finance in production makes possible, however, is new forms of crisis or instability and their possible expansion. Credit, in our example of blue jeans, intervenes in accumulation by attempting to shorten the temporal distance between the production of a commodity and the realization of its value. It is precisely in this way that finance nurtures new possibilities for instability, speculation, and crisis in accumulation. Kojin Karatani has re-read Marx's critique of capital, privileging both credit and what he terms its *salto mortale* (leap of faith) and linking them to crisis:

> Classical economists believe that a commodity is a synthesis between use value and exchange value. But this is only an ex post facto recognition. Lurking behind this synthesis as event is a "fatal leap [salto mortale]." Kierkegaard saw the human being as a synthesis between finity and infinity, reminding us that what is at stake in this synthesis is inevitable "faith." In commodity exchange, the equivalent *religious* moment appears as "credit." Credit, the treaty of presuming that a commodity can be sold in advance, is an institutionalization of postponing the critical moment of selling a commodity. And the commodity economy, constructed as it is upon credit, inevitably nurtures crisis.[3]

Finance and credit, which accompany commodity production in some form, are leaps into the unknown because they are claims on future value that may or may not be realized. I can loan you one thousand dollars to produce jeans anticipating your business will continue to grow (that is, anticipating my claim on your future production will be able to be paid in full), but if your workers go on strike or if a new technology revolutionizes textile production, then I might not get my money back. Thus in the salto mortale between commodity production and selling—a salto covered by credit—lies the potential for finance to generate special kinds of instability. In the late 1970s Mexico borrowed heavily against anticipated oil production revenues, and this same form of potential instability was introduced, but on a massive scale across many actors and national spaces. When Mexico declared a moratorium on debt payments in 1982, the potential instability became a true interruption, a real crisis.

The turn to attempted accumulation through finance in the 1970s, via means such as foreign debt, currency arbitrage, and business and personal lending, seeded in a mass way this kind of instability across all levels of the global economy and national social formations. Finance can result in speculation and predation, but its instability is not the result of behaviors or lack of regulation but rather is structural to finance itself and embryonic within capitalist production. That is, finance is the rise of new ways and means of exploiting through shortening or elongating the gap between the moment of the production of a commodity and the moment of the realization of its value. And because finance involves not the production of value but rather a claim on future value, it generates instability in two ways. First, as a claim upon future value, credit or financial instruments are always subject to potential non-repayment. Second, financial instruments, because of their degree of remove from the commodities or values that underlie them, frequently result in the creation of fictitious value, in bubbles or booms, or a widening gap between the real value of assets and what people are willing to imagine they might be worth in the future or present. Indeed, all of the most important new financial instruments that are utilized in the post-1973 period (securitization, options, swaps, etc.) as well as the new financial *dispositifs* (exchange rate arbitrage, high frequency trading, etc.) end up producing massive amounts of fictitious claims and result in the booms and bubbles that have populated this period both in the global North and South. The turn to finance, wherever it takes places, amplifies the potential for instability, failing accumulation, and crisis.

The potential for instability and crisis is therefore inherent in finance. However meaning must be produced around the instruments and events of finance, and one way this occurred was through an investment in a set of linked terms that adjudicate social decomposition, *crisis* and *caos.* Crisis or instability became a central category through which the post-1982 world and the initial rise of finance was thought; indeed, as Claudio Lomnitz notes, the period after 1982 came to be known in popular discourse in Mexico simply as *la crisis.* La crisis serves as a polysemic figure that names all the effects of finance's rise: declining wages, government corruption, mass unemployment, as well as the experiential forms of shock and uncertainty that pervaded the 1980s and 1990s in Mexico. Lomnitz's work on the post-1982 period demonstrates the newness of this type of (financial) crisis, but also the degree to which this figure spread as a means for understanding the events of 1982: "Until the events of 1982, the term *crisis* was most often used by journalists and intellectuals, usually in the restricted sense of, for instance, 'the crisis of agriculture' or 'the cyclical crises of capitalism.' After 1982, however, when the Mexican government could not meet its debt payments, the use of the term became so widespread that this whole era, together with its concomitant situations, practices, and sentiments, became known as *la crisis.*"[4]

Between 1982 and 1994 the Mexican state undertook all the reforms and institution building necessary for the construction of a financialized economy: an expanded stock market, the issuance of government bonds, and the liberalization of capital controls. In 1994 as power passed between out-going President Carlos Salinas de Gortari and incoming President Ernesto Zedillo, Mexico was rocked by yet another deep, catastrophic financial crisis—this one requiring a bailout administered directly by the United States, which demanded in return further liberalization and austerity measures.[5] It was in this period that another term circulated alongside the figure of "crisis": that of "caos" (chaos). The usage and circulation of "caos" as a descriptor of Mexican social reality can be seen across sites of popular discourse, including in liberation theologist Tomás Gerardo Allaz's 1994 article in *Proceso*, simply titled "Salinas: El caos," in which he writes: "They appear as so many symptoms of the deep decomposition of our society throughout the twelve years of Salinas. This ruler, so imbued with his absolute personal power without limit, will be held responsible by history for having installed the nation in chaos."[6] Caos as an evaluation is a recognition of crisis pushed to its limits, but also at the same time, it is, like crisis, a polysemic figure in which financial and political levels are collapsed, often resulting in the displacement of the economic cause in favor of an analysis of state failure.

In the following section I will take what first might appear as a detour far away from the realm of finance and financial crisis, in the form of a close reading of Jorge Volpi's *En busca de Klingsor.* I do so because this close reading will provide a set of forms, tensions, and ideas that will open back out onto the world of finance, instability and crisis, and the cultural and social transformations produced alongside the rise of finance in this period. I engage deeply with *Klingsor*, first, because it is an exemplary text that turns around the figures of crisis and caos in the form of a sustained meditation on indeterminacy and, second, because it is a site where one can discern a set of cultural and social transformations that move alongside financial crisis. Specifically, I will track how a form of racialized social control exercised by the national popular was reworked—in this case, in a move from representation to ontology—and how it came to be marked by the form of the financial salto or the increasing distance between production and the realization of value.

Klingsor, Hard Indeterminacy, and Moralism

After it was selected for the Biblioteca Breve prize, the novel *Klingsor* established Volpi and the Crack generation as a Mexican and international literary phenomenon. Criticism of Volpi's work more generally, and of the novel itself, has primarily taken place within the larger debate in the field of Latin American literary studies on the limits and/or end of autonomous literary practice, or what Carlos J. Alonso has called "the novel without literature."[7] Within these debates, some readers, such as Cristóbal Pera, have stressed the postnational aspects of Volpi's literary production, while Wilfrido H. Corral and Lidia Santos have questioned the political horizons of Volpi's notion of the literary, and Ignacio Sánchez Prado has positioned Volpi in the context of "strategic occidentalism."[8]

Instead of focusing on the novel's possible or improbable politics of literary autonomy, I locate *Klingsor*'s political intervention on another level, namely, in its concern with indeterminacy, uncertainty, and chance, as it is here that the novel engages with and presents its own articulation of the discursive figures emerging from Mexico's ongoing financial crises. *Klingsor* develops what I term a "hard indeterminist" vision of the natural and social worlds, wherein chance and uncertainty are foundational and overcome any attempt to construct a stable world. For all its emphasis on a kind of totalizing indeterminism, I argue that *Klingsor*, in key moments, reintroduces forms of determinism, in particular as a means of conditioning the political.

I forward a reading of *Klingsor* not in the ambit of the transformation of the literary by "globalization," but rather as a laboratory for the rearticulation of state power and its discursive supports. The twin crises of the state and finance dealt serious blows to the state infrastructural-imaginary nexus derived from the Mexican Revolution and its institutionalization. As Nicola Miller and others have noted, the literary has played an important role in Latin America throughout the twentieth century as a site for the elaboration of state forms of ideology or the elaboration of forms of thought within a state-defined field of literary autonomy. It is no surprise that it is in the literary field in Mexico in the 1990s where we find serious engagements with and attempts at rearticulating and refounding the national popular imaginary. In Volpi this rearticulation will occur in a transition from a system of control based in representation, the sine qua non of the national popular, to one based in ontology, understood in a very general way as a concern with the nature of being or the structure and existence of the material world. The novel's ontological principles give rise to its thinking of the political as a division between those who respect the indeterminacy in the heart of the natural world and those who attempt to overcome it and fall into madness, evil, and moral wrong.

En busca de Klingsor recounts the imbrication of two events: the scientific debates concerning chance and causality after the discovery of relativity and the last days of the Nazi regime. The novel opens with a young physicist, Francis P. Bacon, whom we first encounter as a graduate student studying in Princeton at the Institute for Advanced Study. Bacon, while brilliant, is a melancholic figure, and due to a series of failed relationships which spill over into his professional life, he takes a leave of absence and joins a special U.S. military mission at the end of the Second World War. The mission is to track down Nazi physicists, but it quickly turns into a much more personal and ambiguous task. Once Bacon encounters the German mathematician and narrator of the novel, Gustav Links, the novel turns into a search for Klingsor, a mythical figure who may or may not have been in charge of a series of secret Nazi science programs. The catch is that neither Bacon nor Links knows if Klingsor actually existed or not, and it is possible that Links is playing a double game, either leading Bacon on a wild-goose chase or actually concealing his identity as the real Klingsor. Famously the novel ends without fully ascertaining the identity of Klingsor, leaving readers to dwell on their doubts as to his existence and their suspicions as to his person.

Klingsor draws on both the genres of the detective novel and the novel of ideas, and it is the ideas, namely the discovery of chance, indeterminacy, and uncertainty by twentieth-century physics, that create the conditions of possibility for the detective novel as the indeterminate and impossible search for Klingsor. A good part of the novel is concerned with presenting the opinions of famous early twentieth-century physicists, such as Max Planck, Johannes Stark, Werner Heisenberg, Erwin Schrödinger, and Niels Bohr, as to the meaning of quantum theory. Volpi's presentation of their views, as we will see below, turns around the implications of relativity, Heisenberg's uncertainty, and Gödel's incompleteness theorem for human morality. As a novel of ideas, *Klingsor* spends much time on discussions of what we might call natural philosophy or in more contemporary parlance, ontology. While on one textual level *Klingsor* walks the reader through various modern perspectives on indeterminacy, on another level it illustrates them in a detective story of a failed and impossible search for a shadowy figure whose very existence no one can even confirm.

Indeterminacy, understood as the breakdown of causality and thus of a human ability to produce knowledge about the natural and social world, is foregrounded from the very beginning of *Klingsor.* In the preface the novel's narrator, Gustav Links, a German mathematician, opens by discussing a failed assassination attempt against Hitler in which he participated and for which he was consequently tried. Links, however, was saved from a sure sentence of death when an Allied bombing raid caused a wall to fall on and kill the judge presiding at his trial. A stroke of fate also saved Hitler from being killed by Links and his compatriots' plan, and as Link notes, "On the morning of February 3, 1945, a similar kind of luck saved my own life."[9] Links reveals himself to be obsessed with fate and the connection between these two seemingly random events: "Why do I insist, so many years after the fact, in connecting movements of chance which in the beginning had nothing to do with each other? Why do I continue to present them as one, as if they were manifestations of one single act of will?"[10] The novel sets up here the peculiar tension between indeterminacy and determinacy, or between chance and causality, which it consequently seeks to develop. On the one hand Links, as an early twentieth-century mathematician with close connections to the modern physics community, is a proponent of uncertainty and chance as a foundational part of the natural world. On the other Links also clearly demonstrates a desire or belief that events are not just random, but that there is a hand ("one single act of will") guiding the movement of the world, of history, and of our lives. It is this tension, which we might call *Klingsor*'s paradox or a desire for determinism in a fully indeterminate world, that I want to tease out.

The following paragraph takes this tension and explicitly turns it into a frame for the novel itself, into the very reason why Links has decided to write it, to recount this history:

> If I dare to join apparently unconnected facts, such as the salvation of Hitler and my own, it is because humanity has never been such a close witness to such catastrophic destruction. And our era, unlike other historical moments, has been largely determined by such twists of fate, those little signs that remind us of the ungovernable, chaotic nature of the realm in which we live. I propose, then, to tell the story of the century. *My* century. *My* version of how fate [*azar*] has ruled the world, and of how we men of science try in vain to domesticate its fury.[11]

The history of the twentieth century, then, is that of "azar," which the translator has chosen to render as "fate" instead of the perhaps closer English translation of "chance." But the choice of fate does capture something about Volpi's approach to the concept of "azar" throughout *Klingsor.* What fate captures is, on the one hand, a sense of chance occurrence, that is, of events outside human control and linked by neither rhyme nor reason, but on the other, there is fate as the sense of a divinely preordained plan. These two senses are reflected in how the novel positions indeterminacy as foundational to ontology ("nobody was safe in a world that was suddenly dominated by uncertainty"), while at the same time it registers a longing for, as Links says elsewhere, a time when "the world was an ordered environment."[12]

Perhaps readers whose ears are attuned to the debates in twentieth-century physics or philosophy have started to pick up on a certain slippage in terms. Do not uncertainty, chance, and indeterminacy derive from different sites of intellectual production and pitch themselves at different conceptual registers? They do but this is a conflation that is essential to the novel's presentation of its fully indeterminate "world" as a result of the early twentieth-century discoveries of relativity and quantum physics. To explain why this conflation is so critical to the novel, let's turn to a key passage in the opening chapter of the book's final part, "Laws of Traitorous Motion":

> If, as stated by Gödel's theorem, every axiomatic system contains undecidable propositions; if, as stated by Einstein's relativity, absolute time and space do not exist; if, as postulated by the rules of quantum physics and as a consequence of the uncertainty principle, science can offer only vague and random approximations of the cosmos—then we can no longer rely on causality as an accurate predictor of the future. And if specific individuals possess only specific truths, then all of us—made up of the same material of which atoms are made—are the result of paradox and impossibility. Our convictions can only be considered half-truths.[13]

This passage collapses a number of different kinds of uncertainty and indeterminacy: logical, in the case of Gödel; macroscopic, in the case of Einstein; and microscopic, in the case of the uncertainty principle. In so doing this passage overpowers the local constraints of any of these individual theories and constructs a sweeping vision of the natural and social worlds as radically indeterminate, as a place where knowledge is not just uncertain or improbable, but in fact, impossible.

In order to demonstrate how this is an overinterpretation of the individual theories at hand, I will focus just on the uncertainty principle. Heisenberg's uncertainty principle in its classic form states that it is not possible to know exactly both the position and momentum of a particle. It is a localized statement regarding the limits of the accuracy of observational knowledge on the quantum level. Moreover it is a statement which only has sense when read against Newtonian mechanics. In classical Newtonian mechanics if one knows the position and velocity of an object/particle, one can predict the object's position and velocity at any future moment (assuming a closed system). What the uncertainty principle says is merely that this kind of total knowledge is no longer possible once we are on the quantum level. There are two key caveats here. First, as most early twentieth-century quantum theorists argued, classical mechanics and tools of observation continue to function in the large-scale macro world. Second, the uncertainty principle, on the quantum level, does not mean that no prediction is possible. What holds on the quantum level is not the mechanical causality of Newtonian physics but statistical probability.

Thus the uncertainty principle does not mean that there is no causality nor that we can have no knowledge of quantum particles, but rather that the causality operative on this level and our knowledge of it do not take the form of classical mechanics.

The novel's presentation of the uncertainty principle and of the way it is collapsed with other forms of indeterminacy takes the results of Gödel, Einstein, and Heisenberg far beyond their logical conclusions. As we can see in the passage cited above, the novel's vision of the natural world is of a universe in which neither causality nor knowledge is possible. This is a vision of ontology we might describe as "hard indeterminist." Hard indeterminacy would be a position which believes that any micro form of uncertainty or indeterminacy implies the total cancelation of any form of causality and the casting into doubt of any possibility of knowledge. *Klingsor*'s vision is hard indeterminist in this respect: since the quantum world possesses some degree of indeterminacy, then the whole of the natural, human, and social worlds are radically, irredeemably indeterminate.

Having said this, what makes the novel a complex literary text is that while it is, on the one hand, a novel of ideas that advances or is motivated by a hard indeterminist vision of the natural world, it is also a novel that is very concerned with parsing and delimiting boundaries between good and evil. Thus while the novel advances an ontology of savage indeterminacy, it also attempts to find a ground if not for the securing of moral certainties, then at least for preventing the slide into totalitarianism and madness. In short *Klingsor* is a novel that postulates a world of hard indeterminacy and then attempts to locate bases from which to construct a moral and political order. However, it is important to emphasize this point: while the novel constructs a moral and political order out of its foundational ontology, it does so in a tendential way. That is, the novel does not posit that disrespecting hard indeterminism *always* results in totalitarianism but rather that it *tends* to. The novel does not propose a hard-wired structure between its ontology and political order (that would be too obviously deterministic and a contradiction too easily refuted). *Klingsor*'s method of securing moral order is to reintroduce determinism via the backdoor while always providing an escape hatch of plausible deniability that the novel is in itself not deterministic.

While not all characters who defy indeterminacy end up in totalitarianism, many do, and throughout the novel much of the textual conversation around how ontology and politics are linked is concerned with how a refusal to recognize the indeterminacy at the heart of the natural world opens the door to illiberalism. In one example of this, sticking with the same section of the novel that we discussed above, we read:

> Why are we weak? For a very simple reason: We cannot predict the future. We live in an eternal present, obsessed with deciphering the future. . . .
>
> Amid this perpetual state of confusion, there is always someone ready and waiting to take advantage of everyone else's blindness to assuage his own fears. . . . Fully convinced of his purpose, he toils for the good of his people, his race, his friends, his family, or his lovers (as the case may be), imposing his own faith upon the prevailing uncertainty. All the truth he proclaims is an act of violence, pretense, chicanery. And how does a weak man become strong? Very simple. Any man who can convince other people—other weak people—that he knows what the future holds is a man who will be able to rise above and control his peers.[14]

This is one version of *Klingsor*'s tendential linking of its ontological vision with a political horizon. As we saw above, modern physics' discovery of uncertainty at the heart of the natural world has cancelled all causality. Politics enters in the form of men who convince others that they can overcome the fundamental indeterminacy of the natural world by leading human communities toward a goal, a better land, etc. But in its very gesture of making this connection the novel violates its own principle: in making the point that totalitarianism arises from the failure to obey indeterminacy, *Klingsor* in this moment surreptitiously reintroduces a form of determinism in the form of a conditioning of the political by the ontological. Thus, as much as the novel advances or derives its worldview from a hard, radical, or all-encompassing indeterminism, it reintroduces at key moments deterministic or causal linkages between the natural world and the political in the form of a regulating, moral shorthand. As such the novel reintroduces determinism and order after having banished them, and it does so by having the ontological condition limit the political, or what is possible or acceptable in the political field.

In *Klingsor* only by respecting not our inability to know, but rather the ontological barrier that means we can know nothing can we avoid a slide into totalitarianism. In the world of the novel we cannot overcome this desire, because it is conditioned by the facticity of the world as such; thus, we can only resist the temptation. Politics in the novel is then transmuted into a moral struggle to resist the temptation to counter ontology. Another point wherein the novel weakly distends ontological uncertainty into a catastrophic political tendency is in an interview between Bacon and Erwin Schrödinger, in which Bacon asks if the uncertainty of quantum mechanics was, in some way, a celebration of free will. Schrödinger replies by narrating the story of one Pascual Jordan, a Nazi admirer, who thought it "was man's obligation to go around filling in the holes that nature left empty" by using the force of will.[15] Both men agree that this "tyrannical" notion is a horrifying and unjustified interpretation of uncertainty.

The Nazi sympathizers who accept the indeterminacy of modern physics represent the opposite position to the one that is, generally speaking, positively coded by the novel. They believe in a radical indeterminacy but they think it can be surmounted by the force of will. In this way *Klingsor* constructs a division between those who respect the indeterminacy in the heart of the natural world and those who attempt to overcome it. Those who fall into the latter category are pushed outside the human community and descend into madness, evil, and totalitarianism. The failure to respect this indeterminacy creates an ontological division in the human, marked by an absolute divide. As such, Volpi's sophisticated take on indeterminacy is a literary formalization and philosophical deepening of popular discourses on caos and crisis which circulated after the financial crises in 1982 and 1994. It is an alchemy, one which takes the indeterminacy of finance and transmutes it into something else, namely an immutable feature of the natural world; and as a result Volpi's approach, much like many of the popular discourses on caos as a social real, assumes that the figures of indeterminacy and chaos are somehow diagnostic rather than symptomatic.

This concern with indeterminacy is reflected across many of this period's other key cultural productions, including its perhaps most important filmic one, *Amores Perros* (2000). The film is structured as three separate narratives of individuals wandering through life without direction who are joined by a random, chance occurrence: a car crash at the film's opening. The film's emphasis on its characters' nihilism and the expansive chaos of the city can be read as a figuration of and perhaps commentary on social decomposition. Similar to the hard indeterminism of *Klingsor*, the social space of the urban in *Amores Perros* is structured by its lack of structure, wherein the key event of the film is both catastrophic and produced by chance. Much like in *Klingsor*, in *Amores Perros* a form of illiberal politics defines a line between inclusion and exclusion in a human community: in the film's final scene, the ex-radical El Chivo walks out into the desert searching for a form of redemption that will enable him to finally overcome the politics that separated him from his family and to perhaps in the future reintegrate himself into the world of the family and social.

For a position on indeterminacy which doesn't assume its giveness or immutability as either a natural constant or social fact, we have to turn to Carlos Monsiváis's *Los rituales del caos* (The rituals of chaos), published the year after the 1994 financial crisis and four years before *Klingsor*, which opens:

> The tangled forms—solemn, amusing or grotesque—of life in society are identified in a rather typical way: crowds that are made and remade every minute, anticipated and unforeseen carnivals, the powers of consumption, the pleasure at getting lost in labyrinths of energy or inertia. Here, greed devours everything, resignation sanctifies everything, disarray knows all and nothing at the same time. Seen from the outside, the chaos to which these chronicles allude (in its traditional, pre-scientific meaning) is linked to one of the most constant characterizations of Mexican life, namely its "fierce disorder." If this was ever true, it has ceased to be so. In my opinion, the best description of the present balances the apparent lack of meaning with the haughty imposition of limits. And in chaos begins the perfection of order.[16]

In *Rituales*, Monsiváis, studying the urban context of Mexico City, endeavors to look beneath the chaotic surface phenomenon of the mass city, its multitudes, and their confusion in order to find the capillary forms of subjection that lurk there, but also the possible lines of flight. For Monsiváis, the appearance of caos covers the operations of power and *orden* which pass through, structure, and grow out of the "feroz desorden" (fierce disorder) of contemporary life. If we can see in Monsiváis, contra Volpi, an opening for another reading of the relation between indeterminacy and the political, one which doesn't depend on its conversion into nature, our task is to explain how this indeterminacy and the new ordering that it hides can be explained, not as a social fact that must be accepted, but as the result of a twin crisis of state and capital.

From Representation to Ontology

Frequently the 1980s and 1990s are read under the sign of neoliberalism, wherein neoliberalism signals both the restructuring of the Mexican state and the process of "opening" or "liberalizing" the economy. However, the decades of the 1980s and 1990s were not only the decades of liberalization but also the decades of a global turn toward finance and in Mexico of ongoing financial crisis. The historical argument that I want to advance is that we should see this period as the moment of the reformulation of the national popular state form, but at the same time as the moment of the global rise of finance and forms of attempted financial accumulation, which sets off the national popular's transformation. In the face of decades of financial crisis and recomposition in the national popular state form away from welfare and into warfare, *Klingsor* works alongside and registers a refashioning of racialized technologies of social regulation and distributions of premature death. The turn to ontology, or to speculation on the nature of the physical and social world, that we can see in *Klingsor* responds to a crisis in the primary technology of racialized integration of the national popular state, the management of representation.

Gareth Williams in *The Other Side of the Popular* has described the form of the national popular as, in part, a regime of management of "fictive ethnicity" (a term he takes from Étienne Balibar). The national popular manages the play of representations and images, the construction of the state's fictive, although by no means less real, unity. Williams writes: "Indeed, it is through populism's repeated attempts to convey an image of national community, and therefore through the modernizing elite's attempts to convey the nation as a utopic commonality thought and negotiated from above, that language and race (as 'the most natural of origins' of identity . . .) become foundational protagonists in the construction of the people as a recognizably autonomous group and as the embodiment of the ideal (national) community."[17] We might take Octavio Paz's *The Labyrinth of Solitude* as a quintessential work of social integration via the management of representations. *Labyrinth* famously opens with the other, the *pachuco*, who Paz presents as one of the "extremes" of any potential Mexican identity. In *Labyrinth*, written during the Alemán presidency and during the first turn toward multinational and finance capital, we have an attempt to (re)integrate the social imaginary of the national popular. The fissures, the nonmodern indigenous others and the outliers, the pachucos and *pelados*, are registered at the essay's beginning, and *Labyrinth* then moves on to construct a presumptive people not through a turn to ontology but by managing the play of representations, by caulking, subsuming, or excluding marginal groups into or from a racialized national imaginary.

From the very first paragraphs of the Crack generation's central polemical text, the *Manifiesto Crack*, the sputtering of the national popular machinery of representation is foregrounded. After the destabilizing financial crises of the 1980s and 1990s, the question of cracks and the people returns but in an entirely new form. What the Crack manifesto registers is that the primary threat is no longer splits internal to national popular subjectivity, splits which might undo its coherence, but rather a threat from outside that destabilizes the entire environment of the national popular state and subject. The *Manifiesto* registers this new destabilization of the environment of the nation through a discussion of technologies of cultural production. The old technologies of fictive ethnicity (the written word) are being overtaken not just in terms of market share, but in terms of their fundamental technology. They are two-dimensional, occurring on the plane of representation, while the newest technologies create worlds: "Italo Calvino, I believe, in *Six Memos for the Next Millennium*, was the one to accurately point out the challenges facing the Crack novels. In those pages, Calvino reflected on how literature and, above all, narrative have been losing their potential readers to technology developed for entertainment: video games, mass media, and, most recently, for those who can afford them, virtual reality games through which—oh, paradoxes of development—someone with a very modern helmet and anatomical gloves can see, hear, and even touch the adventures offered on compact discs."[18]

How to solve this problem? One obvious solution would be to leave behind the technology of the book. But the Crack writers will take another: to move from writing that works from identification to writing that constructs worlds: "It is obvious to point out reality itself is multiple, it comes to us as multifaceted, eternal. We need books in which a whole world is revealed to the reader, and can *trap* them. This word has a unique use here. It is not about identification, but the superpositioning of worlds which are being talked about. Using all the metaphorical potential of the literary text so we can say again: 'So here you are, meet one another [*encuéntrense*].'"[19]

This is how I suggest we read *En busca de Klingsor*: as a proposal to move away from the management of the play of representations internal to the national popular to the structuring of worlds and their ontology. This move occurs while the environment of the national popular is being destabilized by new forms of financial crises, and as technologies of social integration are being rendered unviable from within the switch to a financial and neoliberal state form. No longer able to build a national popular subject through a technocracy of images, Volpi moves to ontology, to establishing a fundamental structure of the world in order to produce a vision of social and political order. In place of a technology of images, or of representation management, there is a social physics; in place of the bond, a structuralist functionalism; in place of a decision of whether to participate in the nation, a decision to obey the deep ontological structure of the social and political field. Those who choose not to obey collapse into totalitarianism, violence, and madness, opening themselves up to the full measure of the state's sovereign force. In place of a management of representations we have a morality play, but one whose guidelines are not determined by the fully divine, but rather by its weak theological substitute: the ontological.

From the Boom to the Crack

Tracking macroeconomic transformations can help us as cultural critics to make sense of the Crack writers' complicated relationship to the Boom, which they see as a welcome antecedent and ghostly competitor. The Boom is both what they want to return to (against the debased magical realism of the market), but also, to the extent that the Boom is implicated in a post–Cuban Revolution pan–Latin Americanism, it is something with which these writers want to break. It is this pan–Latin American imaginary that subtends García Márquez's statement on the Boom, "The group is writing one great novel. We're writing the first great novel of Latin American man."[20] Perhaps none of the Crack writers has done more than Volpi to attack this imaginary, and by proxy the national popular and dependency theories that lie behind it.[21]

As Volpi says in one interview, "Cuando nací, el boom estaba allí" (When I was born, the Boom was there).[22] The Boom was always there—that is, its pan–Latin American imaginary and the specific form of national popular politics attached to it and the specific form of integration into the world economy underlying it. However, by the mid-1970s the crisis of global capitalism had already begun, and it would soon bring dictatorships, populists, and pan-Latin Americanists equally to heel. Borrowing against future oil production in the late 1970s enabled the Mexican state to continue its patronage of national capitalists and to support key commodity prices, but finally, after the U.S. Treasury raised interest rates (the famed Volcker shock), the crisis of accumulation came home to roost in 1982. A stark choice had to be made: to continue the turn into finance and socialize the debt onto the working classes and the poor, or go against the grain of the IMF and capitalist restructuring. We know the results of that decision nationally, but what is not often remarked is how this moment is also the end in Mexico of the pan–Latin American imaginary partially created in the aftermath of the Cuban Revolution and with the help of the Boom novels. The declining rate of profit forces a new form of integration into the world market and destroys a fictitious continental unity. As the Boom fades, the cracks multiply, and as the crisis can no longer be put off, the imaginary of pan-Latin American unity and its national popular figures crumble. If it is the case that "when I was born, the Boom was already there," then when Volpi and Crack came of age, the Boom had been backed into la crisis of finance.

The Crack generation and the Boom are both literary movements directly tied to English-language economic vocabulary and by means of this anchor to particular historical regimes, moments of accumulation, and geopolitical imaginaries. The Boom references both the good years and in Spanish perhaps also a suspicion that underlies their effervescence, that booms are more often than not bubbles. "Crack," the English loan word used in Spanish to denote stock market crashes, such as that of 1987, refers to a crisis not of production but of finance: "One speaks of the crisis as . . . in the Anglo-Saxon terms which have taken over the greater part of economic science, the *crack*."[23] As the Boom fades, the Crack surges. From the decomposition of the structure of accumulation that gave rise to booms in production to failed accumulation—that is, the crack—based in government borrowing and financial mechanisms, the imaginary subtending these moments changes as well.

These imaginaries are marked at their root by two different approaches to worlds. In perhaps his most famous essay, "On the Marvelous Real in America," Alejo Carpentier writes, "Because of the virginity of the land, our upbringing, our ontology, the Faustian presence of the Indian and the black man, the revelation constituted by its recent discovery, its fecund racial mixing [*mestizaje*], America is far from using up its wealth of mythologies. After all, what is the entire history of America if not a chronicle of the marvelous real?"[24] In the Boom, the established structure of national popular mestizaje and antiblackness (which forms a stable, recognizable "ontology") produces a politics of representation and the opening for the exploration of the (potentially) utopian difference of the "marvelous real." The worlds of the Boom are spaces in which the play of representation occurs, where the logic of mestizaje plays itself out and where the ontology of the space is not in question. But as the very foundation of the national popular world becomes unstable, in the Crack generation cultural production moves to the construction of worlds themselves as a counter to the instability of financial forms of accumulation and crisis. As in Volpi's *Klingsor* the human community is thought not through figures of hybridity or representational mixing and management but rather through an absolute divide.

Finance, Race, and Division

On the level of the nation *Klingsor* charts and participates in a larger cultural shift away from fictive ethnicity and representation to a concern with restabilizing ontologies and worlds. As Joshua Lund has shown the apparatus of fictive ethnicity, that of mestizaje mixed with antiblackness in the case of Mexico, is at root a racial theory of the nation, even though it is not often recognized as one.[25] If *Klingsor* charts a shift between two regimes of control or processes of racial formation, what happens to "race" as the racial structure of mestizaje/antiblackness is rearticulated under new pressures of finance and surplus population? The literature on shifting forms of racialization in Mexico has seen the 1980s and 90s as marked by the rise of important new indigenous movements and also by a shift in the state ideology of race, from mestizaje to neoliberal multiculturalism or pluriculturalism.[26] *Klingsor* glimpses a different, but equally important

I will argue, response to the breakdown of the system of racialized control which had theories of mestizaje and *lo mexicano* at its heart.

We have seen that the form of division we find in *Klingsor* is one in which subjects face a choice to obey the ontological structuring of the world—if they do not they are marked or tagged as being outside the human community (such as the Nazi sympathizers). However, it is important to note that this tagging is tendential—it comes from somewhere in between the sphere of law (concerned with acts and actions, right and wrong) and the sphere of security, concerned, as Foucault has noted, with probability (not with prohibiting) and with keeping outcomes within a certain acceptable range.[27] In *Klingsor* one is not unequivocally pushed out of the human community for trespassing on the belief in a radical indeterminacy at the heart of the world; rather this distinction is always hovering, like a threat, waiting to be applied, somewhere between a law and a probability. An ontological distinction between groups and the threat of potential exclusion is what marks one part of the new racialized infrastructure of control in Mexico that emerges out of the crisis of finance and the state in the 1980s and 1990s.

Certainly for some readers a form of racialized control based in an ontological division between two worlds will sound familiar, as versions of it have served as a basis for a long tradition of crude popular and state understanding of the relationship between indigenous and/or Afro-descendent and mestizo/ladino communities in Latin America. This then is the recoding in which Volpi's novel participates: in a moment of the decaying of the state racial formation grounded in mestizaje and antiblackness, the novel mirrors a crass racial division that has circulated alongside and that underpinned antiblack/mestizaje discourses and elevates this distinction to the level of a social theory. In this process its roots in a prior process of racial formation disappear, but the category's exposure to state violence and force remains.[28]

In Volpi's text we can register the emergence of a new form of categorization, one based in the construction of a *mobile* ontological divide. This is the imaginary that begins to concretize, in the popular discursive sphere around the same time as Volpi's novel, into the figure of the *delincuente*. In the months after the Zapatista uprising in January 1994, then-President Zedillo was careful in his refusal to follow the lead of other political figures in the employment of criminalization discourses to describe the EZLN, always using instead more neutral terms like "los inconformes." Once the full extent of the financial crisis had hit, Zedillo's language swivelled, and in an address in February 1995, he began using the term delincuentes to describe the Zapatistas and communities supporting the EZLN.[29] Under the weight of multiple financial crises, no longer could indigenous struggles be contained and their violent repression justified by the discursive fields of *indigenismo* and mestizaje. In 1996 Zedillo's government would oversee the passage of the Ley Federal contra la Delincuencia Organizada, modelled after the U.S. RICO law, which increased the penalties for "organized crime" but which also turned this emergent discursive figure into a legal category and allowed the government a new range of repressive powers (wire-tapping, use of undercover agents, and seizure of assets) against any group at which it directed the delincuencia discourse.

Another key moment of public visibility of this new racializing formation was seen on September 27, 2004, when the NGO México Unido Contra la Delincuencia (Mexico United against Delinquency), in association with the conservative business groups Coparmex and Canacintra, brought out over 350,000 upper- and middle-class residents of Mexico City, all dressed in white, to protest "insecurity" and "delincuencia"—making clear the expanded class and racialized work the category had come to do in the intervening years.[30] Unlike previous racializing frames, what these uses of delincuencia show is how it is a discourse detached from both biology (a phenotypical definition of "race") and culture (a concept of "race" based in ethnicity or cultural markers).[31] For who is the delincuente? No one, but also everyone. Everyone, but also conveniently the same groups, the rural and urban poor and indigenous communities, who have resisted exploitation by state and capital throughout the twentieth century.[32] It is a mobile category that can be applied to anyone found dead in the street or anyone accused of organizing against the state—in sum, against anyone whose "morality" diverges from whatever the government names as its own. It is a category that morphs into the figure of *delincuencia organizada,* a phrase that dropped so casually and frequently from ex-President Felipe Calderón's lips as he launched his "guerra contra el narco." As we have seen on numerous occasions—such as the Masacre de Villas de Salvárcar, where sixteen schoolchildren between the ages of fifteen and twenty who were brutally murdered at a party were accused of being delincuentes—"delincuente" is a word whose mere shadow turns even the most innocent into disposable bodies. It is a term that in fact calls forth the "reality" which it purports to name and serves as a new cover for state violence against rising surplus populations, a state violence that now is also more mobile and in some ways less constrained or perhaps differently marked by geographical region and locale.

This is not to say, of course, that there is still no longer a relevant discourse about indigeneity or that racism based on aspirational whiteness and antiblackness has disappeared. Moreover, this is not to ignore the important changes in the state position toward indigenous communities, such as the inclusion of pluricultural language in the Mexican constitution (1992) and allowing for forms of indigenous self-governance (2001 for the majority of states).[33] What we can see in the construction of the figure of the delincuente is another form of adaptation, wherein the form that racist discourse took in its popular, vulgar version in the twentieth century has been extracted and generalized, but also rendered postracial. Which is not to say that this vulgar racist form is still not in circulation, but rather that the state and the far right parts of civil society, especially since the end of the 1990s, are relying more and more on the delicuencia discourse as a preferred means of social control against the poor, marginalized, and politicized. At the same time it is important to note that this shift to a "post-racial" formation is without a doubt driven in part by the success of indigenous groups in the late 1980s and 1990s in forcing open the sphere of representational politics whose closure had been justified by or explained away with the national popular racial formation.[34]

Are delicuencia and Volpi's ontological divide in some way racial structures? They are to the extent that they do the work of race; namely, to produce and police communities and bodies anew that were marked first by biologically or culturally racist discourses and to effect a new distribution of premature death in a moment of rising surplus population. In the twentieth century the racial formations of mestizaje/antiblackness and vulgar anti-indigenous racism produced groups with differentiated access to the means of social reproduction and with differentiated exposure to state violence. These racial formations envisioned certain bodies as forming part of the "nation," as deserving and needing integration into labor markets and capital flows. "Delincuencia" does this work now but it does so, we might say, without explicit reference to a racialized "content," that is, by other means. Those means are an ontological divide which is not fixed (as would be the case if it was merely a legal or moral category), but mobile and tendential, no longer tied (primarily) to nineteenth- and early twentieth-century notions of biology, culture, or territory and no longer entirely governed by an imputed spatial and cultural division between the urban and rural, modern and premodern. One result is that "delincuente"—while most often aimed at the poorest and most marginalized—names a potentially almost unlimited population; having disengaged from biology and culture, this distinction roams across potential bodies and spaces. While Volpi's work discussed in this chapter is not the only source of these new formations that do the work of racialization, his work participates in their construction and is a site where we can register their appearance and, most importantly, grasp how a shift to ontology is a necessary condition of their elaboration and how financial crisis forms a necessary part of the historical matrix of this new racial formation.[35] We could frame this in another way: if one privileged figure of finance is the salto (or the elongation of the distance between production and the realization of value), we can see in the category of the delincuente how this form has pressed upon and shaped racial discourse. As the relation between production and value has become more opaque and probabilistic, so too in some ways has the relation between the category of the delincuente and the individuals whose exposure to state violence and premature death it retroactively justifies.

Catastrophe and Ontology

In Volpi's work we can register not just a new natural philosophy in the turn to ontology but a new theory of history and temporality that flows from it and that is also conditioned by finance's rise and marks a second site of transmission between finance's form and the literary which, as we will see, also opens out onto a wider set of popular discourses. Volpi's contribution to the *Manifiesto Crack* is titled "¿Dónde quedó el fin del mundo?" (Where was the end of the world?). In it Volpi offers interpretations of the main Crack novels through conceptual figures he variously calls the "fifth rider," chaos, or "el fin del mundo":

> The end of the world can be believed and praised, as in *Memoria de los días*; can be reached by car or train, as in *Las Rémoras*; can be recalled and rebuilt in childhood and in the past, as in *La conspiración idiota*; can be cultivated inside oneself to the point of madness, as in *Si volviesen sus majestades*; and can also be granted to others as an infamous Pandora's box like in *El temperamento melancólico*. Be that as it may, in any one of these cases, nobody is free from this last illness, this fifth rider, this plague, and this entertainment: this last state of the heart.[36]

What is the connection between what I have been calling ontology and "the end of the world"? If we return to *Klingsor*, this question can be rephrased as: What happens when history becomes, instead of progress or modernization, a perpetual crisis, a series of false starts, or a set of uncontrollable events that leads not nowhere, but to unsettled endings, nonknowledge, and paralyzation? In a world of stagnating indeterminacy, like that of *Klingsor*, history becomes catastrophic and chaotic, the novel becomes eschatological, and the subject becomes structured not by the other as in Paz but by the experience of disastrous, unplanned events. When events have no causes, when every event is an unexpected blow, history is not over but rather can only be experienced as catastrophic.

In the twentieth century there have been two important loci for the thinking of catastrophe. In the first, moving out of the work of Heidegger and post-Holocaust philosophers like Jean Améry, catastrophe serves as a synonym for the depredations of modernity, technology, and the way they can combine to produce events like the Holocaust. The second is based in the work of Walter Benjamin who argued that "the concept of progress must be grounded in the idea of catastrophe. That things continue to 'go on' *is* the catastrophe."[37] For Benjamin, whose notion of catastrophe was elaborated under the conditions of German hyperinflation, a moment of early twentieth-century financial crisis, the catastrophe is the relentlessness of time continuing to move forward, the angel with its back turned with the debris of modernity piling up against its wings, the fact that no one has yet pulled the emergency break.[38]

Starting in the 1980s in the global North, catastrophe was rearticulated in a new context: the financialized economy. New senses of catastrophe and catastrophic risk emerged out of two parallel financialized shifts that began in the 1970s at the end of the postwar boom and that both produced new forms of risk and new forms of profiting from risk's production. The first shift was from the large-scale pooling of risks common during the welfare state to neoliberal forms of individualized risk—but which brought new systemic risks along with them—such as 401(k)s, individual health accounts, and adjustable rate mortgages. The second shift, very much connected to the first, was the turn to new financial instruments as a means of compensating for failing accumulation—instruments which drew on new ways of distributing risk, for example, securitized mortgages, derivatives, and pension funds dependent for their health on an ever-rising stock market. With these forms of finance, a new theorization of catastrophe emerges and spreads into popular cultural life in the global North: the catastrophic risk of the near future, the black swan.

"Black swan" was a term used in 2001 by Nassim Nicholas Taleb to describe catastrophic, unforeseen events—particularly financial ones—that occur without warning and are characteristic of, and perhaps limited to, areas such as economics, biology, and history, that involve organic and nonorganic matter and that are marked by extreme discontinuity. In Taleb's formulation black swans are events that are nearly impossible to predict based upon known conditions; they are located in a hazy gray area that, drawing on the science fiction genre, one might describe as the "near future."

Taleb's theory—in particular after 2007, though also before—was widely circulated and deployed to explain financial crises and to narrativize their return in the contemporary moment as a consequence of the emergence of new forms of financialized risk. As Taleb and others who picked up the term were quick to note, some of the central instruments that had driven the rise of finance in the global North—derivatives and securitization—attempted to profit from or protect against near-future events. These instruments had the, perhaps unwitting, effect of making the temporal space of the near future an important object of knowledge.[39]

The pace and form of the spread of these new instruments of finance are different in Mexico, however. The dismantling of the pension system didn't begin until 1995,[40] and while derivatives and securitization played a critical role directly before the 1994 crisis,[41] they are not widely discussed or theorized. The forms of catastrophic or unforeseen events that works like *Klingsor* meditate upon and mediate are those resulting not from near-future risk, but ongoing financial crises, as seen in 1982, 1987, and 1994, and this gives the elaboration of catastrophe or disaster as a theory of history in Mexican popular and high culture its special form and feeling. If the rise of finance in the global North is associated with the figure of the near future and cataclysm, in Mexico such disastrous events are less heroic, less singular—instead of majestic black swans we have dreaded ugly ducklings, instead of cataclysmic breakdown, we have perpetual crisis with no endpoint in sight.

Examples of disastrous, unforeseen events proliferate across *Klingsor*, from Bacon's love life to the actual building of the atomic bomb, but one of the most interesting is the already-discussed scene from the novel's preface which brings together the thematics of catastrophe, indeterminacy, and the slide into totalitarian will. The preface takes the form of a letter by the novel's narrator Gustav Links, but it is structured as a short story and opens with a voice saying "Basta de luz!" (Cut the light!)[42] The voice is Hitler's, and the preface recounts not from a first-person perspective, but rather an omniscient one, Hitler, as his regime crumbles around him, watching and rewatching films made especially for him of the torture of the enemies of his regime.

The opening setup of this scene links together political violence (as the antithesis of liberalism) with fanatical, excessive pleasure and repetition: "With the enthusiasm of a child who listens again to his favorite story, Hitler savored for the umpteenth time the show."[43] With the fall of the Reich imminent, Hitler is "obsessed with the irreality of cinema." What is Hitler's mistake; why is he obsessed with "irreality"? Hitler still believes in determinism, in cause and effect, and this is the source of his pleasure in the repetition of this cinematic irreality: "The succession of causes and effects began their ritual cycle, celebrated again and again according to the feelings occasioned in him by news coming from the front."[44] Causes and effects, proceeding from and preceding each other: this is irreality. What instead is the true nature of history? Links illustrates it as he moves from recounting the perverse repetition of Hitler's illiberalism based in the irreality of determinism to history as chance, catastrophe, and "golpes de suerte" (strokes of luck).

The first narrative of chance is a failed assassination attempt against Hitler. The attempt fails because of "a minimal error of calculation—a triviality: one of the bombs could not be activated or perhaps the briefcase was too far from the place where Hitler was sitting—sinking the plan."[45] Links, as a member of the cabal that planned the attack, is captured. However, on the day of his trial Allied forces launch their most intensive bomb attack on Berlin yet, and the trial judge is killed when part of the wall collapses and falls on him. Links brings these two events together under the sign of chance: "On the afternoon of July 20, 1944, a stroke of luck saved Hitler . . . the morning of February 3, another stroke of luck saved me."[46] This presents not just the problem of chance, but a problem of an imaginary as well, of the inability to give meaning to history: "I still don't know how logical—or sane—it is to establish a connection between these two events, but I do. Why do I insist, so many years after the fact, in connecting movements of chance which in the beginning had nothing to do with each other?"[47] Here we have another version of the novel's ontology that reality is indeterminate and that believing in determinism tendentially leads to illiberalism. Moreover, we have a struggle with the desire to make deterministic connections between what are random occurrences, mere golpes or blows.

I want to return to a passage I cited at this chapter's opening to bring out how this ontology of indeterminacy is connected to the figures of catastrophe, disaster, and destruction. If history is nothing but a series of strokes of luck, of unpredictable, chance events that occur without warning, then all history is catastrophe. All events are disastrous, as they occur without warning; even the positive ones, such as being liberated from a certain death penalty by the chance collapse of a wall (the fact that Gustav's introductory letter to the novel is dated November 10, 1989, the day of the "fall of the Wall" should not be missed here):

> Perhaps because other unforeseeable circumstances, no less terrible than these, have forced me to write these words. If I dare to join apparently unconnected facts, such as the salvation of Hitler and my own, it is because humanity has never been such a close witness to such catastrophic destruction. And our era, unlike other historical moments, has been largely determined by such twists of fate, those little signs that remind us of the

> ungovernable, chaotic nature of the realm in which we live. I propose, then, to tell the story of the century. *My* century. *My* version of how fate has ruled the world, and of how we men of science try in vain to domesticate its fury.[48]

The history of the twentieth century, in Volpi's version, is the discovery of chance at the heart of ontology—and the failure to "domesticate" it. As a result, we have not exactly the end of history, but the reign of chaos, of the catastrophic unforeseen. In the same way that chance as the heart of the ontological conditions politics in Volpi, it gives rise to a philosophy of history, one in which all events are disastrous, because they are chance events and occur without foresight, rhyme, or reason.[49] An ontology of chance gives rise to a concern with eschatology because it implies the end of meaning, the end of an ability to see systematicity, that is, those larger structures, as Elizabeth Wingrove has argued,[50] that determine the position of individuals and condition individual consciousness and experience. For a thinking of systematicity as a structuring of historical experience, *Klingsor* substitutes its negation, chaos, catastrophe, and "the end of the world."[51]

Thus in *Klingsor* there is only crisis, which first appears similar to the way near-future catastrophe comes to be thought of in global North discourses as a singularity. There is, however, a key difference; instead of a strictly financialized catastrophe, these unforeseen disasters have a peripheral financial tonality, because the temporality of crisis is different. Crisis or catastrophe is not the near-future singularity as it comes to be thought in the North, as what irrupts; rather it is the horizon of all experience. In *Klingsor* there is only the zero time or the repetition of catastrophe; there are no intermittent long waves of accumulation between the singularities of crises as in the global North. In Volpi's novelistic imaginary crisis is perpetual, failure is assured, and melancholy and paralyzation the dominant affective categories. In the global North crisis is a moment of creative destruction that makes possible a new cycle of accumulation, and as such it is viewed as sublime, as a terror, as what leaves traumatic traces deep in the subject, and as something to be both dreaded and awed. While in *Klingsor* instead of majestic black swans, we have fizzled hopes, ongoing crisis, and searches and investigations that end in frustration, betrayal, and giving up. This difference is the affective specificity of financial catastrophe in the semi-periphery.

We might say that the subjective category of disaster or catastrophe the novel presents is unique in these two features: First, it is generalized, as it sits on the horizon of any social situation. Second, it structures subjectivity, turning subjects into paralyzed figures incapable of acting, ones who are thrown forward by the golpes (blows) that uncertainty rains down upon them, as the characters of Links and Bacon are structured to a great extent by their inability to act and by their paralyzation in the face of unforeseen, disastrous events.

I have dwelt on this part of *Klingsor* because it is here we can register a conception of historical time which has circulated in a subterranean way in Mexico. While the "end of history" has been widely proclaimed (and critiqued) in the global North, the end of a belief in the promises of progress and modernity occurred within a different context in Mexico, that of almost twenty years of financial crisis. Instead of a sense of history as overcome, we have history as disaster and an unending series of shocks—ones that occur without apparent rhyme or reason. Perhaps the circulation of *desmadre* as a popular term of social adjudication reflects this sense of temporal disaster; a high cultural articulation of its sense of unyielding crisis as a metonym for Mexican social reality can be found in Roger Bartra's *Blood, Ink, and Culture: Miseries and Splendors of the Post-Mexican Condition* where he writes: "We can no longer critique Mexican culture in the name of modernity, of a liberal-inspired modernity that raised up the banner of 'progress.' We have to critique modernity from the standpoint I call dismodernity, or better yet—taking a cue from desmadre, Mexican slang for disorder—dismothernity."[52] Reading *Klingsor* allows us to register this specific sense of the end of history and of the ideologies of progress in its context of semi-peripheral financial crisis. It also allows us to ask a follow-up question to Volpi's proposal: that is, whether the only path through these new indeterminisms is to accept their most extreme versions and make a turn to ontology.

The Long Tail of Catastrophe and Ontology

Subjects structured by catastrophe and the concern with ontology do not end with the work of Jorge Volpi; rather they have filtered forward into later cultural work and in particular into the period of the drug war, where neither the catastrophes nor the instabilities have diminished.[53] For example, Sergio González Rodríguez's *El mal de origen* is a kaleidoscopic nonfiction work which turns around notions of the present as catastrophe, urban and ethical disintegration, and the potential for writing to be a critical force. The subject we find in *Mal* is one structured, much like Volpi's, by catastrophe: "In other words, the daily burden of catastrophe, that short-circuit between the human and the inhuman described by Annie Le Brun: at the bottom of every person lies an obsessive feeling of catastrophe, like a distant echo of far-reaching drives, whose extent sometimes we perceive 'with astonishment but whose origin eludes us.' What to do?"[54] While in Heriberto Yépez's *El imperio de la neomemoria*, a book concerned with the links between imperialistic U.S. culture and memory, gives its final pages to ontological speculation; the universe, as Yépez writes, "is not":

> The world is an archipelago in time. Each universe is a macro-island that in its own consistency, pulses. But space-time mutates, and its information is lost forever and where before was its body, there is now another obeying different laws, and between universe and universe, the illusion of fixity. If synchronically there are parallel universes—each ruled by its own laws—also diachronically heteroclite chaosmoses disappear and appear, separated from each other by an uncrossable abyss, by a pulsating irregularity. Science becomes an absurdity if it doesn't heed that principles discovered today will serve only for a certain, indeterminate, perishing space-time, because life is a life always inside another death. All memory is temporary. All laws will perish. All history has limits. All texture, loses its plot.[55]

Whereas *Klingsor* grounds its ontology in indeterminacy, Yépez's vision of indeterminacy is distinct: it is not that there are no rules but rather that the rules can change at any time, that "all laws perish." Yépez's vision both converges and diverges with that of Volpi; it is possible that there could be moments of stability (a given set of laws), but it is equally possible that the universe could be subject to an even more savage version of indeterminacy with its ontology (its "laws") transforming every minute or even every second, all without warning or without reason.

What a reading of Volpi's work demonstrates is the deep roots of the tropes of ontology and catastrophe within a response to financial and state crisis and their continuing importance in both literary and popular discursive spheres. As long as capitalists and states continue to attempt to solve the long downturn that began in the 1970s with failed finance-led accumulation, it appears that in cultural production catastrophe will continue to serve as a theory of history (forming a partial ground for subjectivity) and ontology as a fraught way station in the storm of the national popular's demise and unending financial crisis.

Ontology in Its Historicity

What I have been calling in this chapter, following Volpi, "indeterminacy" is a question that goes to the very heart of the historical formation of capitalist finance, which has always been linked both to states and their war machines and to the science of probability underpinning them and the problems of belief and decision those sciences and states give rise to.

While this is not the place for a full discussion of these relations, it is possible to make a few brief gestures toward a historical account. As Ian Hacking has argued probability underwent the first of many modern revolutions around 1640 as part of a shift to new financial instruments to fund colonial trade and exploitation and the military apparatus to support them.[56] One way of understanding modern probability theory is as the science of limiting chance or as the mathematics of the nondeterministic world which finance and financial speculation require.

That is, moments of finance-led accumulation require, at least in thought that is engaged in supporting this accumulation or deeply marked by its historical conditions, a recognition of some form of indeterminacy as a component of the natural, economic, and social worlds. This recognition, however, frequently leads to crises of belief (of despair over nondetermination and human inability to parse and predict the future) and a turn to decisionism, as states and state reason prefer, if not tightly welded, then delimited yet fungible intellectual formations. Despair over indeterminacy, frequently palpable in moments of financial ascendency, is the antechamber of decisionism.

Carl Wennerlind's superb *Casualties of Credit: The English Financial Revolution 1620–1720* gives us another window into the historical connections between finance, probability, and theories of the natural and social world. Wennerlind's work demonstrates how the movement between "the Renaissance world of credit to that of the [English] Financial Revolution" required "a radically transformed worldview that drew extensively on developments in natural philosophy and political theory."[57] This new worldview turned precisely on questions of probability and determinability: "Leaving behind the traditional notion that mankind exists in a material, social and economic world that is finite, static and knowable, mid seventeenth-century political economists embraced the ideas of infinite worlds, nature's perfectibility, and probabilistic knowledge. With these component parts, they constructed a new worldview in which mankind's purpose was to ceaselessly pursue new methods for the infinite improvement of nature, society, and mankind."[58] This intellectual foundation was provided, in part, by a group of alchemically inclined thinkers, the Hartlib circle, who "believed that wealth was potentially infinite, [thus] they needed to find a way to expand the money stock proportionally to the ever-expanding world of goods."[59] Along with the idea of "money" as a sign of value, rather than a carrier of it, this formed the philosophical foundation for the creation of credit in the modern sense. While the present day has perhaps not seen such a transformative revolution in the nature of credit, nor a radically new intellectual project providing the bases for it, there is a way in which a similar set of connections have emerged between probability, finance, and ontology. But rather than a new ontological vision providing a foundation for financial expansion, it has served as a way station from finance. By way of conclusion I want to draw out how, in the work of Volpi but also across much of the social theory produced in this period, ontology has become a site for working through these new forms of indeterminacy produced by finance.

In the preface to the second edition of their *Hegemony and Socialist Strategy*, Laclau and Mouffe narrate the theoretical impasse of Marxism in the 1970s. In the face of the ongoing restructuring driven by the global downturn, there was an increasing gap between capitalist realities and what the theory could describe. This gave rise in their account to two options: retreat into the orthodox bunker or give an ad hoc descriptive account of the new conditions. Laclau and Mouffe describe their approach as a third, more rigorous option: they seek the preconditions of Marxian categories and new possibilities for their use. Their approach however is not just a rethinking but rather is cast in terms of renewing the ontological paradigm that underpins Marxist categories:

> There is one aspect in particular that we want to underline at this point. Any substantial change in the ontic content of a field of research leads also to a new ontological paradigm. Althusser used to say that behind Plato's philosophy, there was Greek mathematics; behind seventeenth-century rationalism, Galilean physics; and behind Kant's philosophy, Newtonian theory. . . . The ontology implicit in Freudianism, for instance, is different and incompatible with a biologist paradigm. From this point of view, it is our conviction that in the transition from Marxism to post-Marxism, the change is not only ontic but also ontological. The problems of a globalized and information led society are unthinkable within the two ontological paradigms governing the field of Marxist discursivity: first the Hegelian, and later the naturalistic.[60]

What motivates the need for this change of ontological paradigm in Laclau and Mouffe is "structural undecidability" which forms "the very condition of hegemony."[61] As they write: "If as shown in the work of Derrida, undecidables permeate the field which had previously been seen as governed by structural determination, one can see hegemony as a theory of the decision taken in an undecidable terrain. Deeper levels of contingency require hegemonic—that is, contingent—articulations."[62]

The turn of Laclau and Mouffe to ontology has not been an isolated event. All across the realm of social theory, the last thirty years have witnessed with different inflections and temporalities versions of an ontological turn. In the field of political theory Stephen White has noted how the work of well-known anti-foundationalists, such as Judith Butler, William Connolly, George Kateb, and Charles Taylor, do not sustain that anti-foundationalism when it comes to describing the political. White argues that these theorists have recourse to "weak ontology," in a way that is perhaps similar, as we have seen above, to Volpi. As Carsten Strathausen has noted, Hardt and Negri, Badiou, Agamben, and Žižek have all turned in different ways to ontology:

> The term "ontology" occupies an increasingly prominent place in current politico-philosophical discourse. "Political philosophy forces us to enter the terrain of ontology," declare Michael Hardt and Antonio Negri. . . . Ernesto Laclau recently said that he has "concentrated on the ontological dimension of social theory." . . . Giorgio Agamben's critique of the state of exception and of today's concentration camps is intimately tied to his ontological reflections regarding our potential existence beyond sovereign power: "Until a new and coherent ontology of potentiality" has been found, he argues, "a political theory freed from the aporias of sovereignty remains unthinkable." . . . Likewise, Alain Badiou's political writings are intertwined with his mathematical ontology of set-theory, and Slavoj Zizek's exhortation to return to the legacy of Lenin in order to combat global capitalism remains inseparable from his ontological determination of capital as the real.[63]

As Strathausen also notes it is perhaps a little strange to see so many critical theorists grounding their work in ontology, which for a good part of the twentieth century, due to the connection between Heidegger and German fascism, was considered an entirely conservative discourse, anathema to any left, anticapitalist thought. While not all of these ontological turns, either in the form of new ontological thought or as critiques of ontology, engage in the same direct way as Laclau and Mouffe with chance and "undecidability," what we can see in each is a generalized search for a new site of theoretical construction after the decline of the global socialist imaginary—in the face of the long downturn and rise of finance—via discussions and critiques of ontology, whether that be one that privileges indeterminacy, one that heroically argues against indeterminacy's destabilization of modern philosophy, or one that critiques ontologization without opening out of a philosophical frame.[64] Much as in Volpi, left academic social theory faced with the uncertainties of a moment of failed finance-led accumulation and ongoing crisis has had recourse to the way station of debates concerning ontology. There is then a limitation to these new forms of social theory: the force and processes of political economy which has shaped their conditions of possibility and against which their turns to and critiques of ontology occur—that is, the rise of finance—are to a great extent nowhere addressed in their theoretical interventions.

If we pull back for a second from Laclau and Mouffe's self-presentation, we can locate their work in a longer tradition of philosophical Marxism that intensified in the 1970s, starting from the work of Althusser (but stretching back to Lukács, whose late-life project was the volumes published as *The Ontology of Social Being*), which represented a turn away from political economy, of state and capital as a system, and a turn to philosophy, specifically to, as Laclau and Mouffe point out, ontology. Without a doubt there was a crisis of Marxist critique in the 1970s, and much of the work generated out of these turns to, as well as critiques of, ontology has expanded the vocabulary of Marxist social theory. The issue I want to raise, however, is that there is a tendency in this work, exemplified by Laclau and Mouffe, that as ontology moves to the fore, discussions of political economy recede. Precisely at the moment in which global political economy is passing through a major restructuring, at the moment for a redoubling of attention to political economy, it disappears from certain forms of social theory.

The position I want to advance is not that all discussions and critiques of ontology and ontologization are bad, a mistake, or a distraction from the "real work" of anticapitalist theory, but rather I want to draw attention to how, in these turns to ontology or its critique, social theory has had difficulty tracking at the same time transformations in political economy and their implications. Instead of a discussion of how these "new" indeterminacies that have so changed the perceived possibilities of the political are related and conditioned by finance as a consequence of the long downturn, we have a preoccupation with ontology and a postdating of the question of whether such indeterminacies are now eternal (ontological) features of our worlds or potentially transitory, the product of a specific conjuncture of historical conditions.

At the beginning of this chapter, I argued that the presence of finance in production makes possible new forms of crisis or instability and discussed the work of Kojin Karatani who has used the figure of a leap of faith or salto mortale to describe the forms of instability, uncertainty, or indeterminacy that finance generates. As finance came to dominate after 1973, as it became an increasingly necessary component for and supplement to production, the leaps—the saltos—became more and more risky, the temporality between production and realization of a commodity's value more and more disjunct, and the circuits between the productive and financial economy more and more torturous, uncertain, and involved. As finance increasingly extends the temporal distance between the production and the realization of value, making possible new forms of speculation, the turn to decisionism and ontology as either a safe ground or as the ground of a proof that a political subject is no longer possible, intensifies in depth and desire. However, indeterminacy in the post-1973 period is neither as hopeful nor as barren as Laclau and Mouffe and Volpi, respectively, make it out to be. To resist these ontological turns, we will have to see that the salto is a specific figure of finance's rise, and to contest this rise, we will have consider, not how to resolve or postpone the destabilizing indeterminacies that now populate our social and personal worlds, but rather how to address the crises of failed financial accumulation that have given rise to them.

CHAPTER 2

The Failures of Finance

BRAZILIAN URBAN PERIPHERIES AND THE SOCIALIZATION OF CRISIS

> —You said before that you didn't steal anything, you just "carried a few things home." But if you take something that isn't yours, isn't that stealing?
>
> —Well, those things weren't exactly mine, no. But let me tell you something. About a year ago when that store opened, everyone in the neighborhood bought stuff—on the "easy credit plan," they called it. I bought a blender because my wife wanted one real bad. She'd seen some ads and really liked them. I also bought a TV so we could have a little entertainment at home. And then comes this problem of the bad unemployment we're in. I still got no job. So, anyway, I missed two monthly payments and I went down there to explain why. But they didn't want to hear about it, they came and took the television and the blender and everything. And they didn't even give back the eight payments I made. No job and no TV. So I figured they owed me something, and I was just being, like, compensated. But I only took what I thought was fair.
>
> **Ignácio de Loyola Brandão, *Zero*, p. 161**

Though divided by the historical experience of formal dictatorship, what Mexico and Brazil shared in the moment after the debt crisis of 1982 was a breakdown in systems of social and racial control and turns in intellectual and cultural production that were marked by this experience. In the national space of Brazil the debt crisis was inflected by the fraying of money's fiction and accelerated state violence, applied with true brutality in the peripheral zones of large metropolitan areas. These breakdowns led to an upsurge in intellectual and cultural production aimed at peripheral urban areas that refashioned, in critical and complicated ways, discursive and racial formations. While the previous chapter in the context of Mexico registered the fraught leaps finance makes possible, in Brazilian cultural and intellectual production on peripheral urban zones we are faced with the violence that follows finance's failures and the supplements to racializing discourses that spring up in their wake.

In this chapter I build an account of how the emergence of hyperinflation, the fraying social synthesis of exchange, and the socialization of crisis moved alongside increasing police and state violence in urban areas. I do so in order to center the emergence of a set of discourses on the "divided city," in Rio de Janeiro specifically, which helped bring order to an urban space in flux, crisis, and contestation. Through a reading of Zuenir Ventura's work and public security discourses, I argue that the idea of a divided or broken city, marked by an absolute division between two types of urban space and by an absence of the state in peripheral communities, should be read alongside both histories of financial crisis and the foundering of racial democracy, the racial ideology that asserts Brazil as a country without racial prejudice or discrimination. While divided city discourses have already received numerous critiques, my approach will be to think of them in the context of this socialization of crisis and an impasse in forms of racialized control.

Drawing on strains of heterodox Marxist thought focused on the power of abstractions and impersonal forms of domination, I leverage this discussion of divided city discourses to examine how two of the central cultural works that emerge out of this period, Paulo Lins's novel *Cidade de Deus* (*City of God*) and the infamous cinematic touchstone *Tropa de elite*, animate and contest these ideas of urban division. I will also make visible the strange force of these renewed abstractions of urban space and society as marked by an absolute separation and trace the difficulties of and possibilities for cultural texts, in a moment of the fraying of racialized order and the social synthesis of exchange, to escape their pull.

This chapter aims to construct a partial account for such difficulties and potentialities by positioning these works and this moment in a longer history of the rise of finance and ongoing financial crisis and by focusing in particular on histories of hyperinflation. I triangulate between three features shared by many moments of financial crisis—socialization of crisis, popular rebellion and unrest, and racialized state violence—in order to track how the valorization of finance capital requires state and structural violence and to examine how in this moment spatialized discursive figures come to wield the forces inherent in both racialization and real abstraction.

Dictatorship, Crisis, and State Violence

In 1964 the state apparatus in Brazil was taken over by a junta of military leaders, who instituted one of Latin America's longest running dictatorships and who continued in contradictory ways parts of the national popular program of the Vargas era (1930–1945). The Brazilian dictatorship purged "nationalists," especially those on the Left, which represented at least formally a break with national popular politics. In terms of economics the dictatorship largely steered a path between the then–IMF recommended "shock stabilization" and a national development framework. For example, instead of orthodox wage controls, the military government opted for an at first ad hoc indexing strategy to control inflation while at the same time softening the blow of inflation on workers' wages.[1] Though the military government attacked leftists and populists who supported national development strategies, the dictatorship did not move to dismantle large state-run enterprises. Rather they reorganized them and outlined a different version of a "tripod" development plan based, in part, on attracting foreign capital and channeling it into sectors, particularly export ones, of the economy.[2] Thus in Brazil the years leading up to the debt crisis of 1982 were marked by an extension of state-led development policies but with a greater exposure to international capital flows.[3]

In the late 1970s, as the country was hit with waves of illegal strikes and the military government had difficulty winning popular elections in key states, it was clear that the dictatorship, after the economic "boom" years of the early 1970s, was beginning to lose control both in economic and political terms.[4] Much like Mexico, after a period of growth from 1968 to 1973 (in Brazil, GDP grew 7.9 percent per year),[5] Brazil went in heavily on foreign debt, beginning a shift to finance-primed accumulation in the midst of a global economic slowdown and the local impact of rising oil prices after 1973. Contracting debt at an extraordinary rate, Brazil became the largest debtor nation in the world: in 1981 its foreign debt totaled US$61.4 billion with a debt service per year of US$7 billion or 65.6 percent of total exports.[6]

Another key difference between the dictatorship and the strictly national popular period in Brazil was with respect to state violence. While Vargas, once the Prestes rebellion was put down in 1935, leaned on corporatist methods and nationalist cultural projections to control labor and integrate dissent, the dictatorship built a terrifying apparatus of state violence and repression, as both Maria Helena Moreira Alves and Caco

Barcellos have demonstrated. Moreira Alves notes that even before the dictatorship took power it had amassed files on four hundred thousand Brazilian citizens.[7] In *Rota 66* Barcellos demonstrates how in São Paulo the military apparatus that was constructed to defeat the urban guerrilla was transferred to policing the populations of the urban periphery with deadly results. In 1981, four years before the official end of the dictatorship, there were two thousand killings in Rio's Baixada Fluminense, a number of which were thought to be the work of state or state-linked forces; many of the bodies were buried in a cemetery whose gates bore a symbol adopted by police-linked death squads, leading to speculation that the cemetery was a dumping ground for the illegally executed.[8] The expansion of state-directed and state-permitted violence used to control peripheral populations in large metropolises is a distinguishing feature of the dictatorship. While the dictatorship continued to deploy (and contest with left nationalist elements for dominance of) a national popular cultural imaginary, it also partially replaced the national popular emphasis on national culture as the unifying element of the nation with state violence.[9]

The so-called "transition to democracy" was not marked by the dismantling of these systems of state violence. A political scientist and specialist in the legacy of Brazil's military government, Jorge Zaverucha has argued that sociologists and politicians who claim that Brazil has completely exited its authoritarian moment and "consolidated" its democracy are quite mistaken:

> Certainly, [these authors] have forgotten that the National Security Law, the Penal and Military Processing Codes, the decree stipulating that the reserve forces of the Military Police [*polícia militar*] are part of the information network of the army, the Law of the Press, the Statute on Foreigners, and the decree that regulates the saving of data, information, documents and materials obtained by covert means in the interests of the security of society and the state, all continue on the books. And if there hasn't been a show of military strength, it is because the civil authorities have bowed before military pressure when they threatened to deploy the mechanisms of military strength.[10]

While there were attempts in the 1980s in the large metropolitan centers of Rio and São Paulo to reform or restrain police power, by the end of the 1980s these attempts were soundly defeated.[11] As Zaverucha argues, rather than a repeal of the dictatorship's National Security Law, in the "democratic" era we have its continuation which is then paired with a "militarization of public security."[12]

When the debt crisis hit in 1982, inflation spiked and the populations hardest hit by the weakened buying power of their wages and by unemployment began to rebel. On April 4, 1983, a march against unemployment set off a week of looting around São Paulo, including one spree of 3,500 persons in the center of São Paulo who attacked almost two hundred commercial establishments.[13] In September a week of looting involving thousands of individuals occurred in Rio across multiple points in the periphery.[14] After the descent into the debt crisis and the recession that followed, the state was concerned with both these dynamics: putting an end to inflation and controlling the civil unrest in poor urban areas resulting from the devastating unemployment that the debt crisis caused and from the erosion of real wages precipitated by spiraling inflation.[15] The importance of state violence as a strategy of control can be given by a single number: in the year 1992 more people were killed by the São Paulo police alone than during all the years of the military dictatorship.[16] While it has been critiqued for possibly overestimating the number of deaths,[17] R. S. Rose's work convincingly demonstrates a turn to state-sponsored or permitted killing as a technique of social control: Rose finds that deaths attributable to police death squads in the states of Rio de Janeiro and São Paulo hovered under one hundred during the 1970s—by the end of the 1980s they averaged more than one thousand per year and stayed at that level throughout the 1990s for São Paulo and above five hundred for Rio de Janeiro.[18] Rose's work also demonstrates that in these killings black and other nonwhite males and females were disproportionately represented, and Jaime Amparo Alves's recent signal contribution has demonstrated the awful continuation of these dynamics into the present.[19] Even if other estimates of the number of deaths by police and police-linked formations in Rio and São Paulo are numerically lower, they nonetheless demonstrate a consistent and elevated level of state-permitted death differentiated along racial lines.[20] In other words, once the decision was made to not default on Brazil's international debt, some social group had to pay, and as is common, the Brazilian state enforced the socialization of its debt onto the poor and working class and then turned to state violence as one means to ensure the success of this socialization.

Socialization of the Crisis

In Brazil the debt crisis, which dragged on throughout the 1980s and 1990s, resulted in mass unemployment, the growth of informal labor and poverty, and the expansion of "informal" urban areas. The federal government eventually capitulated to the IMF's debt restructuring demands, and Jackie Roddick's assessment of the effects of the crisis reveals the devastation: "By the end of 1983, the average wage had fallen by about 15 per cent since the beginning of 1980. . . . Nationally, there were about four million people unemployed, and another eight million under-employed, none of them receiving unemployment benefit or social welfare payments of any kind. These people together made up about a third of the country's economically active population."[21] Privatization and liberalization of the economy arrived with the election of the governments of Collor and Cardoso, between 1989 and 1997 over one million industrial jobs were lost in Brazil and between 1994 and 2001 average real wages fell by 8 percent.[22] In 1980, 24.3 percent of the population was classified as poor, but by 1988 that number had increased to 39.3 percent,[23] with all the attendant effects on life outcomes, premature death, and deterioration of living standards that lie behind such figures.

There is here an important but often overlooked link between rising state violence and the socialization of financial crisis, or the need to force the working class and the poor, through wage losses and social program cuts, to pay for a crisis they did not create. Thomas Marois has defined the socialization of financial risk, or what I will call socialization of crisis:

> The strengthening of state authorities' capacity to socialize mounting financial risks is one of the most significant manifestations of this shift in capital–labor power relations within the state. This is most evident at times of crisis when the socialization of financial risks is demanded to avoid systemic collapse. Thus, as the Bank of England Governor, Mervyn King, so bluntly put it, the price of 'financial crisis is being borne by people who absolutely did not cause it.' Even mainstream economists cannot help but acknowledge that state-led financial rescues represent a transfer of resources from present and future taxpayers to bankers. . . . Interpreted under a Marxian lens, this form of socialization represents a struggle over the allocation of present and future social resources (insofar as state bonds, or fictitious capital, help cover the costs of rescue) collected by and distributed through the state apparatus.[24]

One way this struggle over the allocation of future resources occurred in Brazil was through the very mechanism of inflation itself. In moments of inflation and hyperinflation capitalists attempt to pass profits lost to inflation onto consumers and workers by raising prices. Workers, on the other hand, attempt to recoup wage losses and decreased buying power through social struggle. Due in part to the strength of working class movements, in 1979 the government of Figueiredo began indexing wages semi-annually to inflation: meaning that wages were, in theory, adjusted twice a year to keep pace with inflation.[25] While the history of inflation, the politics of different forms of indexation, and their link to the socialization of crisis in Brazil deserves a deeper treatment, what is important for the narrative here is that, despite partial wage indexation, the burden of structural adjustment in the years after 1982, whether measured as income distribution or the overall wage bill, fell disproportionately on the poor and working class.[26]

Thus two decades before "Too Big to Fail" became a hashtag (#TBTF) in North Atlantic countries, before bank bailouts in the trillions of dollars, before "quantitative easing," the Brazilian state made a decision (as did Mexico and others) that their federal governments would be responsible for and not default on the debt of state entities and corporations and, in so doing, make the least advantaged social sectors bear the brunt of the debt crisis and then currency crises. This was "Too Big to Fail" before there was a name for it, and this is an example of a form of indirect or structural violence particular to states during moments of financial crisis across the long downturn: Mexico and Brazil were not the first to socialize massive debt onto the bodies least able to support paying for it, nor will those countries affected by the 2007–2008 financial crisis be the last.

There is yet another way we could turn this concept of socialization, putting it into the framework of finance as defined by an elongation or shortening of the passage from the production of a commodity to the realization of its value. As I have argued finance makes possible an expansion of the circuit of M-C-M' (money–commodity–money) and the production of fictitious values in the gap between a commodity's production (C) and its realization as value (M'). Financial crisis, one could say, is a moment in which Cs fail to turn into M's or when M's, which represent claims on future surplus value, are revealed to be just that: claims, assertions, but not value itself. Another way of describing socialization is as the state stepping in to complete the circuit of value production that is in danger of failing. When enterprises take out loans (or banks make bad ones) and the state absorbs their debt or refuses to default on or renegotiate its own and forces working-class and poor individuals to pay (through service cuts, wage de-indexation, allowing inflation to rise, etc.), they have effectively forced the working class and poor to complete a form of the C–M' circuit. As Latin American countries during the 1970s, 1980s, and 1990s became critical sites for the valorization of international financial capital, in order to impose this socialization of debt and complete the failed *saltos* of finance, states have turned to new articulations of racialization and state violence.

The Fiction of Money

As numerous articles in the popular and academic press attest, the intensification of inflation after the debt crisis in 1982 laid bare the fungibility and instability of money.[27] In 1988 the money that in 1986 would have bought a car, would not have been enough to purchase a set of tires. In 1989–1990 inflation was peaking at 2,700 percent per year.[28] Supermarkets began changing prices every week in order to not lose money simply due to inflation, and consumers invented numerous ingenious strategies for attempting to avoid having their money lose value just by holding on to it. While credit cards had penetrated into the Brazilian upper classes by the end of the 1970s, it was during the period of hyperinflation that they became a possible end-around on paper money. Items purchased with a card produced a hidden discount, especially with inflation at 10–20 percent per month, in that one could make purchases at lower prices and then pay later (usually up to forty days) with money that one perhaps did not have the month before.[29] This, of course, was a strategy available only to those earning solidly middle-class and above salaries. While not fully explanatory of its rise, the turn to drug logistics in peripheral communities can be read in this light as well: in a time of hyperinflation, without access to other financial devices, one of the few alternative supplements for poor or working-class communities were the superprofits of the drug trade.

In Karl Marx's theorization, money is a paradoxical object. On the one hand, it serves as a universal equivalent: it is coinage, pieces of paper, bits of data that are used to exchange commodities. At the same time money is itself a commodity; that is, it can be bought and sold, and this is where exchange rates and currency speculation come from. In the first volume of *Capital*, Marx outlines how there is a certain type of capitalist crisis that turns on the paradoxical nature of money. In a normally functioning economy, capitalists pursue money and profit as if it was their only desire—in these moments money is seen as a real representation and holder of value. However, there are moments when the fiction of money is revealed and money suddenly transforms from an agreed-upon holder of value to merely worthless pieces of paper.[30] Hyperinflation and currency crises are two such moments where the fiction of money as a holder and measure of value is exposed and anyone who can trades their worthless paper for something that appears to be a more stable form of value: another currency, commodities, or precious metals such as gold. Crises in which the fiction of money is revealed are both cyclical and disturbing. Without this fiction the simple, repetitive exchanges that are constitutive of sociality (buying groceries, being paid by one's job, taking out credit to make educational or commodity purchases to improve quality of life) and the horizons of stability that make these exchanges possible break down.

The hyperinflation of the 1980s and 1990s in Brazil was a prolonged moment of the denaturalization of money's fiction. An interesting aspect of this moment is that the very basis of this crisis came to form part of the solution. That is, if money was an agreed-upon fiction, what was necessary was a currency that people would believe would be stable (in addition to macroeconomic conditions that would enable it to be). As a result, starting with the Sarney government's Plano Cruzado in 1986, Brazilian governments banked on the idea that creating a new currency along with other appropriate measures would restore confidence in the fiction of money. In 1994 the government of Itamar Franco, under the guidance of then–finance minister Fernando Henrique Cardoso, launched yet another inflation stabilization program, introducing yet another currency, the Real. This currency, pegged to the dollar, along with another strenuous set of measures to reduce the money supply, was finally able to control inflation and remains Brazil's currency to date.[31] While the Plano Real stabilized the currency and inflation, the government was forced to borrow in order to prop up the currency, leading to its overvaluation and high levels once again of short-term debt. This combination of an overvaluation of the currency and dependency on rolling over short-term debt, led to speculative attacks on the Real and a forced devaluation in 1998 and yet another deep financial crisis in 1999.[32]

In the aftermath of the debt crisis there was a breakdown in the reality and stability of the Brazilian currency and the creation of a day-to-day wondering at the failure of exchange and at the fungability of a fundamental building block of commerce and social interaction. For those who were formally employed, inflation meant that their wages, despite formal or informal forms of indexing, were worth less and less. For those who were in the swelling ranks of the unemployed or those in the informal economy, the basic commodities needed to survive were increasingly out of reach. Diminished possibilities for life were met not with increased state support but rather increasing state violence. Thus, the spread of post-dictatorship violence is intimately connected with the post–debt crisis phenomena of inflation and unemployment and the decline of the social synthesis performed by exchange and money.[33]

Space, Race, and Division

As instability and intensified forms of state and social violence spread across urban spaces in the 1980s and 1990s, there were a resurgence, renewal, and recycling of discourses on favelas and peripheral areas as defined by separation or what Alba Zaluar and Marcos Alvito have called "dualism" or "duality."[34] The idea, particularly in Rio de Janeiro, of a split between formal and informal parts of the city has an extensive history, and the notion of peripheral areas as zones of incorrigible criminality has long been used by police and state forces to justify their frequent and deadly incursions.[35] I want to focus here on two discursive nodes drawn from popular journalism and public security which conjured Rio de Janeiro as a divided city, marked by a polarization between two kinds of space and by an absence of the state in peripheral areas. As the range of sophisticated academic work, which mobilized the very different but occasionally linked notions of divided city, social apartheid, and social exclusion, is too vast to summarize and to generalize about, my approach focuses narrowly on these two articulations due to the visibility of their authors. I do so in order to illustrate how these works produce an ordering of urban space strongly marked by polarization and state absence and then turn to cultural works which interact in critical and contradictory ways with these renewed imaginaries of division and separation.

The locus classicus of urban space defined as a divided or broken city is Zuenir Ventura's widely read and debated 1994 book, *Cidade partida.* In August 1993 police forces massacred twenty-one residents of the favela Vigário Geral. Ventura, a well-known journalist and author, spent several months in the favela interviewing residents and accompanying the work of the civil society group Viva Rio in organizing a response to the massacre. *Cidade partida* chronicles Ventura's experiences and theories of Rio as an urban space, and in its opening pages he defines his idea of the broken or divided city:

> Truth be told, during this century, from the reform of Pereira Passos to the Agache and Doxiadis plans, separation, if not segregation was always the program. The city was civilized and modernized by expelling its second-class citizens to the hills and outskirts.
>
> The result of this policy was a broken city. Putting it back together will take perhaps the next century, but we must start now—because the politics of exclusion have been a disaster. Not only moral and humanitarian, but also from the point of view of effectiveness. Its main product, social apartheid, runs the risk of having the fate which racial apartheid had elsewhere.
>
> The fantasy of the final solution—removal and extermination—proved equally as disastrous, iniquitous and impractical. At the end of the last century there was only one favela in Rio; at the end of this century they are more than five hundred.[36]

This passage constellates many of the thematics of Ventura's articulation of the divided city: a heavily spatial view of the urban, as opposed to one focused on differential inclusion or flows of capital, persons and goods; an argument that favelas were zones characterized by an absence of the state, despite frequent and violent police incursions; and a political imaginary of a vaguely defined "inclusion" as the solution to exclusion.

The idea of Rio as a city divided received, as the useful work of Enrique Desmond Arias has noted, an inflection in discourses on public security as well. In his detailed examination of relationships between trafficking groups and the state, Arias names one of the dominant schools of thought on public security and peripheral urban areas, "the 'divided city' approach." His excellent summation of its emergence in the period after the mid-1980s is worth quoting at length:

> The "divided city" approach argues that since the mid-1980s, favelas, as a result of varied and complex forms of state policy failure, have emerged as "feudal" bastions of criminal dominance set apart from the rest of the city. Roberto Kant de Lima, an anthropologist studying security issues in Rio, states, "The bandits do not follow the same norms as the State. They create a state within a state." Rubem César Fernandes, an NGO leader, argues that "organized crime is growing in these regions, imposing on them a regime of unchecked violence." For Fernandes, the "parallel power and tyrannical rule" of these organizations "is impossible to contain . . . without abolishing the division between the civilized center and the margins excluded from civil rights."
>
> Luiz Eduardo Soares, a sociologist and former national secretary for public security, writes: "The territorial control of the bandits subtracts the zones of urban poverty from the national State and creates an archipelago of independent areas, a species of clandestine feudal barony, nonetheless visible, that the rule of law cannot reach, where democratic institutions, the Constitution, and the law do not operate." These observers, and many others, see Rio as a "divided city," where poor areas are separated from the polity and dominated by a premodern form of authoritarian rule.[37]

Arias brings out how these arguments, especially as he notes in their "cruder, journalistic, iterations," depend on seeing favelas and the periphery as areas the state is "absent from and unable to penetrate."[38] Arias argues that this approach produces a deep split between a "dangerous feudal underworld on the city's hillsides" and "the life of the wealthy seashore neighborhoods,"[39] and he makes a dual critique: first, rather than an absence of the state in the favelas and periphery, there are "deep connections" between state officials and traffickers, and second, that the imaginary of absolute division presents a false vision of favelas and peripheral areas as zones cut off from the rest of the city, as dominated by violent traffickers, and as representing an existential threat to the virtuous, law-abiding remainder of the city.[40]

These discourses of a divided city have received numerous critiques in the years since, and in particular Ventura's work has generated a direct and poignant response from Jailson de Souza e Silva, one of the founders of Observatório de Favelas (Favela Observatory) in the Maré.[41] Writing in an open letter to Ventura, he explains that residents of the favelas and peripheries have always had to "circulate" in the city, in search of work, recreation, and cultural activities. Souza e Silva notes that these residents have also had to pressure public authorities to fulfill their obligations. He continues:

> In this case, the city is crossed by a set of practices of circulation that make it, for the poor, not "divided" at least not in terms of their insertion into a territory, in a totalizing way. They seek to live in the city fully.
>
> I think it might be more appropriate to say that the "State is divided" because it, dominated by an interest in serving only specific social groups, does not fulfill its so-called "universal role." Likewise, we have a "divided market," because, dominated by prejudices and narrow views of cost-benefit relations, it has never recognized all residents of the city as full citizens.[42]

If problematic on a conceptual level, the divided city idea has also been criticized on an empirical one, notably in the work of Luiz Cesar Ribeiro. Ribeiro's work demonstrated that the problem is not division but rather the self-segregation of elites and revealed not an increasing polarization of urban space into two zones but rather a pervasive inequality woven in complex ways throughout the city's structure.[43]

While ideas of informal areas or favelas as defined or marked by an idea of separation have a long history, these discursive inflections of a divided or broken city marked by absolute separation and absence of the state appear within a moment of prolonged financial crisis and of a decomposition in a critical piece of the Brazilian racial formation, racial democracy. The argument that I want to advance is that to capture the work that these inflections of formal-informal separation do, especially in their public security form, it is necessary to read them alongside both histories of financial crisis and of a breakdown in forms of racialized control.

During the 1930s and 1940s the Vargas governments, like many Latin American states at the time, incorporated a theory of *mestiçagem* (mixing) into the formation of a national popular culture.[44] Fusing elements of Afro-Brazilian culture (samba, *carnaval, futebol*) into the foundation of a national culture, intellectuals elaborated a theory of "racial democracy," which celebrated Brazil as a country, due to a fortuitous mixing of races, without or with minimal racial discrimination and prejudice. Peripheral urban areas (in particular those of Rio, then the nation's capital) occupied a contradictory place in national popular culture as sites of racialized proletarian exclusion but also as the cradle of a supposed "national" culture.

Toward the end of the military dictatorship, militant black intellectuals began to question the myth of racial democracy, arguing that it was more a technique of social control used to mystify and pacify peripheral populations than an ideal that the Brazilian state was committed to realizing. As Paulina Alberto notes, in the early 1980s black intellectuals broke decisively with "excessively conciliatory" positions on Brazil as a land of "racial harmony."[45] Moreover, Reiter and Mitchell highlight a new wave of research conducted in the 1980s and 1990s that "provided ample evidence that the promise of a racial paradise had not been fulfilled." Tianna S. Paschel's work has traced the turn in this moment to a black politics based in demands for racial equality, while Michael Hanchard has detailed black radical organizing that was done coming out of the dictatorship and into the 1990s.[46] The popular, public security and journalistic inflections of imaginaries based in an absolute division of urban space and society appear and gain force at the moment of the decline and defeat of racial democracy as a means for controlling peripheral, racially othered populations.[47] These discourses, which are directed at peripheral areas and their inhabitants, assist in the re-elaboration of prior material and cultural systems of racialization and division and come to take on a life of their own: more than a simple category, such ideas, like that of a "divided city," become a force, an abstraction that newly spectralizes and comes to partially structure urban space and the social relations found therein.

To understand the force these new discursive inflections take on and how they appear in the cultural work of this period, they need to be put in conversation with crises of race and finance, in particular during hyperinflation and then the 1998 currency crisis, as a moment when both exchange and money as forms of social synthesis break down. These renewed discursive inflections of urban separation, in particular in their popular, journalistic, and public security manifestations, emerged alongside the breakdown of money's fiction in the 1980s and 1990s, which disrupted the regulatory influence of exchange processes, and the movement of racially-othered bodies in urban space in new ways and the collapse of racial democracy ideologies. It is into this crisis in forms of social stability that such discourses on division and separation step, performing a partial substitution to the real abstraction of money and exchange and rearticulating discourses of race. While of course instances of these discourses can carry a critical and diagnostic intent, I want to argue that they perform at the same time an ordering in the way that they produce a new abstraction of urban space in crisis. The rearticulation and intensification of discourses around the favela as part of a divided city or one marked by accelerated separation is a point of transmission between the form of Brazilian financial crisis in the 1980s and 1990s and the site at which cultural works from this period come to engage with the social consequences of finance, but on a terrain that might first appear displaced from finance itself.

The Abstraction of the "Favela"

Most often abstraction is thought, especially in popular parlance, as the opposite of the concrete and as somehow less "real" and potentially more illusory. This usage carries over into certain philosophical discourses, where abstraction is understood as the process by which discrete objects are recognized as sharing a common property or trait (redness, roundness, etc.); in this register abstraction names the movement from empirical real to concept. Marx and the heterodox Marxist tradition, however, have understood abstraction differently; not as an illusion, but rather as a *force* in the world.[48] While orthodox theories of the relation between capitalism and knowledge (unrefined ideology critique and reflection theory) have well-known problems, there are a number of heterodox Marxist thinkers who have attempted a more sophisticated account of how capitalism acts as an invisible, spectral force on thought, space, and social relations. In particular in the heterodox Marxist tradition there is a name for a "thought becoming a thing" or a quasi-objective force that comes to shape social life, a force that is neither wholly immaterial (of the mind) nor simply material: a real abstraction.[49]

This perhaps counterintuitive perspective on the nature of abstraction is central to certain traditions of Marxian analysis where, as Alberto Toscano has noted, "a particular modality of social abstraction can thus be identified as the *differentia specifica* of capitalism vis-à-vis other modes of production."[50] One influential approach can be found in the work of German theorist Alfred Sohn-Rethel, who coined and popularized the term "real abstraction" in his work *Intellectual and Manual Labor* (begun during the Weimer period of hyperinflation, but only finished in exile in 1951 and finally published in Germany in 1972). Sohn-Rethel's argument is that the capacity for abstract thought and thus the ability to abstract scientific laws, to reason mathematically from nonempirical sources, all have their origins in what he calls "the exchange abstraction" or the specific form of universality that money makes possible. When two commodities are exchanged, their use values are made equivalent, and this process Sohn-Rethel terms abstraction.[51] Sohn-Rethel argues that the equivalence produced by exchange and money are needed before philosophers such as Kant can postulate time and space as homogenous, independent categories of experience. The exchange abstraction is "real" in that it is not merely a mental category but rather a pervasive concrete social process that then regulates and shapes the categories of human thought and social life.[52] When exchange processes break down during a moment of financial crisis, it would stand to reason that the real abstractions, the social forms and modes of thought attached to them would as well: it is into this gap that discourses on the divided city step. These discourses do not themselves become a real abstraction, but rather they restore in a regional, local way a certain degree of order and come to take on some of the structuring force of exchange as a real abstraction.

In a moment of urban crisis, in which forms of social synthesis and control are thrown into confusion and contestation, one result of popular and public security discourses of a divided city is to restore a level of coherence, to re-spectralize the favela as an abstraction and an equivalence among disparate spaces and, as such, provide cover for socialization and the state's practices of policing and distribution of death. What becomes difficult to see, invisible, or suppressed in this process is the category of relation or the preexisting ways that nonelite areas are integrated into the larger city: as the site of land for future housing construction (and thus land speculation and attempted financial accumulation) and as the residences of the domestic and other low-wage laborers who make the Brazilian urban environment run.[53]

As many authors have noted, in even a period of relative stability, the "favela" as a category is notoriously difficult to define and groups together areas that are marked by deep differences among themselves and internally.[54] It is in the reproduction of this equivalence or abstraction of the "favela" that the divided city and other dualist inflections become something more than a sign or name; they become a force, a form that mediates how the geographical and social space of the urban is perceived and lived and that conditions the social relations that are found there. It is with the ongoing failure of the integration of surplus populations into capital's productive apparatus and processes of valorization, and the breakdown of money's fiction and the myth of racial democracy that the idea of a "divided city" or an absolute distinction between formal and informal parts of the city reestablishes and spreads itself as a form of common sense. These dualizing urban discourses, as inflections of long-standing imaginaries, play a role in shoring up crumbling systems of racial domination. In so doing they do not come to replace discourses of race, but, as we saw in the previous chapter with Volpi and an ontological rift, ideas of urban space and society as marked by an absolute separation come to rearticulate and supplement the work of race.[55]

Abstractions in Circulation

At the end of the 1990s these discourses concerning urban space and public security mixed with and were met by a surge of new cultural production on and from peripheral urban areas. Texts like Paulo Lins's *Cidade de Deus* and Ferréz's *Capão pecado* (Sinful Capão) famously and powerfully represented the violence of everyday life in the favelas and peripheries of Rio and São Paulo and interacted in complex and challenging ways with discourses of urban separation and division. In what follows I will discuss two rather different cultural objects, both of which have very determinate connections to the matrix of divided city work, Lins's *Cidade de Deus* and the film *Tropa de elite*. With *Cidade de Deus* I will show how a split between the formal and informal city comes to shape the novel's field of possible social relations, while in *Tropa de elite* I examine how the favela as a part of a "divided city" produces the only possible conditions for knowledge of peripheral areas as singularity. What I am interested in capturing is not only how these texts take on and work over discourses of separation but also how they can be seen as participating in the circulation and sedimentation of ideas of urban space as structured by absolute division and state absence.

When new literary productions, such as Paulo Lins's *Cidade de Deus* and Ferréz's *Capão pecado*, began to appear in the late 1990s two characteristics marked their reception and representational modes: First, these works were frequently marketed and circulated as written by authors from marginalized areas; that is by authors who, it was claimed, had access to the "real" of these urban territories. Second, often these works assumed peripheral urban areas as their object and were situated only or almost completely in them. As such, the number of scenes that take place outside these zones or the number of characters who circulate or enter from outside (other than the police) are often relatively few. In this way, these texts work through—at times in a contradictory and critical fashion—a difference between the formal and informal city.[56]

In Lins's *Cidade de Deus*, except for very brief trips to the beach, hospital, and prison, the action of the novel takes place entirely in Cidade de Deus. Moreover, the characters of the novel are figures who, if they do indeed have links (social, familial, or other) or insertions (laboral, intellectual, or other) outside of this space, are portrayed as if those linkages had little to do with their essence as individuals (other than Rocket). Indeed, the only outside linkages that have a structural position in the novel are the arrival of various trucks, which are then robbed, and the arrival of the police who kill, rob, terrorize, and are occasionally killed themselves.

The narrative of *Cidade de Deus* is divided into three parts, with each part covering a section of time ranging from the 1960s to the early 1980s and featuring an overlapping cast of characters. The final section, "Tiny's Story, the Late 1970s and Early 1980s," narrates a gang war that irrupts when Tiny, a drug dealer, rapes the girlfriend of the former military parachutist José or Knockout. This scene sets off a chain of events that leads to Knockout's transformation from a hardworking, low-profile member of the community into the leader of a rival armed force engaged in a fight to the death against Tiny's gang. Knockout is one of the few characters in the novel who undergoes a transformation and who also has experience outside of the favela: "José worked as a bus conductor . . . was finishing high school at night in a state college on Seca Square and played soccer every Saturday afternoon—the only time he was ever around people his own age, because he wasn't really the chummy type."[57]

Knockout's development references the classical novelistic tradition, while the majority of characters in the novel are rendered without significant pasts or futures and frequently with minimal accounts of their interior states of being. The novel, for example, opens with two young boys, Stringy and Rocket, smoking a joint together with Stringy recounting his dreams of becoming a lifeguard. His dreams, however, will not come to pass, as the novel consistently negates at every turn its characters' attempts to connect their present with a desired future and with an exit from the favela's violence (with Rocket being the rare exception). Tiny is another example of this lack of depth or lack of future. After raping Knockout's girlfriend, he comes looking for Knockout. His motivation: "He'd kill Knockout so that what had happened to Sparrow wouldn't happen to him."[58] Tiny's affect and justifications here are reduced to a flat, almost banal, violence.

Knockout as a character is different because he leaves behind the path of a quiet, if not successful, life that bridges in some ways the *morro* (informal city) and *asfalto* (formal city) for one that reconstitutes itself within the violent flatness of Tiny's world. Once Knockout's grandfather and brother are killed by Tiny's gang, Knockout enters into an all-out war with Tiny, building a sizable army of youths and engaging in multiple, long-running clashes with Tiny's forces. In the process Knockout is wounded multiple times and hospitalized, only to come back to try to finish off

Tiny. This is how he is described before the final series of battles that leads to his death:

> His eyes stung, but that's all—the tears did not come, and what good were tears anyway? Crying didn't change a thing. All he could do was allow his desire for revenge to well up. He had flashbacks of the sheet covering Grandpa Nel stained red, Steak-and-Fries with his head blown off, his darling being abused, the wall of his house riddled with bullet holes, his dog full of lead, and now the image of a blood-stained Antunes was about to be embedded in his memory. He reached Miguel Salazar Street, where the morning breeze was stronger, but fuck the breeze and the sun burning his face! What he really wanted was for it all to be an illusion, for his brother to be alive. He caught sight of the crowd. Blood ran down his pants leg and made the inside of his sneakers slippery.[59]

This scene and the opening scene of the novel are crucial—they are the two moments in which those who dream or those who bridge the gap between the "favela" and the outside are brutally forced back inside it. In this scene, the possible narrative path set up for Knockout at the beginning, a path of transformation, possibly leading him to a differing social status, is noted, recalled, and foreclosed.

There is a level of indeterminacy here that any reading must address. Clearly, the novel has difficulty in placing sustained attention on the linkages between the formal and informal, but this can be read as a critique of the violent suppression and diminished opportunities faced by the novel's characters. At the same time it is hard not to feel the impress of divided city discourses here, and one could argue the novel's approach to reading urban space is less a realism and is, rather, deeply influenced by this imaginary. However, we could imagine a critical approach that would take this indeterminacy of interpretation into account and focus rather on how the potential critical force of the novel along this vector (its negative rendering of the connection between types of urban space) depends on a version of urban separation in order to produce a critical operation on it.[60]

One could point to a similar, indeterminate yet structural, connection to ideas of urban space as deeply dualized on the level of character. The flatness of the characters in *City of God* results from their inability to shield themselves from violence and thus from being sucked into the cycle of retribution that structures the novel and its social world. On one level, this flatness or shift from interiority has a critical edge marking the effects of daily violence on social life. This marking, however, also contains within it a negation of the possibility of determinate linkages across the experience of subjects and social locations. Again there is a way of arguing that the novel's aim here is critical in nature, and what I am trying to draw out is neither an argument for nor against that. Rather I am interested in what structures the situation into which the artistic intervention positions itself and how that structure is a—sometimes tragic, sometimes critical—division or profound divide between kinds of urban space.

As a point of contrast, one could cast a look back at earlier representations of the favela and to a key aesthetic work of the 1960s, *Cinco vezes favela* (Five times favela). The short films that compose *Cinco vezes favela* could be said to be significantly about the *relation* between elite and non-elite areas as they show police chasing children hustling in the city center, the homes and lives of rich developers trying to seize land, and the reactions of the hungry poor to the splendor and inaccessibility of commodity culture (just to mention only a few of the relations that are presented). It is a film whose critique is settled squarely within relation and the flows of capital and power across urban space. What I am interested in pointing to in *Cidade de Deus* is how a gap between the formal and informal city takes on a quasi-objective form in the novel; it is both unremarked on but constantly present. This means that, while it is possible to generate a critical edge from it, its structuring force cannot be displaced by such critique. As such, what I want to bring out here is how representations (such as a novel) can participate in a social process of the production of an abstraction (in this case the "favela" is seen as absolutely divided from the formal city). While an individual cultural object may use such an abstraction to sharpen a critique, in the cumulative effect across repeated representations, this figure becomes something more than just a representation; rather it becomes a force, a thing structuring social relations inside and outside the field of representation, and one which, in this moment, steps in to partially shore up the failing real abstraction of exchange and decaying ideology of racial democracy.[61]

In decades that were marked by black intellectuals' and movements' critiques of the ideology of racial democracy, as well as by urban crisis and peripheral uprisings brought on by financial crisis and hyperinflation, the spatialized division between the formal and informal city played an important role in rearticulating forms of racialized control. While both structural racism and racial discrimination in their particular Brazilian forms continue to exist, the rearticulation of the favela–formal city distinction as a "divided city" has come to supplement discourses of racialization and racism itself, which, as Ruth Wilson Gilmore has argued, is the "state-sanctioned or extralegal production and exploitation of group-differentiated vulnerability to premature death."[62] In particular this abstraction of the favela—while it has been used to critical effect within certain cultural productions—has been central in marking (and justifying) the urban areas which will be exposed to the intensified forms of state violence and death dealing deployed in this period to control urban surplus populations and in producing, much like the figure of *delincuencia*, a spatial and criminalizing supplement to biocultural forms of racialization. The zones of Brazilian cities targeted by the violence of the BOPE (Batalhão de Operações Policiais Especiais) and other specialized and everyday police units are those on the wrong side of the formal–informal divide, and as long as this divide remains unremarkable and omnipresent, the violence directed at the populations circumscribed by it will be thought by those living elsewhere to be necessary (if at times excessive), to be an unfortunate consequence of geography, or as having nothing to do with race, capital, or the socialization of crisis in the moment of the long downturn.[63]

A Singular Knowledge

We can see another version of this abstraction and re-spectralization of the favela—this time as creating the conditions for the possibility of knowledge—if we turn to one of the most discussed films of the 2000s, *Tropa de elite*. The film and its sequel draw upon a series of books written by Luiz Eduardo Soares, former national secretary of Public Security for the Lula administration and a well-known anthropologist and political scientist, which have circulated as forms of intellectual knowledge about the favela and peripheral areas and as middle-class best sellers. Soares's work has moved across a variety of media platforms and sites of distribution and, as a result, has become one of the most important and formative set of ideas about security and urban peripheries in circulation.

Elite da tropa, a book cowritten with André Batista and Rodrigo Pimentel which served as the basis for the 2007 film, presents a set of "fictionalized" stories and narratives of the BOPE, a part of the military police of the state of Rio de Janeiro that comprises one of the most lethal and controversial urban operations units in the world. The BOPE was created during the dictatorship in 1978 but took on its current form in 1991, that is, during the democratic "transition," once state and national governments switched from a politics of favela eradication to favela suppression.

As a film *Tropa de elite* was a surprise success. Shot on a shoestring budget, it sold thousands of pirated copies on the street before being re-edited and released in theaters, and it stands as one of the most terrifying and innovative cultural productions from this moment for the way it generates subjectivities for the militarized public security state. The film tells the story of and is narrated by Captain Nascimento of the BOPE and traces two events: Nascimento's search for his replacement from a group of recruits and a major operation by the BOPE to "pacify" the Morro dos Prazeres favela in advance of a visit by the pope to Rio. Nascimento has two potential successors, Neto and Matias, and the film traces their evolution through the initial stages of training as Nascimento's voice-over measures for the audience their weaknesses and strengths and their progress in internalizing the worldview of the BOPE. In both characters we watch the insertion of their subjectivities into the police logic of the state, and we are guided by Nascimento's voice-over which serves as both judge and jury, highlighting for us the positions the faithful servants of the security state must take up. For most of the film Matias is the front-runner in this search, and the film traces his subjectivization in great detail.

Matias, played by Afro-Brazilian actor André Ramiro, is the figure the film uses to stage its condemnation of any thought that is not that of the police, and wherein we can see the force of the idea of an absolute divide or polarization of urban space conditioning not just social relations but knowledge. Matias, in addition to training for the BOPE, is enrolled in law school, which leads to a series of scenes set in comfortable university classrooms where Matias is the only visible Afro-Brazilian. In his voice-over Captain Nascimento tells us that this interest in the university and these people was a failing of Matias, that he was "soft at heart." Enrolling in school is read for us as a personal failing to completely submit to the logic of BOPE, in which there are only friends and enemies, either friends of traffickers or those who fight to save society from them. In a world in which an absolute division between the formal and informal city rules, the logic of the friend-enemy becomes one of the only possible forms of social relation.

The film rehearses and reinforces this absolute division by putting the well-meaning, left-leaning university students who run an NGO in the favela in awkward, embarrassing, or naive positions (especially when confronted with what the film portrays as the harsh, dog-eat-dog reality of urban life). The film goes to great lengths to portray these students as out of touch with reality and troublingly fascinated by the favela (a theme which is repeated in many popular films). In the logic of the movie the students and their NGO are on one side of a divide, a divide that the movie portrays as uncrossable: the divide is real, total, and permanent.

Matias is the principal character who circulates between the world of the BOPE-favela and the world of the middle and upper classes. The film uses Matias to demonstrate that this divide truly conditions all social relations and that there can be no crossing. This is nowhere more clear than in a scene in which, for his law class, Matias has to complete a group project on Foucault. During the group's presentation to the class, the film portrays the students prattling on about discipline, excessive force, and the police as Matias quietly fumes. Finally, he explodes. Matias opens by saying that most police want to do honest work, but then, as some students push back, he changes register and exclaims: "Tem que reprimir mesmo" (There has to be repression). As the other students continue to disagree, Matias invokes his social location, telling them that from their middle- and upper-class homes the true reality of the periphery is not visible—and then the room falls silent. As Matias speaks the discursive field is shifted completely from a debate concerning the limits of sovereign power and the social distribution of the surplus to that of the logic of the friend-enemy. It is clear, though, from Matias's brief discourse that this logic is less that of the "traffickers" than that of the BOPE.

What is most interesting is not Matias's argument per se, but rather how the film has positioned him, as black and as a trainee of the BOPE, as having access to what we might call "the singularity of the favela," with singularity understood in a sense similar to Peter Hallward's usage in *Absolutely Postcolonial.* In this book Hallward essays some of the limitations of the postcolonial theoretical framework which focuses on the singular or events or textual examples which are defined by their particularity and contingency as opposed to their relation to other events or instances. Hallward contrasts this with countercolonial writing that "assumes a world of constituent antagonisms and sharply demarcated interests; it is militant and partisan by definition. Its fundamental terms—engagement, position, mobilization—are necessarily specific or relational rather than singular in their orientation."[64] Hallward's critique of postcolonial criticism avoids some of the usual pitfalls in order to argue that postcolonial criticism's orientation toward the singular undermines its claims to specificity which is inherently a relational category. The "singularity of the favela" can be thought of in this way as a false kind of particularity, a kind of knowledge of social relations that actually has no purchase on the relational.

The reason why Matias's argument leaves the room silent is not that it is better formed or more deeply reasoned. Rather the room falls silent because we are being shown that Matias's classmates recognize the film's "truth": that deep in the heart of the favela there is a singularity and that there are two groups who have access to it. The first are those on the other side of the divide: the racialized others. Matias's classmates do not know he is a BOPE trainee so for them his access to the truth comes from his racialized social location. However, for the film's viewers who know Matias's affiliation, the message is that the only group outside the favela with access to its truth is the BOPE. The film's affective pedagogy is to implant the idea that the middle classes, the intellectuals, anyone from the outside, can never have access to this singularity. This is a spatialized and racialized truth. If public security and journalistic discourses re-spectralized the favela as an abstraction, it is in films like *Tropa de elite* that we can see that abstraction shapes not only social relations but the kinds and forms of knowledge that are possible. In the end, the film reveals how the absolute divide between formal and informal cities has changed the social location occupied by the police: no longer just the perpetrators of state violence, the police have become the guardians and producers of the only legitimate knowledge of the favela as well.

Other Than a Standpoint?

Cultural critics' responses to these literary and filmic works centered on favelas and the periphery have seen in them a return to realism and have tended to fall along two lines.[65] Some examine the ways these new cultural productions function as a form of *testemunho* (testimony) that, as Beatriz Jaguaribe has noted, "articulate their power of representation by positing a vital connection between significant personal experience and testimonial veracity."[66] Others, like Karl Erik Schøllhammer, have sounded cautionary notes that it is occasionally difficult to distinguish between "compromisso social" (social engagement) and "marketing" in these works: "One sees, then, a language in text and image incorporating the rawness of peripheral reality in a pasteurized media representation that dilutes both the content and the problem of how to give visibility to these issues . . . Here, it is clear that it is no longer possible to assess the work's engagement or commitment either by its themes or content since marginal and peripheral realities have long been incorporated into a spectacular desire."[67] While much writing on these novels and films has debated their critical force, what we can see in *Tropa de elite* is that the testimonial structure is easily inverted, which should at least give us some slight pause. If for progressives new cultural production from the favela carries a critical realism in the form of giving space to marginalized voices, *Tropa de elite* shows this belief that only authentic voices can express the truth of the favela, can become a truth or singularity that only the police have access to. At some level this debate over whether these novels are "authentic" cultural products or coopted, spectacularized forms of capitalist cultural production, is undecidable, and rather than getting trapped in it, what I have tried to do in this chapter is show how part of their force lies not in the truth that they speak but in the abstraction that they animate.

At the end of the 1980s and throughout the 1990s there was a debate in Latin American studies about the nature of testimonial literature. The 1970s and 1980s had witnessed an explosion of testimonial writing in Latin America, frequently alongside new forms of political mobilization (the case of Rigoberta Menchú being the most well known). Certain critics took this work as being proof that subalterns could indeed "speak"; while others, particularly after the canonization of this work in the U.S. academy and its commodification in the marketplace, took a more cautious approach.[68] What I want to suggest is that debates on these new works centered on urban peripheries replay in certain ways this prior one about testemunho or *testimonio* (testimony), but also that the idea that social location and access to knowledge are linked has a much longer history, one that is rooted in class-based Marxism stretching back at least to Lukács's *History and Class Consciousness*.[69] In order to move away from the treatment of peripheral cultural production as either spectacularized commodification or true speech, I want to formalize an engagement with a Marxist tradition that locates domination, not in the direct oppression of one class by another—the tradition which gives rise to the undecidable conundrum of testimony, of the truth (or fungability) of the voice of the dominated—but rather in the very form of capital itself, in the impersonal, quasi-objective structures that arise from the production of value.

This line of heterodox Marxist thought which has been concerned with impersonal forms of domination we might loosely define as "value-form theory."[70] In the late nineteenth and early twentieth century, critics such as Eugen von Böhm-Bawerk began to point to a "transformation problem" in Marx's *Capital* and argued that Marx had no coherent way of relating price and value in his work. The Russian author Isaak Illich Rubin, in his *Essays on Marx's Theory of Value*, responded to these kinds of critiques by arguing that Marx was actually not interested in explaining the world through bourgeois economic categories (such as price) but rather saw capitalism as producing a form of social life shaped by the "value form"—in Rubin's case, the commodity fetish.

In the 1970s a group of German theorists, known as Neue Marx-Lektüre (New Marx Reading), drew on works like Rubin's in an attempt to refound Marxist thought after the exhaustion of orthodox Marxist programs. These authors, including Hans-Georg Backhaus, Helmut Reichelt, and Alfred Schmidt, argued that Marx's *Capital*, which had been taken as a text about labor, exploitation, and direct class domination, had been misunderstood. The Neue Marx-Lektüre reading of *Capital* emphasized not labor and the extraction of surplus value, but drawing on the work of Adorno who was the teacher of Backhaus, they focused on how capital produced a world of indirect social domination.[71] Through detailed readings of the first chapter of *Capital*, which many interpreters skip over or dismiss as "dialectical wordplay," they presented a new picture of Marx as a theoretician of the *value form*. As Backhaus wrote in his classic 1968 essay "On the Dialectics of the Value-Form": "In the foreword to *Capital* Marx energetically warns against neglecting the theory of the value-form: 'For bourgeois society, however, the commodity form of the products of labour or the value form of the commodity is the economic cell-form. To the uneducated its analysis appears to turn on minutiae.' 'The human spirit has sought in vain to ground the value-form for more than 2000 years,' the Ricardian school included. From the quotation it follows that Marx claims to have unravelled, for the first time in the history of research, this 'puzzling form.'"[72] For Backhaus, Marx's project was not just the critique of the existence of this "'objective semblance' . . . which constitutes the 'mystical character' of the commodity"[73] but rather an account of its genesis—that is, how these thing-like forms came to define the social world of capital.[74]

The Neue Marx-Lektüre reading of Marx—a critique of most prior interpretations of *Capital*—was also a critique of the theoretical foundations underpinning the workers' movement. Both the German school and subsequent authors influenced by them, such as Moishe Postone, argued that prior forms of Marxism and Marxist theory (whether orthodox or heterodox) were based on labor, as opposed to value—meaning that they were based in the standpoint of labor or a theory of capitalism as defined, primarily, by the exploitation of labor and the production of surplus value. Authors in the value-form tradition hold that capitalism is first and foremost a system of impersonal domination. Postone, for example, argued in *Time, Labor and Social Domination: A Reinterpretation of Marx's Critical Theory* that the standpoint of labor implies that capitalism is seen as a system of two classes where one, through possession of the means of production and a juridico-legal structure based in private property, directly dominates the other. This leads traditional Marxists into a politics based not in the transformation of production, but rather in a redistribution of the social surplus. Postone argues that what the failure of "actually existing socialism" demonstrates is that there can be no redistribution of the social surplus as a "solution" to capitalism; rather the entire system of production must be overturned. As a result the forms of domination that structure capitalism are not, Postone continues, direct or juridical, but rather impersonal and take place through the production of quasi-objective structures.

My desire is not to throw out the lens of class and racial domination, but rather to complement it with a focus on structures of impersonal domination, of which the real abstraction of money and exchange is one such structure. I want to suggest that part of the undecidability of debates about whether cultural productions addressing peripheral urban zones are forms of testimonial realism or spectacularized commodification is that they ignore the importance of impersonal structures of domination and thus tend to over- or under-valorize the contribution of testimonial knowledges. While the critical force of many of these works—especially the literary ones—has been significant, it has been difficult to make visible the forms of abstraction that underpin the reproduction of the "favela" as an object in the period after the crisis of hyperinflation, the breakdown of the myth of racial democracy, and the spread of new forms of state violence. This difficulty then is a limit, a real one, of the aesthetic in a moment of financial crisis, in which the fiction of money breaks down, creating a need for new forms to supplement real abstraction's role in capitalism's impersonal forms of domination. As a result, there is a limit to the kind of work that can be done on a representational level by cultural objects when they are caught up in a moment of the breakdown of real abstractions and systems of racial domination.

However, having noted this limit, we cannot simply fall into the grand hotel abyss (as Adorno was once accused of doing).[75] Rather as cultural producers and critics we must learn to stay in the room with the intractability of real abstraction as a force in our social worlds and not overvalue nor underestimate the work of representation. Part of this staying with the intractability of real abstraction and its partial supplements means recognizing that the structuring of urban social relations and knowledge by the abstraction of the favela or by urban space as defined by an absolute divide has proven a durable one. In particular high cultural production in both São Paulo and Rio de Janeiro focused on peripheral communities has had difficulty escaping from the force field of the favela defined by an absolute division. However, in a 2013 film shot in Brasilia, *A cidade é uma só?* (Is the city just one?), we can see an attempt to break with the forms of abstraction that underpin these discursive formations and to maintain an anticipatory distance from their fields of strange force.

Blending documentary and fiction elements, the film follows three individuals, all residents of a peripheral zone of Brasilia known as Ceilândia. Brazil's capital city, a testament to high Modernist design and planning, contained no residences for the workers who built the city. As a result they settled in informal settlements, and in 1969 the government initiated a massive publicity campaign and program of removal of one such settlement, which sat in the path of international flights landing in the capital. These residents were removed to Ceilândia where they were promised titled lots and infrastructure. There they found neither. Of the three main characters, one, Dildu, is running for *deputado distrital* (district deputy) on a platform that promises to end the institutional racism (in education, health, and employment) faced by those from Ceilândia. Another, Nancy Araújo, is a folksinger who as a young girl participated in a government-run publicity campaign for the removal, singing a song written to convince residents it was their duty to move, "A cidade é uma só." The third, Zé Antônio, is the brother-in-law of Dildu and spends the film alternately helping him campaign and cruising around Ceilândia looking for people who are selling their property.

The film documents three things which are pertinent to our discussion: First, Ceilândia is a current site of land speculation and "re-urbanization," and all around high-rise condominiums are going up. Second, because of the modernist framing of Brasilia we have informal areas being read not only as overly determined "favelas" or zones of informality but within a different frame, occasionally ironically invoked but frequently provokingly so: the utopian promise of one city for all. Finally, the film focuses extensively on transport: many scenes feature the long bus rides Dildu takes to get to his job, Nancy driving to a radio station, or Zé driving around Ceilândia or farther out in the countryside. The film reveals that the line between informal and formal is never static, that it is shaped by the pressures of land speculation and capital accumulation occurring through the construction sector. At the same time the film extracts discourses on peripheral areas from the abstracted forms of the megalopolis and positions the thought of their relation not in a frozen horizon of integration but rather in the yet empty but still potent promise of the jingle "A cidade é uma só."

Perhaps just as important and relevant are the aesthetic means used to accomplish this. The film never formally presents any of its subjects. It also never formally defines any territory or notes a transition between parts of the city. The film operates from an aesthetic that is marked by its indirection and its distance. Never presenting a topic like land speculation or the transformation of Ceilândia into condominiums directly, the film allows these thematics and processes to emerge from the space and the speakers themselves, never wholly, always fragmented, and frequently as an intuition. In one of the final shots of the film, we see in the distance across a barren, red dirt lot an ad for a coming high-rise development. This distance is the aesthetic wager of the film: instead of participating in the abstractions that circle the space like vultures, the film's indirect means of address allows for the possibility of the emergence of a new vision of the urban and a new set of social relations.

Violence, Mediation, and Seizure

In Latin American studies the topic of violence has received a great deal of attention in the last decade. Much of this work has attempted to address the paradox of rising or expanding forms of violence and social war during the transition to and solidification of democratic regimes in the region. Most often the diagnosis that has been advanced is that the fragility or weakness of states has led to the proliferation of state and nonstate violence across the social field.[76] These explanations tend to think of the state and violence primarily in Weberian terms: the state is defined by a monopoly on violence, and if there is violence in the social field then it must be caused by an issue with the establishment or maintenance of this monopoly. As a result in such work, the cause of increasing violence is seen as the lack of strong states which also generally leads to a downplaying of states' roles in the promotion of or participation in violence.

Such arguments often move alongside ones of neoliberalism and the decline of developmentalist states. What a perspective that stresses finance and financial flows can show is how, even at the height of developmentalist ideologies, states performed a mediating function: directing external capital flows, in this case productive as opposed to mainly financial, into a desired developmentalist strategy. In the case of Brazil, perhaps more so than other Latin American countries, this position of the state as a mediator of flows, productive and then financial, is very apparent.[77] The shift of flows from production into financial instruments and devices during the 1970s, 1980s, and 1990s is significant in its difference and specificity, but the position of the state across these historical moments registers a similarity. What a perspective on the state that starts from finance can demonstrate is that there are certain continuities (e.g., of the state as a mediator) on which neoliberalism represents a modulation and not a clean break.

This matters because frequently in theorizations of new forms of or increasing violence in the global peripheries, the assumption is made that less state means more disorder and thus an increase in nonstate violence as states recede, lose control, and shrink. A different, less developmental state-nostalgic perspective would be to start from the state as mediator; thus in the 1970s, 1980s, and 1990s the Brazilian state begins to take on a different mediating function: instead of regulating, directing, and opening the country to international productive capital, it did so for financial capital while also taking on the function of socializing crises and ensuring payment. Once the decision is made not to default, what remains is the decision of which social group(s) will bear the burden of paying for the debt. The socialization of crisis onto peripheral and working-class groups generates the unrest associated with hyperinflation and unemployment, and it was to impose this socialization and to successfully perform its mediating role that the Brazilian state doubled down on state violence, in direct, indirect, and structural forms.

In short, instead of a narrative of shrinking states producing situations of social chaos, this chapter has tracked how valorization (of finance capital) requires violence (of the state and for socialization). At the same time, the ground covered reveals one of the many specific social forms that have emerged from local crucibles of financial crisis: namely, the way in which weakened theories of racial democracy and a failing social synthesis of exchange produced an opening for new spatialized discursive figures, which came to be animated by and to wield the forces inherent in both racialization and real abstraction. Socialization, seizure, and supplements to real abstraction are the terms which define the particularity of this passage through the aftermath of finance's failures. To place this back into more general terms: where there is financial crisis, most often actual or threatened state violence follows close behind and with it the work of race and the sciences of human division.

If one thinks of finance as defined by an elongation of the passage from the production of a commodity to the realization of its value, the socialization of a crisis can be described as the state stepping in to complete the circuit of value production that is in danger of failing. The socialization of the crisis is a way of completing the C–M' circuit of capital, perhaps only partially and depending on the deals cut and the level of resistance. This is why moments of financial crisis are accompanied by those "unpolitical" gestures of marginalized surplus populations: riots and insurrections, seizures and *saques* (looting). The popular measures adopted in a moment of financial crisis are the inverse of finance's failed saltos and the state's socialization strategies: saques are the seizure of what finance makes scarce. The politics of the saque is the politics of a counter-salto, jumping directly from C to C, a refusal of the failed mediation of finance and a recognition that the state is attempting through socialization to close this gap, to complete a failed leap.

Moments of financial crisis, then, are defined by these political poles: seizure and socialization. To protect against seizure and to enforce socialization, states turn to racialized state violence as a material practice, while new discursive forms—such as those of the divided city—begin to move and jostle alongside them, supporting, belying, or contradicting these practices. While racialized state violence can take many forms—some direct and some indirect—unless their connection to the ongoing socialization of crisis during the rise of finance is grasped, these forms of violence will continue to be explained away as, tragically and ironically, the result of states being *too weak*, being failed, or having lost control over the monopoly of violence. Socialization is not a site from which all forms of racial oppression can be thought and dismantled. However, foregrounding its importance in the historical moment of the long downturn is necessary to prevent the continued expansion of these forms of state violence and to make visible the complicated and indeterminate ways, particularly in the aftermath of the 1982 debt crisis in Latin America, racializing discursive structures were supplemented and how apparatuses of state violence were increasingly employed, and to multiple ends, against marginalized individuals and populations.

CHAPTER 3

Anti-Subjects of Credit

FINANCIAL PARA-CORPORATISM AND FRAGILITY IN BRAZIL

E (Elio Gaspari): *Como saideira, Gullar, como é que você vê as perspectivas de socialismo no Brasil hoje?*

F.G. (Ferreira Gullar): A longuíssimo prazo. . . . A longuíssimo prazo . . .

E: *E com juros!*

F.G.: E com juros!

In the early 2000s, the generalized financial and political crisis of Latin American countries began to be "stabilized," and both Mexico and Brazil moved toward a new model of attempted finance and export-led accumulation.[1] In the case of Brazil this model had two key components: personal credit to spur domestic consumption and the export of primary commodities, including oil, minerals, and foodstuffs, to China and other countries.[2] As such, the neo or social developmentalist economic model that emerged in the aftermath of the 1999 currency crisis and during the first and second Lula administrations was a mix of financial and extractive industries. One of the distinctive features of this period in Brazil is the degree to which global capital flows were channeled by the state and banks into personal credit structures and operating capital for corporations, thereby enabling a (temporary) boom fueled by domestic consumption and extractive "national champions," in particular after 2005–2006.[3] If the 1990s were the years in which a new institutional architecture for financial valorization and circulation was finalized in Brazil, but during which international capital flowed fitfully and in crisis-causing stops and starts, during the Lula presidencies, due in part to the low interest rates of the U.S. Federal Reserve and excessively high interest rates in Brazil, capital flowed steadily into Brazil, even after the 2008 financial crisis.[4]

These mostly uninterrupted flows of global capital into the country, coupled with the expansion of China's economy and its need for extractive and other resources, produced a moment of social and political ebullience—a period of plans and projections, many of which, as the specters of economic crisis began to reappear in 2013, were never realized and some of which turned to ruins during the social and political calamity that immediately followed. These flows, and how they were channeled—into credit cards, housing and auto loans, into infrastructure and construction projects which fed political and other forms of corruption—have deeply marked everyday life and political and social formations in Brazil in the last two decades but have not often been placed at the center of cultural and social analysis, which is my aim here. In this chapter I focus on the boom years and their immediate aftermath until early 2016 and trace three transformations that the cultivation and sustained flows of finance into Brazil after 2003 and their domestic channeling have wrought: a form of (failed) financial para-corporatism, a projective structure of feeling, and a specific kind of subjectivization. In each case, my aim is to be attentive to finance's fragility or instability: finance-linked expansions last only as long as the apparent accumulation does. Thus part of what this chapter traces in its readings of an expanded range of discursive materials is how the fading of a financial expansion opens the way for a reliance on violence, policing, and the law in order to control unruly populations, supplement a sputtering para-corporatist machinery, and enforce austerity.

In the opening section of this chapter I chart the expansion of personal credit as a form of financial para-corporatism during the Partido dos Trabalhadores (PT) governments. I also examine some of the principal cultural mediations of credit and the role of Rio de Janeiro as the site of the production of these mediations, in particular the partial transition from discourses of racial democracy to credit democracy elaborated in the 2012 telenovela *Cheias de charme* (Sparkling Girls). In the second part of the chapter, drawing on the work of Raymond Williams, I turn my attention to finance's structure of feeling and the everyday ways finance presses upon and shapes social relations and social life and the political consequences of the fragility of finance. In the final section I examine the kind of subjects that the personal credit expansion has produced. Here I argue that the credit expansion has produced a form of the subject as a pass-through or gateway in which the state is less concerned with subjects' interiority and more with facilitating the seizure of assets or income. This seizure requires a concomitant expansion of militarization and the threat of state violence which further hollows out the subject, producing what we might call "anti-subjects." I conclude by examining the fraught terrain for political struggle opened by the moment of mass credit and the possible futures of its denouement.

Credit and Financial Para-Corporatism

The so-called "new middle class" of Brazil has been the object of countless studies and homages—perhaps to the point of exhaustion and parody. They were called the new *batalhadores* (fighters), seen as a new source of wealth "at the bottom of the pyramid," and heralded as the protagonists of a new era of Brazilian politics. However, what went under-analyzed for many years was the centrality of credit—which is not a wage but rather money one has to pay back and with interest—in this cycle of consumption and the state's role in providing it.[5] Since 2003 Brazil has witnessed an important expansion of personal credit, and while real wages most certainly did rise in the period after 2003, the expansion of credit was also exceptionally strong. As Lena Lavinas notes, "While the wage bill doubled between 2002 and 2013, total credit soared 250 percent, 'the line of credit' allocated to consumer credit was raised by 300 percent, and personal credit nearly quadrupled. Therefore, from 2003 to 2014, personal credit and consumer credit grew at a much faster rate than total wages and the supply of total credit."[6]

What this meant was millions of people paying significant amounts of interest for cell phones, appliances, for new or used cars, or for their homes. However, credit was sold by the governments of the PT in part as a process of (financial) "democratization," of making society more "inclusive," and while it may change consumption patterns and spur domestic growth, mass credit has most certainly made a great deal of money for those holding the loans or those who own shares in the companies that do.[7] In this chapter I build an interpretation of this rapid expansion of mass credit as an attempt by the state to refashion a para-corporatist machinery which neoliberal policies had undercut and trace its accompaniment by a new kind of racialized national cultural imaginary, one which I will call "credit democracy" to emphasize its historical roots in and difference with racial democracy.

In the process of financial liberalization in the 1990s, many Latin American countries privatized their banking systems to various degrees. In Brazil a number of financial institutions remained under state control, such as Caixa and Banco do Brasil and the development bank BNDES.[8] These forms of government control over public money made possible in the Lula era the attempted reorientation of the Brazilian economy around internal demand supported by mass consumer credit and primary commodity exports. Due to its control of large state banks and its regulatory capacity, the federal government can influence and incentivize the amount of personal credit in the market. Under the Lula administration the state went one step further, in essence creating a "new" form of personal credit known as *crédito consignado*.[9] While all forms of personal credit can be thought of in some way as enacting a kind of financial para-corporatism (as the state can attempt to regulate how much credit is being offered by lenders, and the state controls the legal environment defining different credit modalities), crédito consignado represents a more direct form, and a discussion of the rise of this credit modality sheds light on how financial para-corporatism has worked in general during the recent PT administrations.

One of the instruments that have made possible the generalized expansion of consumer credit was the massification of this formerly little used modality of credit, crédito consignado, which began in 2003–2004. Crédito consignado functions essentially as a payroll deduction loan, which means that as long as someone is employed in the formal economy or is receiving their retirement benefits, their loan payment is deducted directly from their paycheck or benefits payment. The creation of crédito consignado forms a part of two deeper historical movements. The first is what Roberto Grün has termed the "financeirização de esquerda" (financialization of the left) in which Brazilian unions, such as Central Única dos Trabalhadores (CUT) and Força Sindical, became financialized by fighting for control of or influence over large pension funds. By 2003 these large union federations, in particular CUT which has close ties to the PT, began undertaking negotiations that would allow them to offer consignado loans to union members.[10] The second is the turn mapped by Lena Lavinas and others of the Lula presidency to a "social developmentalist" model. As Lavinas notes, at the center of this model of accumulation and social policy, as originally theorized by Ricardo Bielschowsky, was the expansion of personal credit to fuel a cycle of domestic consumption.

As part of this emerging social developmentalist model, in September 2004 the Lula government extended crédito consignado to individuals with Instituto Nacional do Seguro Social (INSS) benefits, in effect massifying the consignado credit structure beyond the PT union-linked base.[11] The lower interest rates led to the quick expansion of consignado to INSS recipients and the slow extension of consignado from public employees to some private workers. Crédito consignado thus serves as an example of how the PT governments more generally used all forms of personal credit to promote domestic consumption as part of a social developmentalist strategy.

While much has been written about the Bolsa Família as a poverty reduction program, it amounts to only 0.5 percent of GDP per year.[12] Accumulated credit outstanding to households in Brazil in January 2016 stood roughly at 25 percent of GDP.[13] Credit has been a crucial part of a political and domestic strategy, but it raises the problem, and question, of financial exploitation, as even consignado borrowers—who pay by far the lowest interest rates—can end up, depending on the length of the loan, paying back significantly more than what they have borrowed and those using forms of credit such as credit cards are subject to rates that run as high as 300–400 percent APR.

The 1980s and 1990s witnessed a widening gap between formal and informal labor markets and the increasing inability of the state to mediate the capital-labor relation through traditional corporatist structures.[14] Credit, as a device promoted by the state and which places into relation both workers and the un- and underemployed with financial capitalists, has played an important role in this situation. Credit expansion, as seen in the crédito consignado modality, was a state-supported dynamic in a directly material sense, but also in the sense of the government being attentive to its spread through market means. While in some cases, personal credit was provided by state-linked banks, generally speaking, unlike in classic corporatism, individuals were not organized via credit provision into groups with designated representatives. However, there is a sense in which the state did help to organize individuals into determinate groups, not only for the state but also for the market to access, and in two ways.

In the para-corporatism of credit, financial corporations are given access to groups constituted by the state (for example, retirees, public servants, and union members) who then choose to enter or not into the weak collectivity of debtors. At the same time state concern for the expansion of credit, and in particular state concern with the expansion of credit to individuals inside and outside of traditional working-class sectors (e.g., to the marginally or underemployed), produces conditions in which many of these individuals also become a part of this new collective formation of debtors. As such state participation in and concern for credit expansion underpins the creation of debtors in this period as a weakly bonded group—as individuals who are joined together by their newly common exposure to fluctuations in interest rates, external shocks, government credit policies, and spikes in unemployment. The para-corporatism of finance produces a weak collectivity which, depending on the way the fragile conditions of credit break, might pour into the streets demanding the radicalization of a left government or might silently back a project of austerity or worse.

Thus the expansion of personal credit should be seen, along with the role of police and parastate forces discussed in the previous chapter, as a structure that reestablishes a form of social control beyond the processes of production, outside the traditional form of capital-labor mediation through the wage and corporatist techniques—which is not to say this traditional form of mediation has entirely disappeared; rather it has been supplemented by credit and state violence. The fact that state violence and credit as a nontraditional para-corporatist structure are imbricated in this period is important because the utopian promise of credit, "equality" through consumption, is highly unstable and illusory. Thus not only is the utopia of credit one that leaves critical social relations, particularly those of social reproduction, untouched, it also requires and calls forth new forms of state violence once its shaky promises begin to fail.

A Nova Classe Média (Parcelada)

One way the debate over the social effects induced by the rise of credit and consumption in Brazil played out was through the discursive construction of and contestation over the category *nova classe média*. While both real wages and state income transfers grew after 2003, the key documents which produced and promoted the category of the new middle class—regardless of the problems with their definition of class—depended on the expansion of credit in ways that generally have not been foregrounded.[15] While traditional approaches to the definition of economic classes are based in income, social status, or location in the relations of production, discursive constructions and popular media discussions of the new middle class centered on, or made space for, not only income, but the kinds of objects in a home. Thus, the idea of a new middle class was at least partially defined by what can be purchased with credit. It is this association of the new middle class with consumption (occurring with wages or borrowed funds) which carried over into popular journalism and consciousness and led to the creation of a cultural imaginary of credit democracy.

The idea of the existence of a "new middle class" in this period and its association with consumption was advanced in key ways by two documents. The first was a classificatory system developed in the late 1990s by the Associação Brasileira de Empresas de Pesquisa[16] known as the Critério de Classificação Econômica Brasil or simply the Critério Brasil. The Critério abandonded "the proposal to classify the population in terms of 'social classes,'" that is, only through income.[17] Instead the Critério built classes (into the standard Brazilian system of A–E) through a point system based on consumer objects in the home and the level of education of the "head of household." Here the possible reliance on credit in the definition of the new middle class is clear as both consumer items and frequently education depend on the provision of credit for purchase.[18]

The second document, Marcelo Neri's 2010 *A nova classe média: O lado brilhante dos pobres*, coined the term "new middle class" and argued that 50.5 percent of the population had become by 2009 *classe C*, or "middle class." However, it also gave, if not analytic weight, then descriptive space to the approach of thinking of class as a function of the power of consumption.[19] What is important is how in the Critério, Neri's work, and the flood of popular press and journal articles that followed the publication of *A nova classe média*, this new power of consumption defines, or attempts to define, a new national subject—the new middle class or classe C which would encompass over half the population.[20] As Neri writes, classe C "is the most precise image of Brazilian society."[21] The literature on the nova classe média, in its academic, business, and popular flavors, produced a new national, weakly collective subject, one not just of production (of labor, the wage, and the worker), but of finance and consumption, and more specifically, of credit. The discursive framing of equality through consumption, which was then amplified in various mass cultural products, defined a new imaginary, not of racial democracy, but rather of what could be called "credit democracy."

From Racial Democracy to Credit Democracy

As discussed in Chapter 2, during the 1930s and 1940s the Vargas dictatorship, like many Latin American states at the time, incorporated a theory of *mestiçagem* into the formation of a national popular culture.[22] As the Vargas state merged elements of Afro-Brazilian culture into the foundations of a Brazilian national culture, intellectuals elaborated a theory of "racial democracy," which celebrated Brazil as a country without, or with minimal, racial discrimination. Peripheral urban areas (in particular those of Rio de Janeiro) were, in the emerging national popular culture, spaces of contradiction, doubling as sites for racialized proletarian exclusion and national cultural production. This apparatus for the distribution of resources and premature death via a "racially democratic" national culture began to break down in the 1980s and 1990s for two sets of reasons. First, the 1982 debt crisis, increasing labor militancy, and the implementation of neoliberal reforms meant the corporatist structures which had underpinned this infrastructure were weakened. Second, starting in the military dictatorship, militant black intellectuals began to question the myth of racial democracy and began to see it as a technique of social control.[23]

With the "stabilization" of the Brazilian economy in the 2000s and the coming to power of the PT, the state began to use credit provision as a para-corporatist technique, which instead of integrating laborers into corporate bodies under control of the state, grouped individuals into weak collectivities tied, but less directly, to the state's control over and regulation of financial resources. In the discourses around the nova classe média we can see the beginnings of a new imaginary, growing up alongside and as an inseparable part of the means and techniques of credit provision, which represents not a return to racial democracy, but rather a turn to what I will call credit democracy. Rather than replacing ideas of racial democracy or forestalling the apparatus of state violence traced in the previous chapter, credit democracy has had a shorter shelf life, functioning primarily as a central discursive node during the PT governments. While academic and government-linked discourses around the nova classe média begin this process of articulation, it is in mass cultural production where the new subject positions and horizons of this formation have been fashioned and disseminated.[24]

These cultural productions, much like the national cultural productions of the Vargas period, are often set in or based on Rio de Janeiro, which continues to serve as a backdrop for the creation of national cultural imaginaries. In the following I discuss one such production, the 2012 telenovela *Cheias de charme*, and its generation of an imaginary of credit democracy. If racial democracy was concerned with producing forms of cultural common sense that obscured real structures of racial and class domination, the imaginary of credit democracy posits a false equality of consumption which obscures very real differences in access to goods and services as well as forms of inequality inflected by race, class, and gender that cannot be overcome by credit or consumption. At the same time *Cheias* reveals the imaginary of credit democracy to be an internally fragile one, as the dreams of social accession in the telenovela itself cannot be realized through increasing wages or credit access but rather require the deus ex machina of pop music stardom.

Cheias de charme tells the story of three women—Maria da Penha (Taís Araújo), Maria Aparecida (Isabelle Drummond), and Maria do Rosário (Leandra Leal)—employed as domestic workers, who form a music group, "As Empreguetes," and become an overnight sensation. *Cheias*, a Globo telenovela, was on the air from April 16, 2012 to September 28, 2012, and while not the most successful Globo telenovela of the moment (that would be *Avenida Brasil*), its narrative of lower-class upward mobility became a point of reference for the changes in and debates over the new Brazilian "middle class."[25] *Cheias* articulates the presumptions and horizon of credit democracy, in part because its plot turns around the very notion of equality and the overcoming of differences between social classes.

In the telenovela the lives of the three Marias are turned upside down after their self-recorded song and video go viral. Their accession to pop music stardom makes them into the social equals of their former bosses and enables them to enact fantasies of consumption: they buy houses and apartments, rehab them, and fill them with appliances.[26] The show then does not specifically focus on credit, but rather on the credit-form or the fantasy of equality via credit-based consumption. That is, credit exists in the background, occasionally motivating the plot or appearing in moments of consumption, while the show itself models the fantasy of credit-enabled consumption, namely the ability to transcend or suspend one's socioeconomic position. This mix of the belief in potential equality through consumption and the obscuring of structural class and race differences through their (temporary) suspension are what define the cultural imaginary of credit democracy.

Cheias is a form of Latin American telenovela which has become very popular and lucrative in recent years. By making telenovelas that center on fictional pop groups (the Argentinean telenovela *Rebelde Way* was among the first in this genre), media companies have been able to add additional revenue streams, including CD and single sales of the songs made popular on a show, concert tickets, etc. While *Cheias* itself was popular, part of its wide cultural dissemination was its utilization of multiple media platforms, including the singles spun off from the show and contests in which actual domestic workers were invited to submit their own videos with a chance to win a guest appearance on the show. The first single from the group, "Vida de empreguete," condensed a series of cultural concerns, perceptions, and aspirations over the new middle class and credit expansion—which can be seen in part by the number of parodies and remakes the single has received in different cultural mediums, in particular on the internet video site YouTube. This single mixes references to credit-enabled consumption with class-based revenge fantasies against cruel employers and their ungrateful offspring. In short, the song combines affects resulting from structural position with the aspirational content of this position's suspension.[27]

Cheias and the song "Vida" draw on academic and journalistic accounts' framing of the rise of the nova classe média as a narrative of the production of equality through consumption. In the lyrics for the single, forms of equality, such as "um dia compro apartamento" (one day I'll buy an apartment) are linked to the suspension of the domestics' structural position, marked here by the phrase "um dia" (one day). This positioning and the song's narrative are determined by the division of labor of social reproduction, of who does the dirty work of "passando pano" (mopping) and "botando a roupa pra quarar" (putting clothes out in the sun) under the arbitrary power of others, and by the experience of those who rise early and use substandard transportation: "Todo dia acordo cedo / Moro longe do emprego . . . Tá sempre cheia a condução" (Every day I get up early / I live far from work . . . The bus is always full). However, the song's reference to the figure of credit-enabled consumption (buying extensions "da parcela" or on a credit payment plan) cannot realize in a tangible way all the desires forwarded by the song "Vida" nor by the show itself, as the plot of its opening episodes is partially driven by Penha's mounting credit card debt. Thus the only way to actually make good on credit and consumption's promises of equality is through the external device of pop music stardom: only after they become famous singers can the three Marias live out the fantasy detailed in "Vida" and desired from the show's opening. Thus even the narrative universe of *Cheias* appears to lack faith in, or demonstrates the limits of, credit's ability to change structural conditions. This is the contradictory imaginary offered by credit democracy: the belief in the possible overcoming of one's position in a certain set of social relations (or the belief in equality through consumption) accompanied by the suspicion that this overcoming will only be temporary or might be impossible.[28]

There has been a tendency for cultural objects in a moment of credit (such as *Cheias* and news reports on the nova classe média) to focus on those individuals whose position is most disadvantaged within the division of labor. Domestics, cooks, and sex workers all attract attention in this moment as subjects of economic and journalistic reports. I would argue this is because credit promises equality but is, in fact, most adept at delivering the temporary suspension of one's socioeconomic location. The concern with figures positioned at the very low end or in the most socially marginalized zones of the division of labor is driven by the impact of the suspension that can be realized there. Domestic workers buying sofas and houses—the sudden traversal of this distance in consumptive power is the sublime equality effect of credit and generates a good deal of the affective impact of *Cheias*, as well as of journalistic pieces that pushed the (false) equality of consumption.[29] In *Cheias* this equality effect of the credit-form also affects an erasure of race: domestics in São Paulo and Rio de Janeiro are predominantly women from Afro-Brazilian backgrounds, while in *Cheias* only one is visibly Afro-Brazilian (Maria da Penha, played by Taís Araújo). In this way, the form of credit democracy produced in *Cheias* has the added effect of making race recede as a central problematic of Brazilian society.

The aspirational form of credit which underpins the imaginary of credit democracy presents itself as inheriting a prior progressive or social democratic imaginary of the wage as a mechanism for the redistribution of the surplus. The promise of wage redistribution was not necessarily the promise of a structural change in or overthrowing of the relations of production, but it was certainly one of an equaling of social outcomes. Credit cannot realize either redistribution or structural change; it can only deliver a temporary "equality" in (certain) patterns of consumption, which also deepens financial exploitation (i.e., the creation of debt and claims on future wages). Even so, equal consumption of refrigerators or airline tickets does not mean equal income, equal rights, or equal access to more prestigious or valuable goods (e.g., homes, education, pensions, or state services or protections). Discussions of credit in the mass media from this moment frequently appropriated the aspirational language of left social movements for the ends of sculpting new discursive worlds and subject positions; credit is a net positive in these accounts, because it democratizes consumption and creates a more "inclusive" society. While for many years this was the dominant discourse of credit, its reality, which is perhaps more tangible now, is that it is a site of extended financial exploitation in that this money has to be paid back eventually.

While the state has fostered the spread of credit and the production of an environment in which consumption has been sold as a new form of equality, the state does not get to choose how this environment comes to be mediated culturally—though it tried to influence this as much as possible. Through its promotion of discourses of the nova classe média, the PT state attempted to massage the framing of credit expansion as a net positive; as we can see in *Cheias*, however, the cultural imaginary of credit and consumption has come with suspicion built into it. To the extent that state-promoted ideologies, such as racial democracy, attempt to both work around and produce real differences of race, class, and gender, such formations have always been in contradiction with the structural conditions out of which they were developed. The difference between racial democracy and the kind of credit democracy or promise of equality through credit-enabled consumption seen in *Cheias* is that the latter is a discursive form that appears to not entirely believe in itself.

Finance, Fragility, and Feeling

While the expansion of personal credit has not received as much critical attention as it has perhaps deserved, the rise of finance as a social and economic phenomenon has not gone untheorized. One common approach within the ambit of critical literature in Brazil, which includes the work of Francisco de Oliveira and others, has been to think of the effects of finance on the level of classes or class fractions, which enter into alliances or competition with each other, battling for control of the state or leadership in a hegemonic project. Approaches that focus on the level of classes and fractions, while grasping critical aspects of the transformation the rise of finance has wrought, can miss how this rise has been justified and its expansive set of effects on everyday life and social relations. In this section, after delving into one of Oliveira's arguments concerning finance, I expand on the suspicion found in the formation of credit democracy to explain the deep-seated connection between finance and unstable structures of feeling.

Francisco de Oliveira's insightful and acerbic essay from 2003 on the trajectory of Brazilian underdevelopment, "Duckbilled Platypus,"[30] argues that the international position of Brazil continues to determine much of its political and social formation. Oliveira notes, however, an important change from the developmentalist period to the present; namely, the emergence of a new class wherein "the upper layers of the old proletariat became, in part, what Robert Reich called 'symbolic analysts.' They are the administrators of the pension funds that originated in former state enterprises, of which the most powerful is Previ—the fund of the functionaries of the still state-owned Banco do Brasil."[31] Oliveira continues:

> It is this that explains recent pragmatic convergences between the PT and the PSDB [Brazilian Social Democratic Party], and the apparent paradox that Lula's government is carrying out Cardoso's programme, and radicalising it. This is not a mistake, but the expression of a genuinely new social stratum, based on technicians and intellectuals doubling as bankers—the core of the PSDB; and workers become pension-fund managers—the core of the PT. What they have in common is control over access to public funds, and an insider's knowledge of the lay of the financial land.
>
> The formation of this class in the periphery of globalized capitalism—Reich's theories are essentially concerned with phenomena at the system's dynamic centre—needs closer scrutiny. For not only is there a new place for it in the system—above all in the financial sector and its mediations in

> the state—which satisfies one of the Marxist criteria for defining a class; there is also a new class 'experience,' in Thompson's terms.[32]

Oliveira's analysis of finance is helpful and revealing in many ways—it captures with particular acuity internal transformations of the PT—but encounters a limit in its focus on the level of classes and fractions and on finance as creating new sites of power and as modifying existing class relations. What lies outside the purview of such a Gramscian or class-based approach to finance is the everyday ways finance presses upon and shapes social relations and social life and the fragility of finance's shaping. From Oliveira's inquiry we can derive part of the story, that of classes and fractions, but the level of the everyday, and the kinds of social relations, mental habits, and collective sentiments that finance produces, remains to be narrated. Such an account requires a different frame, in particular because such relations, habits, and sentiments are always fragile and fugitive: due to finance's inherent instability in this period, these elements are never able to fully form themselves into a durable social formation—or in the terms of Raymond Williams, the social forms of finance exist as a "structure of feeling," never quite solidifying into full institutions or ideologies. Finance is a fragile construction because its effects last only as long as the flows of credit and its moments of calling to account are its moments of fracture and failure.

There is a special relation between certain forms of finance and feeling.[33] Since financial flows are always to an extent temporary, the social forms of finance are riven by contradiction and are exposed to collapse. As Jonathan Flatley notes, Raymond Williams used the term "structure of feeling" to describe this kind of social and cultural formation that is more transitory than ideologies or institutions: "Williams conceived of the term, however, in a very specific sense. He initially describes the term as useful not only because it enables us to talk about the sociality of affect, but because it enables us to describe those structures that mediate between the social and the personal that are more ephemeral and transitory than set ideologies or institutions. The problem with most forms of social analysis, Williams notes, is that the 'habitual past tense' that such analysis falls into creates a set of 'finished products'; it fixes the social forms in which we participate."[34]

Structures of feeling are, in a sense, what finance traffics in; finance is never long lasting but rather a crisis waiting to happen, especially in the contemporary period. Existing below the level of institutions and ideologies, structures of feeling can give us access to "impulses that are not yet organized as movements"[35] and "social experiences in solution."[36] Moreover, Raymond Williams's approach to them (in particular in *Marxism and Literature*) was a way of making more supple, and critiquing, Gramscian approaches to culture through the category of hegemony, which can reduce the social to "fixed forms."[37] Thus the term is well situated to provide a supplement to approaches to finance as a matter of classes and fractions, which have difficulty tracing the ephemeral, noninstitutional, and fragile collective forms of meaning and sense making that proliferate in a moment of finance.

The structure of feeling of this moment of Brazilian finance is a mode of anticipatory assessment, which I call "projection." In the following I will define projection as an opening onto the near future's promises and possibilities or as a movement between a set of material conditions and their projection into a future moment. I will argue that it is in this appearance "in solution" of projection that one can track finance's shaping of contemporary social relations, habits, and feeling. Neither merely the space of class fractions contesting for power, nor that of capital's colonization of subjectivity, finance's structure of feeling straddles the psychic and social.

As such, the structure of feeling of projection is marked by the political economic form of finance in a very particular way. As discussed previously my understanding of finance, and credit more specifically, follows the work of heterodox Marxists, such as Annie McClanahan and Joshua Clover, who have argued that finance and credit are best understood as a claim upon future wages.[38] Credit and other forms of finance, as a claim upon future earnings, are a form of extraction that extends the moment of value's realization into the future. As we saw in Chapter 1 with the theory of history as catastrophe, the near future can become a site of speculation and theorization in certain moments of finance, because the ever-receding "near" future is where claims against future wages will either be paid in full or defaulted on. Thus the control, monitoring, and shaping of this temporal space becomes an object of concern. Projection as a structure of feeling of finance in Brazil is marked by a similar relation to and referencing of the near future, where the promises or failures of finance will be realized.

In the following, I examine three relays through which the current wave of finance has passed into the everyday social world of post-2003 Brazil: personal credit, the shift of corporations to financing through the stock market, and a state-sponsored construction and infrastructure boom. I trace examples of how the expansion of finance in each of these relays has been accompanied by a refraction of finance's projective structure of feeling. In so doing I draw on a corpus of recent financial, sociological, and journalistic writings to read these pieces (occasionally against the grain) for the fleeting glimpse they give us of finance's fragile social formation. I do so with the aim of leveraging this theorization of finance's fragility into a contribution to discussions of the June 2013 protests that swept across Brazil.

Postdating, or Social Relations of Credit

In a 2005 talk at the Twelfth Congresso Brasileiro de Sociologia, Larissa Pelúcio discussed a phenomenon that emerged in 2001–2002 in which men who frequented *travesti* sex workers, began crafting a new identity for themselves as "t-lovers." "Travesti" is a Brazilian Portuguese word and category for defining men who dress and/or live as women and have frequently undertaken feminine bodily transformations (especially by hormones and silicone) but who opt not to have sexual reassignment surgery.[39] The term "t-lover" is derived from the U.S. English term "t-girl," and in the early 2000s, as the internet entered more and more into daily life in Brazil's large cities, the t-lover as an identity spread across blogs and chat rooms used by men who interacted with travestis on the sexual marketplace.[40]

One part of Pelúcio's talk narrates how a loosely knit group of individuals, frequenters of the t-lover blogosphere and chat boards, started organizing days in 2004 and 2005 in both Rio and São Paulo, where they would gather at a bar or club, usually frequented by travestis and their cliental for the purposes of business, in order to have a day celebrating travestis as "muses." These days of "celebration" occurred during the first years of the mass expansion of personal credit into Brazil discussed in the opening part of this chapter. What interests me about Pelúcio's account of these days is how we can begin to register at this site the slow infiltration of the form of the credit economy into social relations.

Interestingly, the "celebrations" organized by t-lovers had one defining rule: sexual and economic transactions were forbidden. Pelúcio writes: "Kisses and a date-like atmosphere are not uncommon in meetings, but according to the implicit code of conduct of the São Paulo t-lovers meeting, you cannot have sex, nor cause embarrassment to travestis with persistent assaults or invasive actions such as running your hands over their bodies. Attitudes of this kind have already led to the expulsion of some members."[41] The rules for these gatherings were very strict: no sex, touching, or lewd talk and clear consequences for the violation of said rules. What is intriguing about these events is how they mirror in certain ways the tropes we saw earlier in *Cheias de charme*, in particular an interest in marginalized figures combined with a sudden, unsustainable change in their circumstances (from "sex workers" to "muses" in this case), but with an additional twist.

The t-days attempt to open a different space for social relations, but one that is created not from an overthrowing of the hierarchies and the economic exploitation of service work, but rather from their momentary cancellation or postponement. That is, the t-days were a space of social relations generated by a temporary postdating of relations of exchange and the money-form (buying of services) wherein the "celebration" takes its semantic force from a momentary displacement of prior conditions of a social relation mediated through exchange (but not a complete break from them, which would be a politics). What we have then is a celebration not of travestis in and of themselves, as complicated, actual individuals who face systematic forces of life-threatening violence, but a celebration and an eroticization of a momentary departure from the conditions of "real" existence. The t-days were celebrations, not of "muses," but of the very power to defer for a moment economic realities, which is exactly what finance and credit make possible: to postdate or to project material conditions into the near future.

It is the way this particular social situation turns around a suspension of economic conditioning that I want to define as characteristic of the structure of feeling of projection. Projection, or this gesture of displacement or orientation toward a possible near future, in this example generates a frisson at the momentary cancellation of market relations, a cancellation which must necessarily in some future moment collapse. If credit is understood as a claim upon future earnings or as turning the space of the near future into an object of concern, then the very form of projection, postdating, or suspension can be seen as inherent in credit as a modality or instrument, and in the case of the t-days we can see the form of credit passing into social relations.

Moreover, instead of an increasingly market-based sociality that one would expect under neoliberalism, what the t-days demonstrate is a form of financialized social relation, one shaded with a projective structure of feeling wherein pleasure and excitement are derived from cancelling, however briefly, the economic structuring of everyday life. My claim is that variations on this form come to shade social relations, assessments, and collective sensibilities in this period and that this structure of feeling is tied specifically to finance, not to marketization or neoliberalism. In the following two sections my aim will be to trace the spread and subsequent collapse of this structure of feeling at two other critical sites of financial expansion in this moment: the stock market and the state-linked construction sector.

Eike, Projection, and Speculation

One of the defining features of finance in Brazil has been the use of high interest rates to attract excess global capital flows, both before and after the 2007–2008 financial crisis in North Atlantic countries. Brazil avoided many of the effects of this crisis by doubling down on credit and finance—increasing the amount of capital and credit flows in different sectors of the economy—and this was possible in part because money that had been invested in North Atlantic stock, housing, and personal credit instruments was searching for untapped sites of investment. One of those sites became the Brazilian stock market. In 2007 the Brazilian stock exchange was home to Initial Public Offerings (IPOs) totaling US$26 billion.[42] In 2006 and 2007 alone Brazilian companies, through IPOs and debt issuances, raised more capital than they had in the previous twenty years combined.[43]

No figure was more representative of how finance and extractive capitalism mixed in this period than Eike Batista. Between 2005 and 2012 Eike's EBX group of companies captured US$26 billion in funding, primarily through the Bovespa, the Brazilian stock exchange.[44] As a result Eike's net worth, tied to his ownership of various EBX companies' stock, soared to US$30 billion, making him the seventh wealthiest person in the world, and led him to state his ambition to overtake Bill Gates at the top of that list. In 2015, after the collapse of his companies' stock prices, Eike became Brazil's first "negative billionaire" with a net worth of US–$1 billion.

One way that Eike's story has been read is as an exemplary case of hubris or as a cautionary tale; Eike's own reading was that he was the victim of "bad luck." However, these kinds of readings can't explain why people once believed Eike's companies were worth investing their money in, nor how, in a moment of stock market inflows and global pressure to find profitable sites of investment, they came to be seen as the doorway to a different economic future in Brazil. To explain this we have to name the structure of feeling which accompanied Eike's rise and fall.

Eike's empire was centered on the petroleum extraction company OGX. The company was created in 2007 and captured US$1.3 billion through a private offering of shares. Its IPO—the largest in the history of the Brazilian market—captured another US$4.1 billion in 2008.[45] All this was before the company had produced a single drop of oil. As Eike relates in his 2011 memoir-cum–business self-help guide, *O X da questão*, there was so much demand for OGX that another US$40 billion was invested.[46] Eike's empire crumbled when drilling began and it was then revealed that OGX's projections of the amount of oil they would be able to extract had been vastly overestimated.[47] In 2010 OGX was worth R$74 billion; by April 2013 it had lost 94 percent of its value.[48]

It would be possible to simply say Eike is representative of the speculative impulse of financialized capitalism, but such a critique would be both too easy and would miss the specific form of anticipatory assessment which underpinned Eike's rise and which concerns the ability to project. In *O X da questão*, Eike writes: "The fact that exploration activity and production in Brazil had a success rate of 50%, while the global average was only 18%, called my attention to the possibilities of an undertaking here. That is, I would have three times more chances of finding oil here than my American colleagues might have had a century ago. If the business was already fantastic with only an 18% chance, it would certainly be spectacular with 50%."[49] Projected production is not actual production. So in fact what people were investing in was a possible future.[50] This is what happens when there is an excess of capital and fewer and fewer sites of investment capable of producing returns—bets begin to be made on the future, on probability, on predictions. What is important to note, however, is that this is not just pure fantasy or speculation as frequently is intimated in some literatures on finance.

The structure is more precise, in that it is not just any kind of company that underwent a spectacular rise and fall, but an oil company. And what is specific to oil (and construction) companies and what can make them sites for asset bubbles in certain moments of finance are that they possess "reserves" or "land banks." In both oil and construction companies a key asset, beside the actual barrels of oil or homes they sell, are the pieces of territory that they have bought but have not yet exploited. A land bank or set of territorial reserves is the location of future value production in these industries—but their value is always only a projection. This then is the specific form that OGX and Eike sold: not entirely a fantasy but rather a projection linked to material conditions and one that would be verified only in the future. "Our initial estimates were incorrect" is a statement which will have less variation when it concerns an assembly line where the variables and inputs are more or less known. What makes possible billions of dollars of investment in a company that has produced nothing are three things: an excess of capital in global markets; a site of investment with an opening into the near future; and the normalization of and familiarity with projection as a kind of mental habit.

The inflection of finance's projective structure of feeling as it passes through the lens of the stock market is a type of assessment, judgment, or anticipatory knowledge concerning unknown future value. Thus in this case it is not that finance is entirely speculative, that its promises are completely arbitrary and disconnected from the real economy, but rather that the spread of finance in the contemporary moment in Brazil has brought with it a projective, anticipatory form of assessment. Similar to the t-days example, projection here takes the form of a departure from a set of material conditions and a putting into relation the present with a possible near future. Both in the t-days and with Eike and OGX, projection forms an essential part of a social complex, while it also operates at a level beneath those of ideologies or institutions, appearing more as a tendency, "sense of things," or gesture which evades attempts to fix it or pin it down into a conceptual structure.

PACs and Contradictory Waiting

Starting in 2007 and continuing in the aftermath of the financial crisis, the Lula government released a significant amount of funds and credit into the financial system and into industrial sectors, in particular the construction sector. This was done through two instruments: The first was the Programa de Aceleração do Crescimento (PAC) which aimed to release R$619 billion into the Brazilian economy between 2007 and 2010, primarily into infrastructural projects.[51] The second was the Minha Casa, Minha Vida (My House, My Life) program, begun in 2009, which set aside R$34 billion for housing construction primarily aimed at low- or middle-income sectors of the housing market.[52]

In an article written in 2012, "Waiting in the Ruins: The Aesthetics and Politics of Favela Urbanization in 'PACification' Rio de Janeiro," Mariana Cavalcanti describes how PAC program funding had been used to remake the urban landscape of Rio, in particular in the run-up to the World Cup and Olympic games. Cavalcanti explains how PAC funds paid for highly visible infrastructural projects (such as the Rocinha pedestrian overpass or the Alemão cable car) which, she argues, created the spectacle of (as opposed to real) integration of favela and formal city. The latter half of the article examines PAC building projects in the Manguinhos region of Rio, concluding that many of them were poorly built and quickly descended into ruins. These new urbanization projects, as well as the UPP (Unidade de Polícia Pacificadora or Police Pacification Unit), the new public security project of placing police stations in informal areas, were heralded as a return of the state to marginalized zones of Rio. Cavalcanti complicates this perception and concludes her piece by describing residents' "sense of waiting": "Manguinhos residents share a tacit sense of waiting for something to happen. Signs of change seem to be closing in on them. As the remote effects of the UPP program entwine with the transformation in the physical landscape of Manguinhos, the sense that a rupture is looming on the horizon colors the imaginations of residents. And yet on a daily level, these changes end up being experienced as an intensification of what is already known. . . . The sense of imminent change itself has, moreover, endured for over three years, thus becoming yet another contradictory part of daily life itself."[53] Change (PAC construction, UPP implantation) appeared to be occurring all around the residents, but these changes resulted in merely an "intensification" of the known (i.e., ruins). Moreover, this sensation of pending change or of the anticipation of change endured for over three years, which marked the period from the beginning of PAC construction in Manguinhos (2009) to the writing of Cavalcanti's article (2012). Cavalcanti describes a contradictory sensation of waiting, which represents what we might call a form of collective disposition on the part of residents as to the possibility of an anticipated change's arrival. Here finance's projective structure of feeling is refracted through a form of collective or group perception, and the contradictory nature of this sense of things or disposition is a measure of the structure's fragility.

Jumping ahead three years to 2015, we can find also in Manguinhos another example of the legacy of this projective form—but now in the fading of finance's power. In 2008 the periodical *EXTRA* published what was to become a celebrated photo on its front page of a young boy, Christiano Pereira, "swimming" in drainage from Cedae, Rio's water and sewage utility. Then-President Lula, moved by the photo, promised as a part of the PAC program to build a swimming pool for Christiano, whose dream, reported by the news media, was to be a professional swimmer. When Lula came to Manguinhos in 2008 to inaugurate several of the PAC works, including a swimming pool, there were multiple photo ops of Lula and Christiano together which were published by traditional media and spread across social media. In July 2015 Christiano, now fifteen years old, passed away in mysterious circumstances, which many news outlets took as an opportunity to update Christiano's story and that of the impact of the PAC on Manguinhos. *EXTRA* was most direct: "Christiano foi o símbolo da esperança num futuro que nunca se concretizou" (Christiano was a symbol of hope of a future that was never realized).[54] By 2015 many of the PAC works, including the pool, were abandoned. Instead of a contradictory waiting whose outcome was still undecided, what had materialized was a perception or collective sense that the projected infrastructural future never arrived, that it was a possible future that "nunca se concretizou" (was never realized).

The anticipatory feeling produced by the spread of finance-enabled PAC construction, one dependent upon a suspension of present material conditions or their projection into a near future, had resolved into its opposite: instead of anticipation, disillusion. If one aspect of projection as a structure of feeling is its creation of a collective sense of the possibility of a shifting of present material conditions, when those material conditions do not change, what this projective structure of feeling leaves in its wake is a perhaps more long-lasting set of feelings and dispositions: namely that of failed and disappointed hopes, an affective structure for which there is no quick or easy resolution. It is the collapse of this projective structure of feeling, which left in its wake disappointment and disillusion, that serves as a partial, yet often unacknowledged, background to the 2013 uprisings in Brazil.

In this instance, finance produced a projective structure of feeling, which I have traced through each of the primary sites of finance's cultivation in contemporary Brazil. With this structure of feeling, as the financial boom weakened, the initial pleasure at or permitting of projection faded into suspicion, complaint, and resentment. Finance's projective structure of feeling is fragile in that its promises and propositions never seem entirely convincing; that its anticipations always require a partial suspension of belief; that its postdating of economic realities always feel a bit too easy. Because of this incompleteness or instability, finance's sustenance through feeling has to be supplemented with state or structural violence once its crisis begins to shake out. This is the importance of focusing on levels other than the institutional, for only by focusing on the fragility of finance's affective structure can we account for key aspects of the political forms that have emerged in its wake.

This is nowhere more apparent than in the interpretations and analyses of the June 2013 wave of protests (Jornadas de Junho) that swept across Brazil.[55] The interpretations and debates over this sequence of events are too varied and numerous to summarize, but the vast majority share two features: first, a recognition that the protests represented a profound disaffection with the PT governance cycle, and second, that many of the participants formed part of a new set of political actors. One axis of debate has been whether the protests were evidence of a new middle class or new proletariat making their first demands on the state or whether the lack of or nature of the demands voiced in the protests pointed to these actors as being naive youngsters or politically inexperienced individuals.[56]

A polarization, however, between middle-class or new proletarian demands and inexperience misinterprets the meaning of the demands that circulated in the streets during those months, which centered on improved health, education, and transportation systems and infrastructure.[57] These were not merely the ingenuous demands of the politically inept or of "new" classes, but rather demands that registered the fragility of the financial boom underpinning the state policies of the prior decade. The calls for infrastructure and public services represented a demand for the state to materialize something solid, something that would endure out of the bubble of credit that it had inflated for almost ten years. These were demands that, at least in part, emerged out of the downslope of finance's affective structure, of a moment in which the realization that the projections and promises of finance were more faux than firm and in which the sensation of contradictory anticipation was being resolved into resentment and frustration. Given the subsequent austerity program pushed through by the Temer government—parts of which were initiated by former President Dilma—it would seem these demands were anything but naive.

In "Lula in the Labyrinth" (2006), which continues his analysis of the rise of the PT, Francisco de Oliveira argues that contemporary Brazil is marked by "a novel combination of neo-populism and party stratification, shored up by social-liberal handouts, on the one hand, and government graft, on the other," which "has helped to forge a new form of class rule in Brazil that could be characterized as 'hegemony in reverse.'"[58] Revisiting his earlier analysis Oliveira compares Lula's Brazil to a duck-billed platypus, combining "external dependency with casualized labour, truncated accumulation with an unremittingly inegalitarian social order; despite thirty years of democratization."[59] In Oliveira's argument, this new social class—a social class with access to and control over public funds—has not been able to unify the bourgeoisie, leading to "hegemony in reverse"—wherein the oppressed masses appear to gain moral leadership of society (via the PT's election) but in fact what their "ascension" to power makes possible are ongoing and, perhaps more rapacious, forms of exploitation.

Oliveira's expansive and masterful account moves well beyond a mere explanation of financial transformation—finance is rather one piece, though an important one, of the larger narrative he constellates. His approach to finance tells one part of the story particularly well—namely, what happens at the level of class fractions—but what needs to be added to this level of analysis is the critical and expansive role played in the last decade by financial para-corporatism and a fragile structure of feeling of projection. It is not surprising that the first political form at the tail end of the current financial and credit inflation included a call for the government, which had skillfully ridden the boom, to produce something other than financialized forms of exploitation (e.g., housing debt, crédito consignado, public debt from unfinished infrastructure projects, etc.). What Oliveira's argument does help us understand is how these demands moved alongside and then cathected strongly to calls to end the "corruption" of the social class with control over public funds. However, to capture the always partially obscure origins of the disappointment and disillusion which fueled the expansion of the protests and their demands, our analysis needs to make space for the failures of finance and the collapse of the structure of feeling of projection.

What is visible in the subsequent turn to austerity is an arc that has played out over and over again across the long downturn. The crisis of the long downturn, which began in the 1970s with the declining profitability of capital, has yet to be solved, and financial flows and attempted financial accumulation can only delay, postdate, and avert the crisis's reappearance for so long. When the flows slow and the bubbles begin to deflate, para-corporatist financial states find there is nothing left to give, no more projections and anticipations, no more credit, and they turn to the familiar devices of austerity and state violence to enforce or prepare a socialization of the crisis onto any group but their own. Once the fragile structure of feeling begins to crumble, all that remains is repossession, repression, and the eventual struggle over yet another round of the crisis's socialization.

Anti-Subjects of Credit

The third transformation, beyond failed financial para-corporatism and unstable feeling, which finance has wrought in Brazil concerns the subject. In *Discipline and Punish* Foucault discusses modern disciplinary procedures as producing the "modern soul."[60] With the rise of disciplinary apparatuses and institutions of enclosure, disciplinary techniques came to reform the soul instead of merely punishing the body. They did so, however, through a complex set of processes aimed at the body, among which were the art of distributions (placing bodies in enclosed, portioned spaces), the control of activity (of time and gesture), the organization of "geneses" (various forms of training), and the composition of forces (tactically combining individual bodies into larger "machines"). Working in concert with the disciplinary techniques of hierarchal surveillance, normalizing judgment, and examination, these operations on the body were part of a historical process giving rise to the individual and its "soul."[61]

If the subject as we have known it since the seventeenth century has been created by "subject[ion] to someone else" and/or through the production of "a conscience or self-knowledge,"[62] the specific environment of credit expansion in Brazil has required a shift in this apparatus, from a concern with monitoring the interiority of individuals to turning the subject into a pass-through or gateway to an asset or into what we might call an "anti-subject." In the moment of personal credit the state has become less concerned with the "souls" or interiority of subjects, and instead a legal environment has been prepared in which the subject serves as a gateway for repossessing or seizing assets and income. As we will see below, this legal environment, which exposes individuals to the threat of state violence and privation in new ways, was a necessary requirement for the expansion of personal credit in Brazil.

This approach to the subject and credit differs from what has been so far the most in-depth work on the relation between the subject and finance, Maurizio Lazzarato's *The Making of the Indebted Man*, which tracks the asymmetry of power inherent in debt. Drawing on a rich philosophical tradition of thinking on debt (including Nietzsche, Marx, and Deleuze and Guattari), Lazzarato makes an argument for debt and debtor-creditor relationships as the "archetype of social relations." For Lazzarato this means society is based in "an asymmetry of power and not on that of a commercial exchange that implies and presupposes equality."[63] Debt implies the production of a subject who secularizes Christian guilt, promising to repay and to keep his or her promises.[64]

My position is that credit, in general, but also specifically in the way it has been massified in Brazil, requires a commitment on the part of the state to defend a narrower definition of property and collateral and to threaten or allow violence to seize assets. That is, credit as a social relation is not only defined by a direct creditor-to-debtor relationship but is shaped by and requires a new social environment, one which blends very specific legal characteristics and public security institutions and apparatuses. To "convince" banks to lend to individuals has required giving them the ability, authority, and means to repossess whatever the credit was used to purchase, to seize future income, and/or the assets posted as collateral. In short credit requires the readying of a legal environment where repossession is swift and difficult to contest and in which the state or parastate forces signal their readiness to do or support the work of repossession and to defend intensified notions of private property. In this way credit represents an important site of imbrication between the militarized security state and the financial para-corporatist state. This legal environment, due to new linkages between repressive and institutional state apparatuses, produces not subjects with "modern souls," but rather subjects whose interiority becomes less of a concern and who serve, within the social relations of credit, primarily as a pass-through or gateway to assets or income to be seized.

The readying of this social environment and the threat or sedimentation of force necessary to sustain it can be described as the new security logic of credit. To take one potential example among many, Ana Carla

A. Costa and Joao M. P. De Mello, in "Judicial Risk and Credit Market Performance: Micro Evidence from Brazilian Payroll Loans," present an argument for the creation of this new environment: "In recent years, the literature has built a near consensus that 'sound' institutions are congenial to good economic performance. . . . Institutions, insofar as they determine the economic environment agents operate in, should be important for explaining economic outcomes. Quite often, the specific mechanism through which institutions influence economic performance is protection from expropriation. In environments in which expropriation is likely, agents underinvest (from a social perspective) relative to more secure ones. In the end, a plethora of suboptimal micro-economic decisions amount to a poorer aggregate economic performance."[65] The environment that must be created then is one in which *lenders* are protected "from expropriation." The legal framework of repossession and bankruptcy was the subject of a great deal of change in the early 2000s in Brazil: repossession of vehicles was facilitated, bankruptcy made less complicated, certain kinds of creditors given priority over others, and the use of future income as collateral for crédito consignado loans was defended by the state in court.[66] The central aim of these changes was making the seizure of collateral and repossession and resale of assets easier, and this was done primarily by removing rights and legal remedies from debtors.

The argument advanced by policy makers was that making repossession easier and allowing payments to be deducted directly from individuals' income (which we might call by the less uplifting name of wage or income garnishment) would deepen credit markets. A version of this argument is offered in Juliano Assunção, Efraim Benmelech, and Fernando S. S. Silva's "Repossession and the Democratization of Credit." The authors analyze the changes to vehicle repossession law and the market for auto loans and echo the idea that changing the nature of "property" by making it more available to seizure would increase access to the equality of consumption offered by credit:

> On one hand, increased recovery of collateral induces banks to offer larger loans with lower credit spreads and longer maturities. On the other hand, however, increased recovery rates enables riskier borrowers who were previously rejected and rationed out of the market to obtain credit. . . .
> We show that the reform brought about an expansion of credit, enabling riskier, low-income borrowers to obtain loans and purchase newer, more expensive cars. We refer to this effect as the "democratization of credit," in which the strengthening of the ability of lenders to foreclose, repossess, and sell assets increases the supply of credit to those who need it most.[67]

Changes in repossession, credit, and bankruptcy laws reframed both the importance of private property and the legal understanding of ownership. Generally speaking, individuals' property (or "collateral" in the form of wages) became less "private," more fungible, and easier to seize, and the importance of repossession and seizure to the existing social order became more pronounced. If credit forms a part of the process of "democratization" and a key part of extending credit is the easy repossession and the direct seizure of income which drives profits up, then the state and para-state agencies who enforce these laws have a mandate to effect, threaten, or defend seizures using the means deemed necessary. The more they become discursively associated with democracy, corporate property rights become increasingly sacred—to the extent that upholding these property rights becomes a part of upholding the very institutions of democracy.

In Althusser's famous "Ideology and Ideological State Apparatuses" essay, he initially argues that there is a dialectical relation between the repressive and ideological state apparatuses (RSAs and ISAs, respectively). However, over the course of the essay it becomes clear that, like most theorists in the moment of corporatist or welfare states, Althusser is most interested in the ISAs, in particular in those aimed at the young (indeed the "Ideology" essay was born out of a larger project on the French school system that had been abandoned).[68] Foucault's genealogical analysis of regimes of sovereign, disciplinary, and biopolitical power breaks with Althusser's emphasis on ideology, in part by turning to the body (discipline) and population (biopolitics). But while attentive in many respects to both corporeal and incorporeal violences, in Foucault's work there is still little room for an accounting for state and para-state violence.[69] However, in a moment of finance-led accumulation, when new forms of the repressive state apparatuses come to permeate the social field, it feels important to find ways of tracking and explaining coercion as something other than merely the loutish older sibling of consent, discipline, or *méconnaissance*.

What makes it difficult to talk about subjects of credit in this context is that this is a subjectivity which does not privilege interiority.[70] In his later work Foucault pushes beyond Althusser's theory of interpellation to examine the ways in which the subject performs its own subjection by self-surveillance. If the rise of mass credit produces new imbrications between the legal conception of property and the state power to enforce that conception, what does it mean for the subject and subjection? Clearly we are at a distance from those great disciplinary institutions of the welfare or national popular state, and instead of self-surveillance or the monitoring of interiority, we have the subject as a pass-through. Subjects of credit, particularly in this social formation, are hollow because the new regimes of property and seizure care little for their particularity, care little about cultivating their interiority; rather, the subject is a gateway to the seizure of an asset or income. Contra Lazzarato and the interpretation of credit or debt as guilt, when it comes to credit connected to a tangible, resellable asset or an income stream, the guilt of the subject lessens in importance. What matters is the ability to seize, garnish, and resell or, critically, the threat and power to force the "free" circulation of collateral and assets. If you can't pay someone else will purchase the good that you have already made a number of payments on; or if you have no goods and your future wages or income have been pledged as collateral, it doesn't matter if you feel guilty enough to pay—the state and financial institutions will seize your checks. From this perspective on credit, there is perhaps no "subject," rather only a door, passage, or gateway to an asset or income stream.[71]

Thus my argument is that the legal environment that undergirds the expansion of personal credit in Brazil has required a new imbrication between the threat of state or state-sanctioned violence and the production of subjects. We might call these subjects "anti-subjects" due to how their production breaks with the disciplinary and pastoral tradition of monitoring, assessing, and cultivating interiority and exposes them in new ways to the threat or possibility of state violence. This is the case both because credit is inherently unstable as a para-corporatist formation and structure of feeling (thus leading to the use of state violence as its supplement) and because the state commits itself to defending a new, more rigid conception of private property as well as to using force to seize assets and income as the credit bubble expands, contracts, and then deflates.

A Fragile Collectivity

What I have traced in this chapter are the ways that fragility has inhered in each of these transformations—as para-corporatism, feeling, and in the formation of anti-subjects—that the most recent expansion of finance, in particular as personal credit, has wrought in Brazil after 2003. I have also drawn attention to how credit expansion has moved alongside militarized public security and how the expansion of finance requires the threat of state-sanctioned violence to structure its legal environment and to deal with the political subjects that result from the end of projection.[72] If certain forms of personal credit imply a turn away from the interiority of the subject, what the structure of mass credit in Brazil has left in its wake is an ambiguous para-corporatist formation. The denouement of the experiment with massifying credit in Brazil has yet to fully play out, and it remains unclear if the high levels of indebtedness will burst into a full-fledged crisis or if families and individuals will, while suffering through rising unemployment and failing wages caused by a turn to austerity, manage to find ways to slowly and painfully pay down their debts.

One way of picturing the fragile para-corporatist collectivity called forth by this moment of credit is by focusing on those whom credit has made most vulnerable, which can be done by extrapolating from national and city-level data. First, on a national level Serasa's 2014 "Mapa da Inadimplência no Brasil" revealed that populations with the most difficulty managing their credit are the urban poor, with 23 percent of "Jovens Adultos da Periferia" (young adults from the periphery) and 17 percent of "Massa Trabalhadora Urbana" (urban workers) having one credit account in default by thirty to ninety days.[73] A 2015 Data Favela study revealed that "48% [of residents of informal areas] had loaned a credit card to parents or to friends," and a 2014 study found that three out of four people who loan their names (so family members or friends can take out credit because they are unable to) had delinquent accounts.[74] Nationally in March 2016, 41 percent of the population over the age of eighteen had at least one credit account that was behind payment, and of these, 77.2 percent earned up to twice the minimum wage, with 40.0 percent receiving between one and two *salários mínimos* and 37.2 percent living on less than R$880.00 a month (roughly US$270).[75]

We can draw a perhaps obvious conclusion from this: adults in lower-income communities, whether in Rio or Recife, are the group with the greatest need for credit to fill in what their wages are unable to provide. They are also the group with the smallest margin of error when it comes to paying money back. A few missed weeks of work or a lost job and individuals can become stuck, if they were not before, on a treadmill or under a mountain of unpayable debt. Second, if the economy continues to contract these will be the first people thrown out of work, which makes them among the most vulnerable to forms of economic decision making, such as having to decide to pay down their debt or pay rent, buy food, or subsidize a child's education, which will affect their ability for self-reproduction.

Much media and institutional discourse around credit has seen it as a net positive, as opposed to being a form of financial exploitation, and the ways in which credit exacerbates marginalized individuals' already significant vulnerability has been often overlooked. In a situation in which the state has decreased the credit supply and in which many individuals are already behind on payments, it becomes harder to avoid default by rolling over or transferring debt. If the financial wave continues to ebb, the state's most readily available means to enforce debts, socialize crisis dynamics through austerity measures, and keep financial extraction running are forms of physical, legal, or structural violence which will find their most likely target in those who are already significantly socially marginalized.

The only certainty of the political future in Brazil in a context of global economic contraction seems to be the difficulty of entirely rolling back austerity measures, and if austerity measures in some form continue, then with respect to the resolution of the most recent wave of finance and consumer credit, there seem to be two potential outcomes. In the first austerity measures advance, unemployment continues to rise, the credit supply shrinks, but individuals sacrifice and suffer and unevenly pay down their debts, while sectors of the population are exposed to routinized, direct or indirect forms of state violence, whether in the streets in moments of repossession, or as the result of the militarization of everyday life, the continued criminalization of poverty, and the spread of extremist, fascist, or law-and-order politics. In the second, the difficult, fraught, and complicated work of organizing and politicizing some segment of the fragile collectivity of debtors, alone or as a part of or alongside other groups, results in a politics that, among other anti-austerity demands, calls for not merely the restoration of the flows of credit, but for their abolition and the advancement of other means for the provision of the goods necessary for survival and full lives. Here in the arc between repayment and repossession, a path divides into two: on the one side a politics of repression and austerity which would complete the movement between lending and repayment, and on the other a politics against the subtle, obscure, yet shattering forms of exploitation called forth by finance. While historically we have seen that the former possibility has most frequently overcome the latter, in repetition lies the potential for variance and the hope—no matter how dark the times—that this time the outcome might be other.

CHAPTER 4

Voided Collectivities

CULTURES OF CIRCULATION IN CONTEMPORARY MEXICO

> The human being is in the most literal sense a ζῷον πολιτιχόν [political animal] not merely a gregarious animal, but an animal which can individuate itself only in the midst of society.
>
> **Karl Marx, *Grundrisse*, p. 84**

If Brazil's path in the aughts through the new financial architectures created in the 1990s resulted in a credit and extraction fueled boom, Mexico's path through this stage of the long downturn involved a turn not to credit, but to circulation. Though both Mexico and Brazil moved toward export-oriented strategies coupled with new forms of financial integration, one difference is that Brazil's exports were primary commodities flowing to China and elsewhere, while Mexico's non-oil exports have mainly been from maquiladoras and manufacturing for export.[1] As has subsequently become clear, the maquiladora had a structural weakness in that assembly plants along the border imported both parts for assembly and capital goods. The importation of inputs and capital goods meant that the maquiladora did not lead to the expansion of the national productive economy but rather to a dependency on importation across the manufacturing sector.[2] As a result, Mexico has often run a current account deficit in the manufacturing sector as a whole, which the federal government has attempted to offset by courting financial inflows.[3]

With respect to finance in Mexico, there was no attempt to grow domestic consumption with a massive influx of personal credit, and as of 2012 only 35.5 percent of adults had a bank account and roughly only one in four adults had a credit card.[4] However, the mass of overaccumulated capital in the global economy does find ways of entering, especially after the 2007–2008 crisis and after the collapse of oil prices. These points of entry pass primarily through corporate borrowing and the state, as the total debt of the federal government climbs from 1,738.23 billion pesos in 2007 to 7,851.30 billion pesos in 2016.[5] While Brazil turns to extraction and consumer credit as a form of financial para-corporativism in a moment of "stability" in the midst of the long downturn, in Mexico these years are marked by death and destruction. This chapter advances two reasons which can contribute to an explanation of this difference—without pretending to be an exhaustive account. In Mexico the economy turns not just to finance, but away from production to circulation, and the state turns from corporativist and para-corporativist techniques to state violence as a primary infrastructure of social control.

Enrique Dussel Peters has described this period as one not of export-oriented, but rather "import-oriented industrialization."[6] Picking up on and extending Dussel Peters's insight, I will argue that instead of export, the dominant political economic form in these years has been one of circulation, which I understand as a set of new articulations between the spheres of production and circulation. Marx, in *Capital*, volume 1, divides capitalist economies into two spheres: production, where goods are produced, and circulation, where value is realized, usually through the conversion of commodities via prices into money, and where people purchase the commodities necessary for their survival.[7] The sphere of production is the location of factories, labor, and the site of the production of surplus value, while the sphere of circulation is the location of enterprises like logistics firms and banks which move commodities and money in order to facilitate the realization of surplus value. What I argue is that many of the most important transformations in the Mexican economy in the post-2001 period are marked not by an overcoming of production by circulation, but rather by new articulations and relations between the spheres of production and circulation.[8]

We can see these new articulations in the maquiladora and other product assembly operations: they are focused on the "assembly" of parts made elsewhere, and as such they expand the definition of "production" to involve circulation in new ways. In this chapter, however, I will concentrate my attention on three processes which represent critical articulations between, or limit cases of, production and circulation: the drug trade, which is a logistics operation that moves commodities into the high-value consumer zone of the United States but which does not control their sites of production; migration, primarily into the United States, which involves the circulation of bodies and induces capital flows back into the nation not tied to its productive apparatus; and finance, which has taken on two important forms, the first being a switch to forms of financial speculation by large nonfinancial corporations and the second, government borrowing.[9] All three are processes that have their roots in the sphere of production of commodities, labor, and factories, but that are also marked either by new (or renewed) imbrications of circulation and production or by attempts at producing the appearance of accumulation in the sphere of circulation. Moreover, each of these areas represents an important and sizable sector of economic activity, and each is a channel for the acquisition of U.S. currency or foreign exchange.

For my narrative here, these areas which turn from production onto circulation are also critical, because they have furthered the breakdown of the state mediation of the capital-labor relation. It is estimated that roughly 60 percent of economically active Mexicans are in the informal economy or exist on the fringes of the capitalist apparatus of production.[10] These are individuals who do not benefit from many of the state mediations of the capital-labor relationship, including the minimum wage, standard workday, etc. The turns to drug logistics and migration have exacerbated this situation of state disintermediation, producing arguably intensified, but certainly more visible, forms of unfree labor where force, domination, and exposure to death are the rules of the day.

We have seen a switch in Brazil in this period to techniques of financial para-corporativism along with state violence and how this calls forth new subjectivities. In Mexico there is no comparable turn to consumer credit; instead state violence and state-permitted violence increasingly become a primary vector of social control for surplus populations who either remain, attempt to emigrate, or circulate through the nation-space. The turn to state violence can be registered in two different forms. The first is an increase in the amount of money spent on the police and military: the defense budget in Mexico has increased from US$2 billion in 2006 to US$9.3 billion in 2009,[11] while the U.S.-funded Merida Initiative funneled 2.35 billion into the Mexican military and policing between 2008 and 2014. This is a vast increase in the amount of money flowing into the repressive apparatus. The second form has been the redefinition and reclassification of roles, the most important being the use of the military for policing functions.[12] For example, in 2008 policing in Ciudad Juárez was turned over to the Federal Police, a militarized police force, and the military, and in 2009 the Mexican military reported that it had 48,750 soldiers involved in combatting organized crime.[13] As a direct result of these shifts, the number of dead or disappeared in Mexico between 2007 and July 2016, according to one widely cited count, stands at 221,468.[14] It is impossible now to know how many of these individuals died either directly or indirectly as a result of state or para-state forces, but only the most cynical would argue that the state has had no role, either in directly dispensing death or in providing cover for it, given after Ayotzinapa, Tlatlaya, and Tanhuato the clear demonstration of state forces' involvement in high-profile killings and disappearances.

Post-Developmentalist Social Theory

As theorists from Marx on forward have noted, capitalist modes of production and social formations tend toward producing collectivities, for example, of workers and capitalists (in a moment of industrialization) or of surplus populations, the formally employed, and capitalists (in a moment of deindustrialization and/or circulation), which then under certain conditions have the possibility to come into conflict with one another. This tendency toward the production of collectivities which have the potential to be politicized has meant that states and capital have frequently concerned themselves with preventing, forestalling, or channeling the growth of these collective groups. Indeed, much of Foucault's work tracks the proliferation of individualizing processes linked to the rise of the modern state and attendant and expanded forms of governmentality and how these individualizing processes break down prior collective forms (the crowd, for instance, in *Discipline and Punish*), but also how they allow these newly produced "individuals" to be grouped together into weakly collective units (the army, "workers," etc.).[15] What we see in the post-developmentalist or postnational popular period in Mexico is the slow breakdown of these linked processes of individualization and collectivization. What is occurring now, due to the turn to circulation—that is, away from the productive capitalism that was the foundation of the developmentalist state's infrastructure—represents a limit case of the breakdown of these processes which have held sway since the late nineteenth century.

In the national popular or developmentalist moment in Mexico, the state assisted in the shaping of a series of individualizing and collectivizing processes, which atomized individuals and then pooled them into nonrevolutionary collectivities, creating and defending certain formulations of the "people," the "worker," and the "campesino," as well as a gendered imaginary of social reproduction (*amas de casa* [housewives]). The production of subjects and their summation into limited collective forms was a central means of control in this period, as the state, in particular through corporatist infrastructures, linked a range of subjectivizing processes with collective figures of the nation and national capital. In the turn to circulation the state, because of its shift away from corporativist and other infrastructures to ones of state violence, is no longer able to produce either processes of subjectivization or meaningful collectivities to mediate the splits between the increasing surplus population and the remaining individuals who are connected to or who control the productive apparatus.

Cultural works in the period before, but most intensively after, 2006 register and respond to this shift as the military-policing apparatus comes to supercede the corporativist and other infrastructures of the developmental state. In the following I track this registering and response along two main lines. First, by focusing on the "drug war" film[16] *El infierno* and the poetry of Dolores Dorantes, I trace the transformation of two key sites for producing collectivity, labor, and death. I then turn to cultural objects that directly address the conditions of surplus population in a moment of circulation to demonstrate how they pivot on the production of new forms of relation between the individual and the collective. At a most general level I read all these cultural works as involved in thinking through the end of the developmentalist problematic: that is, their critical valence is no longer how to preserve agency in the face of, or to break with, overwhelming or administrated structure but rather to limn the possibilities of collective reproduction and defense in a world rendered unlivable by state and capital.

The Failure

The failure of the state and capital to produce inhabitable lifeworlds and forms of collectivity can be registered in the cultural objects that deal with the drug war, in part because during the developmentalist period in Mexico labor was a privileged site for the production of subjectivity and collective identities and these cultural objects index how little labor serves that function today.[17] These objects reveal that in a moment of surplus population and a turn to circulation, what was once a site for the generation of subjects is now one of interruption of these prior individualizing processes. However, in many cultural objects which meditate on the "drug war" there is still a connection with labor, which means we have not passed beyond all forms of subjectivization, unlike, as we will see, in cultural works on migration; rather we remain at a stage of interruption. This interruption is conditioned by the specific nature of this labor, which is connected more to circulation or logistics than to production and which no longer results in the creation of the grand, depoliticized collectivities of the developmentalist state-capital relation.

The drug trade, as Luca Rastello notes in *I Am the Market*, is at the cutting edge of contemporary logistics. That is, the drug trade is not conducted by mules swallowing forty condoms filled with heroin at a time but rather by moving hundreds of tons of product into high-value northern markets.[18] In the South to North American trade cocaine is the primary source of profit, even though this is a situation that is in flux.[19] In this trade the Mexican drug logistic groups primarily control the transportation (as opposed to production) of product. This is due in part to geography (Colombia, Bolivia, and Peru are not their home base), but also to a shift in the structure of modern megacorporations involving the rise of global logistics which the Mexican organizations mimic.[20] The new corporate form produces very little; rather it is a condensed core of upper and middle management controlling a global supply chain. Profit is made by exploiting the international division of labor and moving products into a high-value consumer area (like the United States) where their price undergoes a substantial markup. Jasper Bernes has analyzed this new production model:

> As opposed to the older, "push production" model, in which factories generated massive stockpiles of goods that retailers would clear from the market with promotions and coupons, in today's "pull" production system "retailers share POS [point-of-sale] information with their vendors who can then rapidly replenish the retailers' stock." This has led to the functional integration of suppliers and retailers, under terms in which the retailers often have the upper hand. Massive buyers like Wal-Mart reduce their suppliers to mere vassals, directly controlling product design and pricing while still retaining the flexibility to terminate a contract if needed. They gain the benefits of vertical integration without the liability that comes from formal ownership.[21]

Mexican drug logistics groups, while lacking just-in-time production and POS informational systems, echo and emulate this model—although many groups have a potentially more diverse set of relations to production (i.e., they might transport cocaine while also producing methamphetamine, etc.). While certain drugs are produced in Mexico, for example marijuana and heroin, some authors see these as short-term financing for the more capital intensive cocaine trade, and in the cocaine trade the logistics organizations directly control very little of the production.[22] Centering the idea of logistics in the recent period of drug-related violence cannot explain all facets of it and its terrible consequences, but it can provide a window into several dynamics, in particular those concerning labor, which have been picked up in contemporaneous cultural production.

One way that a logistics frame can be useful is that it allows for tracking how the control of the points of entry into the high-price consumer zone of the United States is now an important site for profit generation. Profits are "discovered" not only in the exploitation of labor, but in the markup, in the space of circulation, and in controlling the transition between exchange rates and national spaces. Through a mastery of logistics and this new corporate form, these organizations are able to realize the superprofits of logistics:[23] they battle over a monopoly not of production, but of the supply chain. The labor of drug logistics is touched by this predominance of circulation in two ways: first, it is a site where the state has shifted from mediating between capital and labor to burrowing into and siphoning off superprofits from the drug trade, and second, drug logistics (and its laborers) exist outside the enclosure of the factory.[24] Logistics in this case is concerned with the defense of a territory through which commodities pass, wherein laborers are exposed to new forms of death and force.

Perhaps none of the cultural productions in the aftermath of the "drug war" has addressed these conditions as devastatingly as Luis Estrada's *El infierno*. The film opens with its main character, Benny, played by Damián Alcázar, being deported from the United States where he has spent twenty years working as an undocumented laborer. His return, in the middle of the U.S. economic crisis, highlights a transition between two moments of foreign currency flows to prop up Mexico's current account and two different destinations for surplus population: from migrant labor to labor in the drug trade. Moreover, the film spends most of its time, particularly in its first half, detailing the specificities of the labor regime of low-level drug logistics workers.

Upon his return, Benny quickly realizes that San Miguel de Arcángel has changed greatly in his absence: few people, many guns. Due to pressing financial concerns, Benny becomes caught up in the drug trade to which he is introduced by his childhood friend Cochi Loco (Crazy Pig). Once Benny joins the trade the film passes into an episodic mode, with Benny being shown the ropes by Cochi. As Benny quickly learns, the labor of narco logistics has a different specificity from even migrant labor as it is even less mediated by socially necessary labor time and the state. As Cochi Loco notes, "La vida del narco: muy buena lana pero no es fácil" (Narco-life: good money but it's not easy). And it is not hard work because it is physically demanding (indeed, Cochi and Benny spend most of their time driving from place to place in a truck or in bars partying), but psychologically so. Benny and Cochi are always on call and cannot refuse any task (their partying is frequently interrupted by cell phone calls from their boss, demanding their immediate presence or attention). Their only site of resistance is that common to logistics and transport workers: namely, pilfering—in their case, taking money and drugs that the boss will never know are missing.

If *El infierno* is a film about labor, at least in part, what is it that Benny and Cochi actually *do* in the film? Their labor we might say has two sides: first, handling logistical operations (delivering product, meeting suppliers, collecting payments, etc.) and second, and increasingly as the film descends into a full-on war between capos, killing other low-level drug logistics laborers. However if one compares *El infierno* with other cultural productions of the narco moment, including films such as *Miss Bala* or novels such as *Entre perros*, it becomes apparent that while all traffic in violence and the representation of violence, *El infierno* grounds this representation in a presentation of narco life as labor, from which it derives a good deal of its black humor and critical force. The critical force of *El infierno* is contained in its ironic commentary on labor as no longer being a site for producing national subjects. For example, the film's running gag is to present Benny and Cochi as just two normal guys doing their jobs—which includes placing festive sombreros on bodies, etc. As Benny and Cochi travel, frequently at high speeds, from one point in the film's underinhabited landscape to another, to enforce a debt or exact revenge, the film's scenes of spectacular violence are offset by its ironic emphasis on their labor as labor: as Benny responds to Cochi honking outside his house early one morning, "Este trabajo no respeta horarios" (This job doesn't respect a schedule).

Foucault's work on the great systems of individualization and the production of subjects in the long sweep of the rise of the state and governmentality turns around institutions and enclosures: barracks, schools, hospitals, asylums, factories, and prisons. We can immediately see that the work of drug logistics takes place not in an enclosure. The critical spatial figure in *El infierno* is the *plaza* or the territory which one controls and through which contraband passes. Instead of the body being inserted within and produced by an institution, one's labor takes place within a territory, is tied to this territory, and is directed toward the control of this territory. It is this move from enclosure to territory that occasions the interruption of prior forms of subjectivization, and these interruptions, I will argue, all turn around the transformation of a discontinuous anthropological limit which defines the subject and body.

El infierno tracks this process of interruption and the testing of the anthropological limits of the subject, especially in its attention to Benny's attempts to normalize himself to the demands of the work. After his first day on the job, sitting in a strip club, his coworker, El Huasteco, asks him, "Qué le pareció la chamba?" (What do you think of the job?) To which Benny replies, "Pues como todo, no más es cuestión de agarrarle el modo" (Well, like anything else, it's just a matter of getting the hang of it). However, the film demonstrates that there are many parts of the job for which Benny's subjectivity has not been prepared. In the next scene Benny is having sex with a sex worker during which he repeats to her his lines from earlier in the film ("te voy a sacar de trabajar" [I'm going to get you out of here]), originally spoken while having sex with his love interest, Lupe. While Benny's masculinity is adapted enough to the present to allow him to engage in these activities, it requires him to disavow his reasons for doing so and connect them to a prior formation of labor, masculinity, and social reproduction. This activity is interrupted by Cochi Loco—the *patrón* has called and needs them immediately. In the car ride there, Cochi gives Benny a packet of white powder, as they can't appear before their boss in an inebriated state. Benny's body again requires adjusting. Benny is then present as the leader of their logistics group (Don José Reyes) cuts off the tongue and hands of a former employee (for being a snitch and thief respectively). Benny faints and in the next scene we see him sitting alone at his kitchen table taking shot after shot of tequila. Lupe (played by Elizabeth Cervantes), enters the room and Benny shows her his hands, still shaking. She rubs his shoulders and says, "A ver mi rey, en esta vida a todo se acostumbra uno, menos a no comer" (Look here honey, in this life you can get used to anything, except for not eating).

Each of these moments represents the interruption of a prior subject formation and an attempt to refashion Benny's subjectivity into an instrument adequate to the labor of drug logistics. The point of the film is that, with Benny, the subjectivization carried out by drug logistics labor does not stick. The film demonstrates that of the hired hands of Don Reyes it is only the two members with military training (El Sargento and El Sardo) who have successfully completed the transition to the subjectivity demanded by the labor of drug logistics—cutting up bodies, torturing, etc.—without a visible response.[25]

If the film depicts logistics labor as interrupting prior processes of subject formation, it shows that also in this moment labor no longer serves as a site of collectivization. Instead of a figure of the worker which binds individuals, what the film presents is the absence of any form of collectivity among the logistics workers. The primary social relation among members of Don Reyes's network is distrust and suspicion: everyone is always potentially a *soplón* (snitch). When Benny turns to the government to trade information to protect the life of his nephew and Lupe, it is quickly revealed that the government officials are working for Don Reyes as well. The film repeatedly demonstrates how little it takes for individuals to switch sides and begin playing for the other team. Thus, instead of the grand figures of the campesino, the noble proletarian *pobre* (poor), or the *mujer abnegada* (self-sacrificing woman), in *El infierno* we have a gallery of distrust and deceit, interrupted processes of subjectivization that know no limited collective sublimation.

At the same time the need to control territory (as opposed to the means of production) has meant that the interruptive effects of drug labor are not confined (primarily) inside any "institution" (such as the factory, the office, etc.), but rather roam across the social field. This leads to forms of force (e.g., the display of dead bodies) as a means to control a given territory and those forms of force deployed in the moment of drug logistics labor escape from any enclosed space and impinge on the lives, bodies, and affects of neighbors, passers-by, or anyone who circulates through the territory. The labor of drug logistics constitutes an interruptive process not just for Benny as a novice laborer in the mines of circulation but for those who live or work in or adjacent to its unenclosed territories. Both of these processes, tied to control of territory, break down old forms of enclosure and interrupt or deinstitute prior forms of subjectivation.

It is the failure of this structure that Benny confronts in the film's final scene. At a celebration of the Mexican *bicentenario*, Benny walks in slow motion through a cheering crowd. Once at the front he pulls out an AK-47 and still in slow motion, proceeds to kill the ruling class of San Miguel, from the priest to Don Reyes and his wife to mid-level government functionaries. Benny is not just exacting retribution for the murder of Lupe, which would imply a more limited selection of targets. Rather his total negation of the current symbolic trinity of the Mexican elite (state, church, and drug logistics) is exacting revenge for the failure of a system at large, which encompasses both state and capital. However, in *El infierno*, unlike later cultural works, this failure is not complete: as Benny walks through the crowd we see that there is a large population for whom the symbols and structures of the state are still functional, in an ideological sense at least: those who respond as Don Reyes waves the flag and chants "¡Viva! ¡Viva México!" The state, and its processes of subjectivization in *El infierno*, still carries a trace of its past functionality—not as a hope for the future but as an ideological substrate of the present. *El infierno* marks the limit of the functionality of the state apparatus but for all its negative power does not speculate on what might come to substitute for it. To begin to see beyond it, we have to turn away from labor, which is still strongly associated with production, to another key site for the production of subjects and weak collectivities: death.

The Cadaver

In a 2012 blog post the poet Dolores Dorantes writes of her book *Querida fábrica*:

> Comencé escribiendo ese libro con la idea de un personaje enamorado de la fábrica, de la industria, de su lugar de trabajo y las situaciones a las que la vida laboral lo somete, en los recorridos de una rutina dentro de esas naves industriales típicas de la frontera y, supongo, típicas ya del mundo entero. Las naves industriales son ahora para el desarrollo de los países, como los iglús para los esquimales. No sé en qué momento el amor por la fábrica se convirtió en el amor fascinante hacia un cadáver. No sé en qué momento, la fábrica con sus tonos metálicos y procesos sincronizados y automáticos; con sus riesgos calientes y el pulso de una vida sujeto a los motores, se volvió un cuerpo muerto descomponiéndose ante la mirada del amor.
> [I began writing this book with the idea of a character in love with the factory, industry, their place of work, and situations that work life submits one to, in a routine within those typical industrial buildings of the border and, I suppose, typical now of the world in general. These factories are now to the development of countries like igloos to Eskimos. I do not know at what moment love for the factory became a fascinated love toward a cadaver. I do not know at what point the factory with its metallic tones and synchronized and automated processes, with its hot risks and the pulse of a life subject to its engines, became a dead body decomposing under the gaze of love.][26]

As Claudio Lomnitz has shown in *Death and the Idea of Mexico*, death is not a stable cultural category but rather one used "as a conceptual field with which to think through the national question, and indeed as a metonymic sign of Mexicanness itself."[27] Lomnitz demonstrates how after the 1982 debt crisis representations of death changed from indicating a common ground shared by all humanity or "a universal that provided ironic distance from the artifice of everyday hierarchy" into a "form of social differentiation." He continues: "Here death is not a form of ironic distancing, but rather a way of exaggerating inequalities, all wrapped in the punch of a highly developed macabre humor that has its own long tradition in Mexico. The skull, then, serves to exaggerate social difference and to extrapolate it to its final consequences in a kind of grotesque. Whereas for Posada skulls were a sign of fundamental equality and communion (and were subversive for that reason), in the crisis period they are deployed to uncover inequality."[28] Death, much like labor but in a more popular rather than state register, has been a site for articulating forms of collectivity (either in consonance, critique, or dissonance with state-produced forms). For Lomnitz the resurgence of Day of the Dead imagery and cultural practices after 1982 is linked to a need to name and note growing inequality. This represents a marked shift from the national popular mediations of death where it is a category that reveals or names an equality and common being among all social subjects. Before the 1982 crisis the subversive power of death was in its claim to a fundamental equality; after it is the skull (*calavera*) which exaggerates social difference to the point of a grotesque critique.[29]

What does it mean, with the present historical period no less in crisis than the one Lomnitz examines, to focus—as a wide range of cultural works do—not on the skull as metonym of inequality or the figure of death as common ground, but on the cadaver or corpse? The shift from death to the skull to the cadaver marks a transition between a modern period defined by production, labor power, and grand state collective forms to a world of crisis and growing inequality after 1982 to the present defined by surplus population and circulation. To the extent that in the years after the 1994 financial crisis one of the key vectors of change in the social sphere is the spread and proliferation of circulation, its intermingling with production the cadaver, which inhabits a space somewhere between the living and the dead, between material and immaterial—becomes a key site of cultural reflection and articulation of an ambivalent collective form.

To give an example: one of the first poems in *Querida fábrica*'s opening section "Condúcenos" inserts the cadaver into a complicated signifying system, one defined by two parallel worlds predicated upon immateriality. In this poem there are references to an "estrella tras la quemadura" (a star behind the burn) and "cada paisaje hirviendo" (each landscape boiling), which are both moments of state change, of flicker, of an undecidability as to the state of a being's substance.[30] We find as well an image of parallel lines of cadavers: "hay que alinear los cadáveres con los que te pretendo hay" (one must align the cadavers with those that I claim to you are there).[31] This image also serves to index two different orders of being: the "real" cadavers and those with a less defined ontological status. In this poem there is an accounting of what is there and what we hope, expect, or pretend is or might be there. The aim of these multiple gestures to cadavers, stars, and fire is revealed in a phrase from one of the final lines—"para alcanzar la carne de un corazón" (to reach the flesh of a heart)—as not that of making the immaterial material, that is, to make it flesh, but rather of reaching the materiality of the immaterial, the flesh of the spirit.[32]

There has been a tendency—identified by Leigh Claire La Berge—in humanities criticism to describe finance as "abstract" or the historical turn to finance as involving increasing "abstraction." La Berge convincingly demonstrates how critics, even Frederic Jameson, have relied on under-theorized notions of abstraction to describe finance.[33] I would argue, as Annie McClanahan also has, that part of the issue here has been a tendency to separate finance from production, turning it into the abstract of production's concrete.[34] Throughout this book I have traced how finance emerges out of and works in concert with production and how finance represents a temporal elongation of the process of value realization that has its roots in production. I believe it is necessary to bring the same critical lens to bear on Dorantes's work and the figuration of the cadaver as an immaterial materiality. Much as finance is not merely a making "abstract" of concrete processes of production, the cadaver is not simply a dematerialization of material bodies, but rather the production of a new set of relations between the material and immaterial or a reconfiguration of their relation in a particular moment of finance, circulation, and drug logistics.

It is important to differentiate the use of "immaterial" here from both its usage in cultural criticism as a figuration of the abstraction (or nonmateriality) of finance and also from the post-workerist theorization of "immaterial labor." The post-workerist usage of the term "immaterial" has its roots in Marx's *Theories of Surplus Value* and other nineteenth-century political economic texts where it is used to describe the product of service work (as an "immaterial" product versus the "material" products of industrial production). There is, however, another genealogical tradition—one that appears in post-workerism in certain moments—that extends back into medieval Christian and Arabic philosophy (Augustine and Averroes particularly), where immaterial is used to designate the soul as a *substance* which is not merely mental nor merely corporeal. My usage of the term—following what we have seen outlined in the work of Dorantes above—will draw on the earlier medieval figuration which stresses the materiality of the immaterial.

Of course, the cadaver in Dorantes cannot but help to refer to, on one level, the more than two hundred thousand dead and disappeared in the ongoing "drug war." But focusing only on drug and state violence would miss the longer cultural salience of the cadaver in Mexico, as well as a part of the specificity of Dorantes's description, namely the passage beyond production, the passage from the factory to the cadaver ("No sé en qué momento el amor por la fábrica se convirtió en el amor fascinante hacia un cadáver" [I don't know in which moment love for the factory became a fascinated love for a cadaver]). As we saw above the cadaver in Dorantes is not merely the brute facticity of the corporal but rather a figure of the immaterial, the not nonmaterial, a paradoxically substantial shadow world. As such the movement into the world of the cadaver can be read as referring to the dead of the drug war period and also to the move to circulation understood as the specific form of a parallel substantial immaterial world, which, I will argue, links the present period with the prior 1980s–1990s moment of financial crisis and condenses features of the present period's form of financial crisis, namely that of second-order finance or derivatives (as the trigger of the 2008 financial crisis). The figure of the cadaver as that which is suspended between two worlds indexes a turn away from production in two ways: by referencing the dead of the drug logistics trade and the immaterial-material forms of value produced by new financial derivatives operations.

Indeed, the salience of the cadaver has a history in Mexican cultural production that predates the drug war. As Claudio Lomnitz notes, the early work of the multimedia and performance artist Teresa Margolles from the 1990s "mobilizes" traces from anonymous victims in Mexico City's morgue.[35] Amy Sara Carroll has pointed out that Margolles's work is concerned with "the life of the corpse" and is composed primarily of the waste matter, stains, and traces of corpses. Discussing Margolles's 2002 piece "Vaporización/Vaporization" in which disinfected water used in the washing of corpses in the Mexico City morgue was run through a fog machine, Carroll writes, "in this regard, Vaporización/Vaporization initially might be understood as allegorically charting an ontological transformation in 'national allegory' proper. Like the body, which is transubstantiated, but not disappeared."[36] Margolles's work—which extends back into the late 1990s and thus predates the start of the "drug war," but which is located comfortably in the turn to circulation—is concerned with both the cadaver and the immaterial (as that which is transubstantiated but not disappeared).

To understand how this immaterial-material world emerges out of not only death but new forms of finance and financial crisis, we have to take a brief political economic detour. During the 2008 financial crisis numerous Mexican companies lost hundreds of millions of dollars as bets they had made on derivatives went bad. The *grupo* Cemex used backing from the Mexican government in order to avoid bankruptcy, even though now it realizes only 16 percent of its sales in Mexico.[37] This moment revealed that many large, nonfinancial corporations, that is, those whose profit making ostensibly occurs in the productive sector, had incorporated forms of financial speculation to maintain their bottom lines and that much of this speculation had occurred in derivatives markets. The "real" economy in Mexico was revealed as having become increasingly dependent on the failed forms of accumulation found in finance or the sphere of circulation.

The emergence and spread of derivatives has its roots in two processes resulting from the long downturn beginning in the 1970s. First, with the growth of multinationals moving profits between currencies became increasingly important. However, with the end of the fixed exchange rates of Bretton Woods, moving money across currencies became more volatile precisely at the moment that it became essential to international accumulation. Second, beginning in the 1970s investment banks began to put competitive pressure on traditional banks, and companies began turning to instruments other than bank loans to finance their operations.[38] Both of these processes led to the usage of new financial instruments, derivatives among them, first as a means of controlling or hedging currency volatility and second to generate new revenue streams for traditional banks and financial firms.[39]

Derivatives have since become not only a big business but part of the fabric of everyday economic life (in 2017, the value of outstanding contracts in the global derivative markets was estimated at US$542.4 trillion).[40] The simplest explanation of a derivative is that it is a financial instrument whose value changes in response to a change in the price of an underlying element. The underlying element can be truly almost anything: a commodity, an interest rate, a group of assets, the weather, a catastrophic event. Thus derivatives exist at a remove from an asset or underlying element, but the most common type of derivatives is a contract concerning future actions or events.[41] For example, a very common type of derivative is a futures contract in which a corn producer might agree to sell a specified amount of corn on a certain future date at a certain price—in effect, locking in that price against its potential decline.[42]

Derivatives open a parallel world of immateriality, a virtual world of possible futures, but importantly futures with a relationship to the actual. It is a world of confusion between price and value, a world that exists at one remove from and which emerges in the decline of production. This parallel world is an immaterial one, in the sense of the term I have been developing here: it is tied to the actual but also blurs into a multiplicity of possible futures and possible future prices. This immateriality becomes a form, an effect, a shadow cast upon social life after the expansion and spread of this means of finance.[43] One might think that derivatives are too esoteric a financial instrument to have any real impact on cultural life other than in a mediated way in a moment of crisis. I want to argue that it is possible to register the conditioning of cultural categories and production by the immaterial materiality of finance in the period after

2001, precisely to the extent that immateriality indexes and participates in a general rise of circulation in the Mexican nation-space. The specific immaterial materiality of circulation cultures, which encompasses both derivative finance and drug logistics, is that of a shadow world linked to, but also just beyond, production.

To return to Dorantes: the landscape of *Querida fábrica* is a barren zone ("al asomarme a este desierto y ver todo calladamente gris" [looking out at this desert and see everything quietly gray])[44] that harkens back to the world of *Pedro Páramo*. But unlike *Pedro Páramo* this is not a world of ghosts (that is, those who are more spirit than matter) inhabiting what would be a *ghost* town, but rather the reverse: the space of *Querida fábrica* is the immaterial linked to the actual, the ghost *town*. Jean Franco has argued that *Pedro Páramo* is a novel about the fragmentation and comingling of capitalist and precapitalist forms of social being. On Franco's account it is money which causes the breakdown: "In *Pedro Páramo*, money dispenses the overlord from any personal confrontation, absolves him from the moral consequences of his actions . . . The Mexican society of *Pedro Páramo* is a feudal and tribal structure onto which has been grafted a money economy which is connected with the existence of a bourgeoisie."[45] If *Pedro Páramo* maps the transition to a money economy, whose primary effect is the move to impersonal structures of social relation, Dorantes's *Querida fábrica* maps the move to an economics of derivative finance and circulation, whose primary effect is the immaterialization of life, its blurring of the present into possible near futures. But here enters the other side of circulation, that of drug logistics: futures for whom? For the already dead, not in the form of ghostly spirits, but rather as immaterial cadavers.

While the landscape of *Querida fábrica* might be barren, it is, however, saturated with social relation. In the final chapter of *Death and the Idea of Mexico*, Lomnitz reads the rise of the Santa Muerte cult in the 1990s as a consequence of the receding of the state which is replaced by Death as "the ultimate sovereign."[46] The cadaver in Dorantes has a different valence, namely that of a particular kind of possible commonality: the cadaver is not the sovereign, but rather what we all (potentially) are and also what bears within itself other bonds. In one of the final poems of the book's opening section, we find a speaker interpellating another subject from a grave: "Te había puesto de espaldas en la tierra / Te había puesto conmigo, *amor*" (Had put you on your back in the earth / Had put you with me, *love*).[47] The common position they share is not that of the worker, campesino, or ama de casa, but rather the speaking dead, the immaterial material cadaver. Different than Posada's calaveras, which are "a sign of fundamental equality and communion," the position of the cadaver is marked by a surfeit of possible relation—something that distinguishes Dorantes's writing in general, which weaves webs of pronouns into complex relational forms.[48] Threaded through the cadaver are forms of potential minor collectives and forms of possible social relation, signaled by repetition ("me gustabas" [I liked you]) and by images such as "Para que florecieras conmigo en la fosa" (So that you flowered with me in the grave).[49] We might even go so far as to say that *Querida fábrica* is a world without individuality, as rarely in the book is a subject indicated without it being placed into relation with another. If for Lomnitz the Santa Muerte cult marks a withdrawal of the state, perhaps Dorantes's work speculates on what comes after the state and capital: pushed out from the factory into the surplus of the speaking dead, the book searches for fragile forms of collectivity which might house or bear new forms of social relation inside itself.

In the landscape of the decline of production—that of the spirit-flesh world of immaterial materiality, the parallel but linked universe of circulation, of the production of future claims on value and the violent contestation for the control of flows of contraband through plazas—Dorantes's work would seem to indicate that all we have left is this tendential linkage to the material substrate of our bodies, the cadaver, wherein we are neither alive nor dead. If death was a figure of equality in the developmentalist moment, and one of a critique of social inequality in the neoliberal transition, then the cadaver is what lies on the other side of the developmentalist state. It figures neither a shared commonality nor a potentially antagonistic critique but rather, as Dorantes writes, "*Algo más entero que yo / es lo que viene*" (*Something more whole than I / is what comes*).[50] The cadaver is a figure that marks the possibility of social relation itself—a figure that holds open the possibility, in a world which has annihilated them, of the production of social relations in some undetermined future. At the edges of the state and against unmediated financial and drug war capitalism, we find the undead in a parallel world of immaterial materiality looking for a way out, the undead saturated in living relation, pronouns circling around each other in an attempt to enact a different kind of collective body.

The Surplus

If *El infierno* and the poetry of Dorantes show us what happens to sites for the production of collectivity emerging from the developmental state, it is in cultural works concerned with migration and state terror where the failure of capital and the state to provide inhabitable lifeworlds is most directly registered and contested. Mexico-based cultural productions about migration, concerning either Mexican or Central American migration into the United States, frequently present migrants as surplus populations, as existing outside the apparatus of state and capital.[51] In these cultural objects, but especially in filmic productions, migrants attempting to pass over walls and through deserts into the United States are portrayed as existing outside all enclosures. Even when they succeed in crossing, they frequently continue to be represented as part of the informal labor market or "gray" market areas where there is little state mediation (other than state violence). Thus, many migrants, at least from the perspective of these cultural works, remain at best at the edge of the capitalist and state apparatus of subjectivization, and in the moment of crossing they pass between two state formations, both of which direct excessive amounts of violence toward migrants. Filmic cultural productions on migration, such as *Norteado* (2009) and *La jaula de oro* (2013), reveal how the interiority of the subject fades once it moves to the periphery of these great historical systems of subjectivization and collectivization.[52]

In *Discipline and Punish* Foucault discusses disciplinary procedures as the production of the "modern soul," and as we saw in the previous chapter with the rise of disciplinary apparatuses and institutions of enclosure, techniques like imprisonment came to "reform" the soul instead of punishing the body. They did so, however, through a complex set of processes aimed at the body, giving rise to the subject's interiority. If subjectivity since the seventeenth century has been produced variously by hailing, integration into the productive process, or submission to disciplinary procedures, cultural works on migration register the dissolution of a specific component of such forms of subjectivity: interiority. Surplus populations are controlled by state violence, not by the disciplining, policing, and regulation of their "souls." In cultural works from this period we see that once the state and capital let up on these individualizing procedures and switch to violence and force, interiority begins to fade. Its absence makes space for the emergence of something else: a form of individualization (not interiority) which derives from a collectivity instead of the other way around.

For example the 2009 film *Norteado* follows Andrés, an Oaxacan migrant, and his attempts to cross the border at Tijuana into the United States. The film opens with him leaving the Oaxacan sierra, traveling by bus to the border, and then crossing into the United States with a *pollero* (smuggler). The pollero abandons him in the middle of the desert, and close to succumbing to the heat, he is picked up by the border patrol. Returned to Tijuana he eats in a shelter and then attempts to call his cousins in the United States. He gets a disconnect signal and speaks his first words of the film, "Bueno, bueno" (Hello, hello)—at the eighteen-minute mark. Andrés then begins working for a middle-aged woman, Ela, who runs a small store, and he slowly becomes a part of the social group that passes through the store, which includes Asensio, an older gentleman, and Cata, a younger woman who works in the small store as well. The film and Andrés continue in relative silence; not until the film's halfway mark does Andrés finally have a full conversation with another individual (with Ela in a bar, where she is trying to hook up with him), and even this one is halting, monosyllabic, marked by the exchange of only the most basic personal information, even though it is filled as well with care and sexual desire.

In "The Subject and Power" Foucault outlines his argument that the modern state appropriated and built on the pastoral power innovated by the Christian church. Foucault writes that among the characteristics of this "very special form of power" is that "it is a form of power which does not look after just the whole community, but each individual in particular, during his entire life," and that "this form of power cannot be exercised without knowing the inside of people's minds, without exploring their souls, without making them reveal their innermost secrets."[53] The lack of dialogue in *Norteado* marks a break with this kind of subject formation, founded in recounting and explaining interior states of being. The film presents us with a hollowing out or absence of interiority—but which does not imply the absence of or inability to form social relations. Rather, what we see is that the link between confessing or giving an account of one's self and the state or pastoral power which cultivates this specific type of subjecthood or interiority has been broken.

A similar process is at work in the 2013 film *La jaula de oro*. Three friends (Juan, Sara, and Samuel) begin a journey out of Guatemala to the United States. The first seven minutes of the film, as they get ready, meet up, and then journey to the Guatemala-Mexico border, pass without them exchanging a single word. After they fail to hop a train, their group is joined by a young indigenous man, Chauk, and the others begin to have limited conversations (discussing travel, counting money, etc.). Again, this is not to say there is no "emotional" or affective life, but rather that it passes through a different apparatus. Having been sent back by the Mexican border patrol, the group decides to make another attempt at crossing. Juan, the de facto leader, says anyone who wants to should turn back now. Samuel decides to not continue on. Juan asks him "¿Por qué?" and Samuel does not respond verbally but the two hug. He then proceeds to embrace, with tears in his eyes, each of the other members of their group. Thus it is not that there is no connection, no affective or social relation here, but rather it no longer passes through the language cultivated by processes of interiority. The question "¿por qué?" that calls the individual to give an account of him or herself has an answer that no longer lies within that domain of accounting. The subject still understands the question; the memory of that prior system of subjectivization exists, but Samuel's current lived practice is other, which is the mark of the rise of surplus population outside the enclosures of state and capital.

One might counter that surplus populations in migration are actually attempting to integrate themselves (differently) into the state and capitalist apparatus, and it is true that some individuals do manage to do this, and outside the universe of filmic representation, that both the Mexican state and Church have developed mechanisms for tracking and managing migratory populations.[54] *La jaula de oro* also shows that this reintegration, at least in the example of the film, is never complete. The passage through the field of surplus population follows and marks individuals even after their reintegration into systems of production and (partial) state mediation. For example, the final thirty minutes of *La jaula*, as Juan and Chauk cross into the United States and Chauk is shot by a Minuteman-like sniper, contains no dialogue other than brief commands. Interestingly, right before passing into the United States, they are waiting in a drainage tunnel, and the film employs a device that it has not used up to this point: the interior monologue. It gives each character several lines in their native language, expressing their emotions on crossing over. But this feels less like a return to the interiority of the subject than a farewell. In the next scene Chauk is shot and Juan is now alone, the only survivor of the journey (Sara had been kidnapped earlier in the film and never returns). The final scenes of the film show Juan working in a meat processing facility—sweeping up the remains from underneath the cutting lines—and then walking home in the snow. His face betrays no emotion as he works without speaking and then walks in the cold. In the final shots of the film we see him standing underneath a streetlight watching the snow fall, and then the film ends with a long shot of the camera pointed up at the blank night sky, the snow cascading down. Instead of Juan's reintegration into the subjectivization of work, there is only blankness. Instead of the finite depth of the subject, the profound infinity of night.

Part of what Foucault describes as disciplinary measures in *Discipline and Punish* is a series of techniques that limit the possibility of the appearance of the crowd. Under earlier regimes of punishment, the condemned would plead their case to the assembled public and occasionally would be rescued by it. Foucault describes this as a form of "popular illegality," which includes a whole range of manifestations, from demonstrations to riots.[55] Part of the aim of modern disciplinary apparatuses' individualizing focus is to prevent the emergence of such crowds, riotous multitudes, or "illegal" publics.[56] Foucault also notes that states, especially the military, need to coordinate large groups and derive a significant part of their power from the ability to concatenate individuals into operationalized masses. As I argued at the opening of this chapter drawing on Foucault and Marx, states do so by first individualizing and then collectivizing elements into depoliticized groups. This process inverts the relationship between the individual and the collective that one finds in the crowd. In the crowd it is the collective which gives or produces a limited, nonpastoral individuality, while disciplinary structures first individualize and then form these elements into nonvolatile combinatory forms (though the potential for a politicization of these forms is always there). What we can see in migration or surplus population films is a return of the forms of individual-collective relation found in the crowd, but of a very specific kind; so it is worth attempting to trace this carefully.

As the characters in *Norteado* slowly congregate around the shared center of Ela's *tienda*, the film reveals that what first appears as a random group of individuals joined by happenstance are in fact all conditioned by the experience of migration. Both Ela and Cata have husbands who left for the other side and stopped contacting them. From a set of shared absences they begin to construct a new mesh of social ties among themselves. Ela first establishes her interest in Andrés, taking him out drinking one night. However, Cata also has a clear interest in Andrés. It is only after he attempts to cross (yet again) and is sent back that their intimate relationship is constituted. They go to the same bar to which Ela took Andrés. The film thus sets up what is a traditional plot of melodrama: the love triangle (with the addition of Asensio as the jealous fourth wheel). As they are all living and working in the same small store which doubles as their living quarters, the viewer waits for the powder keg to explode. But it never does. Instead they all work together on a plan to get Andrés across—building an armchair in which they hide him while Asensio drives him across the border in a pickup filled with other miscellaneous household items.

This is not to say that demands emerging from desiring self-interest or a form of emotional life are not present and articulated by the characters. Ela in particular does not want Andrés to leave. Sitting in her car after a day spent working on the armchair, she tells him, "Yo necesito alguien que me ayude. Yo no puedo sola con todo" (I need someone who can help me. I can't manage everything by myself). Andrés for his part extends an offer to Cata to cross with him (it is unclear if he means to start a relationship with her or only to help her cross). The way the film diverges from traditional romance plots is that these demands or desires are stated but they do not interrupt the form of collectivity that has been generated (or the collective process of its generation). There is never a moment in the last part of the film in which it feels like any of the characters will break their bond with Andrés and stop assisting in the plan to help him cross. Nor does the film present a moment of Ela and Cata engaged in competition or attacking each other to win Andrés to themselves. What the film never calls into question is the group, even though it is nonidentical to itself and does not suppress forms of individuality or emotional life inside it.

Norteado sketches a form of intimate groupality based neither in codes of friendship nor marriage as a contract,[57] because it is not compartmentalized individuals who confront and negotiate the terms of a relationship with each other. The film presents not individuals entering into state- or capital-sanctioned forms of groupality but rather the emergence of a collectivity in which individuality takes place. It is important to note that the film's ending perhaps pulls the narrative back into a more traditional romance register (Andrés gives both of the women dresses which the film shows them trying on as the pickup waits to enter the United States), and that it is the women who (once again) are left behind when Andrés crosses. However, for an extended period, the film traces a different relationship between collectivity and individuality. Instead of individualized elements that must then be combined into larger forces and structures, we have a form of collectivity, of intimacy, that does not pass first through the individual but rather produces individuation along with and inside itself. The film demonstrates that this form of collectivity or crowd cannot be broken (by the melodramatic device of the love triangle) because, unlike in the collectives of the developmentalist state and capital, the individual has no meaning outside it.

The Void

As previously argued *El infierno* is a film concerned with the normalization of subjectivity to the demands of drug logistics labor or the testing of the anthropological limit on what a body and psyche can be expected to withstand. As it has slowly and painfully become clear, in particular after the state disappearance of forty-three students from Ayotzinapa, how much "drug war" violence has been state-legitimated, permitted, and inflicted, later cultural works in this period have turned their attention explicitly to the effects of state violence or state terror as a means of social control aimed not at producing a new normalization of bodies, but rather at interrupting or voiding any form of collectivity which might oppose the very terror of state and capital.

In contrast to the great twentieth-century definitions and meditations on terror (Arendt, Merleau-Ponty) or twenty-first-century reconsiderations of its Jacobin legacy (Žižek, Badiou), state terror in Latin America, and in Mexico and Central America specifically, has been transformed by counterinsurgency tactics into a tool for disciplining populations, which it does by displacing anthropological limits on physical or psychological force. Terror as state-sponsored or legitimated violence operates in one of its forms by exceeding thresholds on the limits of what is thought to be "acceptable" force.

There is a longer history of how states came, through counterinsurgency practices, to incorporate specific forms of community terror into their apparatuses of control that I can only gesture to here.[58] The counterinsurgency techniques deployed and developed in the 1970s and 1980s, particularly in Central America, were aimed at social destabilization and terrifying populaces into submission. These techniques were designed to break down forms of collectivity and communal, ethnic, or familial solidarity or identification, and they did so by deploying force that exceeded permitted limits on the use of violence against civilian populations. In addition to the death and displacement these techniques inflict, the use of excessive, grotesque, and public forms of violence leave deep traumas that are linked to this exceeding of normalized limits on uses and degrees of force and to the disintegration of communities and collectivities. Emerging out of this historical matrix, contemporary formations of the Mexican state and military have operationalized terror as a technique of discipline and as a tactic for interrupting processes or forms of producing collectivities.

The films of Amat Escalante have been exemplary in their attempts to wrestle with and make legible these conditions. For example, *Los bastardos* (2008) traces the strange form of temporary collectivity that emerges between two undocumented workers in the United States and a suburban mother whose house they are hired to break into before a moment of horrific and unexpected violence irrupts into the plot. However it is Escalante's "drug war" film *Heli* (2013) which plunges deep into the set of conditions we have been discussing in this chapter, as it traces how neither family nor work provides a form of livable collectivity and how the state has shifted its role from mediator of the capital-labor relation to purveyor of direct force as a form of control.

Heli works at a car assembly plant on the night shift and has a strained relation with his wife, Sabrina, who hasn't felt comfortable having sex with him since the birth of their child. On a deserted, desert road near the factory, they live in a house with Heli's father, who works the day shift at the plant, and Heli's younger sister, Estela, who is twelve and seeing an older teen, Beto, who is in the military. Beto hides a packet of cocaine in their water tank which Heli discovers and throws away. Heli punishes his sister and any emergency appears to be averted when their front door is suddenly knocked down by militarized police, who shoot the father dead, take Heli and Beto to be tortured by local "gang" members, and leave with the younger sister.

Like Escalante's other films, the narrative is constructed to place maximum emphasis on the suddenness and unforeseen irruption of violence into a space which has not been normalized to it, in this case the family and the family home. In the aftermath of this event, Heli returns to work at the car assembly plant but is fired once the insurance payout of his father is finished and when he turns to the legal system for help finding his sister, they accuse his father of being involved in an illegal union movement. The film registers the abandonment of two critical sites of subjectivization and collectivization in the developmentalist period: labor and the family. At the same time, in scenes of contact between Heli and the state, the film demonstrates how state terror functions as a form of domination. In one visually stunning scene the military personnel return to Heli's house, solely to threaten him with their presence. The shot's composition places Heli's body in relation to the looming military truck: Heli's head barely rises above the hood, as the truck, outfitted with a machine gun, towers over him.

Much as in the migration films discussed previously, there is very little dialogue throughout the film, and in this scene Heli stands mute in front of the military vehicle, the institutional apparatus of the paramilitary state pitted against his slight frame. The composition of the shot establishes a relation between Heli as an individual and the state's military apparatus, which appears as a classic moment of subjectivization, of interpellation, but with an important difference or addition: the military returns to *remind* Heli of a moment of terror that was lived collectively inside of, and which has disarticulated, the family structure. Terror produces here not merely a process of subjectivization, but also a negation that destroys prior forms of collectivization and replaces them with the outline of a voided collectivity composed of all those touched by this event of terror. The military vehicle returns because the terror hasn't stuck, because Heli continues to search for his sister, and the police return to say: remember the terror. The message for Heli of the unspeaking, threatening militarized vehicle is that his social relations are only negative in shape and that he must stop trying to make an operation upon the negative form of the voided collectivity of terror.

The film, however, is not narrated from the perspective of the state, and so its conclusion makes more room for an exploration of what kinds of operations are indeed possible on the voided collectivity of terror or what can be done with the realm of pain and suffering generated in recent years. At the end of the film Estela returns, walking up to the front of the house by herself. She does not speak, and we are informed by a doctor that she is several months pregnant (which is how the film alludes to the sexual violence done to her). In the final scene of the film Heli and Sabrina have sex again while Estela lays on the couch curled up with their infant son. The sounds of Heli and Sabrina can be heard in the background as the wind blows forcefully, pushing the curtains and light into the room where Estela and the infant are lying in each other's arms.

The scene is jarring: the reconnection of Heli and Sabrina and Estela into what was the space of the family grates against the framework of a scene in which Estela listens to them while holding their child. Perhaps this scene can be read as an imperfect exploration of what can be done in the wake of terror, an investigation into the possibilities for turning a collectivity voided by terror into something else. The position the film seems to adopt is that the terror cannot be escaped; it will (initially at least) always be present, and before this moment the outlet Heli's trauma finds is rage and physical intimidation toward Sabrina. Thus, the film registers in the ominous tonality and strangeness of this scene the existence of a collectively lived trauma, the interpersonal violence it gives rise to, and its complicated afterlives. The film's not entirely successful wager appears to be that to create a different set of social relations from the void left by terror, one will have to acknowledge and engage it, to enact an operation, a displacement upon it.

Heli and Sabrina are able to encounter each other again as individuals while working through the possibilities of a new collective form, and Estela is also located again as an individual within this matrix. What we can see in *Heli* is an operation on voided collectivity which inverts the traditional state collectivization-individualization relation. If in the twentieth century states produced individuals in order to then build nonrevolutionary collective forms, in *Heli* we witness that on the other side of a collectivity voided by terror stand forms which do not sum individuals but which produce individualization within the shape and space of their collectivity. What brings Estela, Heli, and Sabrina together at the end is not (simply) that they once formed part of a kinship structure, but that they were marked by an experience of state terror. This process of interrupted structuring both destroyed and recoded the relations among them and made necessary the production of a new form of non-state-sanctioned collectivity. In the final scene the film points to the project of the present: namely to the need, in a moment of transition from developmentalist collectivizing and individualizing structures to one of voided collectivity and the de-subjectivization of surplus populations and state violence, for creating new forms of collectivity as a shelter and citadel against state and capital.

These artistic works are not alone in their thinking about forms of collectivity in contemporary Mexico; in fact, they take place against a background of or within a larger set of cultural, theoretical, and political meditations on and practices of producing collectivity outside of the state and capital. From among these processes stand out the Zapatista experience in Chiapas, some governance in Oaxaca (and other states and localities) by *usos y costumbres*, and early formations of *policía comunitaria* (community police) in the state of Guerrero. These experiences, and the cultural and theoretical productions which have accompanied them, were part of a wave of indigenous-led resistance and organizing that first spread across Mexico from the 1980s into the early 2000s. At the center of these movements was the notion of autonomy—which received various theorizations and was the subject of much debate—but at whose core are ideas of self-governance and popular control of economic resources.[59]

These artistic works, in particular *Heli*, take up such collective processes in a much different environment than that of the 1980s or 1990s: namely, in the midst of the violence of the state-sponsored "drug war." Since the attack on the Ayotizinapa students on September 26, 2014, in which six people (including three students) were killed, forty were wounded, and forty-three students were disappeared by Mexican state and state-linked forces, how we understand the relation between the "drug war" and state violence has definitively changed. As Ivonne del Valle has written: "Ayotzinapa and the way the authorities have handled the investigation of the students forcibly disappeared by members of the state have revealed what many people already 'knew': that there is hardly any—or no—difference between rule of law (the juridical, military, and executive state apparatus) and criminality (drug cartels, illegal forms of accumulation—in the form of bribes, payoffs, 'gifts,' etc.). Law and criminality are two sides that collapse into each other."[60] Ayotzinapa marks a definitive turning point in our understanding of contemporary Mexico in that it is now difficult to argue that the state and the "narcos" are separate forces and that the military and police forces are not involved at every level (and across every branch) in state-sponsored violence, extortion, kidnapping, forced removal, and drug logistics.[61]

In this situation one is struck in these artistic works by the fragility of the forms of collectivity that are traced—how exposed they are to state violence and how asymmetrical is the balance of force between the state and these collectivities. In Chiapas, Cherán, Ostula, Xochicuautla, and many other places around Mexico, autonomous forms of governance have been successful in preventing or limiting state violence, even during the most intense moments of the "drug war."[62] However, we also know that long-term state campaigns of violence and criminalization have often been historically successful in disarticulating, limiting the spread of, or severely curtailing these kinds of autonomous movements. There is a congruence between the fragility of the forms of collectivity seen in these artistic works and the complicated and difficult attempts to sustain autonomy against state violence on the ground, in particular after 2006 and Calderón's declaration of "war."

While the last thirty years have seen the state turn away from the generation of nonrevolutionary collectivities via corporativist infrastructures to the control of surplus populations via state violence and terror, in multiple registers and social locations we have seen the development of powerful new means for the production of collective formations. We have also seen the successful disarticulation or destruction of these new forms of collectivity by state violence. This is the fragile limit traced by works like *Heli* and *Norteado*: the limit of the contemporary is that we can imagine and bring into being new collective forms but are unable in many cases to sustain them against a fully militarized state apparatus.

Circulation and Necropolitics

Within cultural circles perhaps the most common concept used for thinking the "drug war" period, its consequences, and impacts has been not that of circulation, but rather applications and repurposings of Achille Mbembe's necropolitics. The concept of necropolitics as a site for thinking about the contemporary and its cultural manifestations received an articulation in an early essay of Cuauhtémoc Medina and then in a 2009 edited volume on Teresa Margolles's work *¿De qué otra cosa podríamos hablar?* (What else could we talk about?). It has since expanded to be employed by many highly visible authors, including Marta Lamas, Diego Osorno, and Sayak Valencia.[63] By way of conclusion, I want to examine how the arguments developed in this chapter might bend toward a reading of Mexico as a necropolitical situation.

Achille Mbembe's notion of necropolitics draws on the work of Michel Foucault on the difference between biopolitical and sovereign power. For Foucault biopolitics emerges with the reformulation of medieval sovereign rule which was founded on a power over life and death. Biopolitics represents a different kind of power, "the power to foster life or disallow it to the point of death" aimed not at the individual, but at large groups, at what Foucault terms "populations."[64] Mbembe's intervention is to argue that biopolitics fails to explain the expansion of violence and death in the postcolonial present and thus the peculiar contemporary "relationship between politics and death." In his "Necropolitics" Mbembe traces how contemporary forms of sovereignty, states, and parastates are produced, not through "inscribing bodies within disciplinary apparatuses" but by killing them.[65]

Mbembe draws out the constitutive structuring of sovereignty as a state of exception and its connection to the instrumentalization of death:

> This essay draws on the concept of biopower and explores its relation to notions of sovereignty (*imperium*) and the state of exception. . . . My concern is those figures of sovereignty whose central project is not the struggle for autonomy but *the generalized instrumentalization of human existence and the material destruction of human bodies and populations.* Such figures of sovereignty are far from a piece of prodigious insanity or an expression of a rupture between the impulses and interests of the body and those of the mind. Indeed, they, like the death camps, are what constitute the *nomos* of the political space in which we still live.[66]

One point at which capital does appear in Mbembe's analysis is in the section on contemporary African states and the emergence of nonstate actors ("war machines" in Mbembe's terminology). These actors emerge as state power begins to break down:

> War machines emerged in Africa during the last quarter of the twentieth century in direct relation to the erosion of the postcolonial state's capacity to build the economic underpinnings of political authority and order. This capacity involves raising revenue and commanding and regulating access to natural resources within a well-defined territory. In the mid-1970s, as the state's ability to maintain this capacity began to erode, there emerged a clear-cut link between monetary instability and spatial fragmentation. In the 1980s, the brutal experience of money suddenly losing its value became more commonplace, with various countries undergoing cycles of hyperinflation (which included such stunts as the sudden replacement of a currency).[67]

These actors are predators and resource extractors—that is, part of their specificity is how they interact with a contemporary turn or return in global capitalism toward the extraction of natural resources. Mbembe describes them as "war machines" that are "highly organized mechanisms of predation, taxing the territories and the population they occupy and drawing on a range of transnational networks and diasporas that provide both material and financial support." Their "extraction and looting of natural resources" moves parallel "with brutal attempts to immobilize and spatially fix whole categories of people or, paradoxically, to unleash them, to force them to scatter over broad areas no longer contained by the boundaries of a territorial state."[68]

There are the seeds here—in this iteration of Mbembe's analysis—of a critique of the relationship between necropolitical transformations and capitalist ones. A contribution this chapter has sought to make is to push on this nexus of Mbembe's analysis in order to provide an avenue for thinking about the role capitalism might play in this new relationship between politics and death in Mexico, by centering in our analysis political economic transformations and their subsequent social effects during the period of the long downturn. That is, this chapter has aimed to bring capital back into our understanding of states and sovereignty and the turn of states away from producing collectivities to disrupting their formation via state violence and death dealing. We have seen how Mexico in the contemporary moment has been marked by a turn to circulation and by new articulations between production and circulation. The turn to circulation has been driven by a lowered rate of profit and has as well produced a significant surplus population in Mexico and globally. The state, which once directed much of its attention to the production of nonpoliticized collectivities of individuals interpolated into or excluded from the productive apparatus in specific ways, was confronted with a growing population outside all traditional means of control—to which it has responded by an unprecedented militarization and state-enacted, -sponsored or -legitimated death and destruction.

Mbembe's most recent work, *Critique of Black Reason*, moves into and engages with many of the additional registers explored in this chapter: histories of capitalism, discussions of finance and "superfluous humanity," and above all an emphasis on thinking being-in-common. As he writes in the epilogue, "But as long as the retreat from humanity is incomplete, there is still a possibility of restitution, reparation, and justice. These are the conditions for the collective resurgence of humanity. Thinking through what must come will of necessity be a thinking through of life, of the reserves of life, of what must escape sacrifice."[69] It is toward these ends of common-being in the face of capitalism's imbrication with forms of state violence that I would turn the genealogy of necropolitics in order to bring it into the Mexican present.

Surely, a new relationship between death and politics lies at the center of the present in Mexico, but in a way that could benefit from the opening of necropolitical thought onto circulation. Rather than only, mainly, or primarily an erosion of state capacity, the constitution of modern sovereignty by the state of exception, and the expansion of biopolitical practices into the realm of death, the forms of death and destruction witnessed in contemporary Mexico have been driven by a need to solve the twin problems of surplus population and surplus capital. This difference matters in particular when we specify what exactly it is that the state is doing when it commits or permits acts of state or para-state violence. In a necropolitical frame, the state or para-state actors are reenacting the fundamental constitutive nature of sovereignty (the state of exception) on a perhaps new terrain (no longer the planation, colony, or camp, but the present of the postcolony). If, however, we include in our analysis how the long downturn has produced an ever growing surplus population, state violence in Mexico takes on a different hue: it is at once more specific (directed at certain sectors of the population, i.e., those no longer necessary for capital accumulation) and rooted in the specific historical conditions of a turn to circulation (with this etiology shaping the specific forms and means this violence has taken).

Moreover, this difference in emphasis matters, once again, when it comes to thinking about how we might exit this situation. An analysis based solely or mainly in necropolitics will lead us to focus primarily on the state: on how to engage sovereign power, reform the state, or defuse the state of exception. Whereas the inclusion of circulation and the problem of the long downturn confronts us with the facticity of how a surplus of labor and capital emerged in the same historical moment and how necropolitical state violence mediates between them. It is a situation that admits no easy solution but which requires holding on to the dual histories of state and capital throughout this period's downturn and dissolution. Here I think we could do no better than to echo Mbembe's thinking of commonality, mutuality, and reciprocity, for it is only in some form of collectivity which could withstand these dual forces and their terrible histories that an alternate future might lie.

CODA

If the 2007–2008 global financial crisis demonstrated anything, it was that the forms of financial crisis which structural adjustment programs and neoliberalism had cordoned off in the global periphery had come home to roost in the countries of the North Atlantic. The ongoing crisis—whose first iterations were Latin American ones—was now fully global. Perhaps it is not surprising then that one of the most succinct, quietly devastating summaries of the dynamics that this book has attempted to capture comes from a Spanish film, *Mercado de futuros* (Futures market, 2011). Three years after a disastrous housing bubble and financial crisis swept through the country—throwing millions out of work and leading to the political formations of *los indignados* and Podemos—*Mercado de futuros* mixes scenes from the world of finance (a housing show, trading desks, a leadership conference) with those of the informal economy (flea markets, junk sellers, the marginally employed). The film is a meditation on memory—and the lack of it—as its images reveal how only three years later many of the same practices which produced the financial crisis continued apace, but now alongside an expanded sector of displaced people and discarded goods.

Similarly in Mexico and Brazil one does not have to look very hard to find continuations into the present of finance's failed forms of accumulation and its deleterious effects, either from the role it has played in the Lava Jato scandal in Brazil or recent reports from Mexico that Grupo Elektra manipulated markets to inflate its share price or that workers' pension funds have been used to invest in businesses of associates close to former presidents.[1] Turning to the IMF's own 2017 *Global Financial Sta-*

bility Report will find more of the same: they warn that low global growth rates are leading banks and other lenders to take on high levels of risk and that the ending of quantitative easing programs (which the U.S. Federal Reserve began in earnest in 2018) has the possibility of drying up financial flows into "emerging" economies.[2]

These are examples of the level—in between moments of crisis—at which finance most often appears in daily life, as scandal or unease. This book has tried to connect such instances into a larger narrative of finance's rise and to trace some of its effects on cultural production, subjectivity, racial formations, and state violence. It is this systemic level that I want to return to by way of conclusion. I began this book with an image taken from the work of Mexican political cartoonist Naranjo, one of a worker stabbed by knives of "devaluation," and I want to close it with another, deftly painted by *Mercado de futuros*, of a world in which massive amounts of surplus capital exist side by side with struggling surplus populations. Between these two images we have the historical sharpening of forms of crisis in Latin America and elsewhere and the political challenge of the present.

The reality of surplus capital existing alongside surplus populations is a contradictory and troubling one. Troubling because it is not difficult to see all around us an accelerating divergence between wealth and misery, and contradictory because it raises questions such as, "Why can't this capital just be invested in production?" or "Why couldn't we just put these people to work?" In volume 3 of *Capital* Marx attempts to explain how such a situation, where surplus capital confronts surplus population, can arise during the "normal" functioning of capitalism and also why such a situation, which seems to have an obvious solution (put people to work, invest money in production), can be so resistant to resolution.

Perhaps the fundamental insight of the Marxian corpus is that surplus value comes from the exploitation of workers. Marx also saw that in the process of competition, capitalists try to gain an edge on each other through the introduction of new machines and technologies into the labor process, which allows fewer workers to transform a greater number of inputs. Thus, in the pursuit of higher profits, there is a tendency for technological innovation, whether in industry or agriculture, to expel workers from the production process. If labor is the only source of surplus value, then as new technologies eliminate workers, this has the potential to lead to a declining rate of profit across each production cycle. A contradiction emerges: as productivity rises, the rate of profit can fall. In other words, capital is driven to increase productivity by replacing human labor with machines, but this process eliminates the very thing that gives capital life and its surplus, that is, human labor.[3]

Under such conditions, if the rate of profit declines and competition between corporations and industrial groups sharpens, at a certain point there will be some sort of creative destruction: Due to competition or crisis, some firms will become no longer profitable and will go under. The bankruptcy of these firms will allow the rate of profit to recover until the next inflection point of crisis. What has happened in the present, for reasons that are still contested, is that the period of "creative destruction" has not occurred, not even in 2007–2008. This has resulted in a depressed rate of profit and global overcapacity in many sectors, meaning that there are fewer and fewer profitable outlets in which the accumulated surplus can be invested. Nonetheless this surplus, along with the forms of fictitious capital produced in the financial sector, have continued to pile up, leading to a mass of surplus capital that now confronts a mass of surplus population.[4]

In this world of surplus capital and humanity thrust outside the process of production, finance has played a double role. Occasionally it has served to prop up wages and buying power (whether in the form of credit cards, briefly inflated home or land prices, or pensions and retirement funds invested in stock markets or government debt), but it has also pulled capital out of production and in moments of crisis destroyed lives, wealth, and individuals' and communities' prospects for survival. The creation of elaborate systems for failed financial accumulation in Latin America has contributed, as seen in crises such as those in 1982, 1994, and 1998, to this process of the production of surplus populations and the deepening of the contradiction of a world in which unimaginable wealth confronts impossible immiseration.

In the face of such conditions there are two programs or proposed solutions that have been common, both involving the state. The first calls for the regulation of finance in the hopes of reducing or containing surplus capital and volatility. There have been arguments for the re-regulation of financial markets globally since they were first liberalized in the 1980s and 1990s, but this has proven difficult, in part because of the degree to which political and business elites' interests have imbricated themselves with financial flows and accumulation and in part due to ongoing problems in production. The second calls for a return to an interventionist state, a state which would bring surplus capital and labor together at sites of production and perhaps alleviate the crisis. Part of the paradox of the present, particularly in Latin America, is that one could argue that the *marea rosada* was precisely such an attempt, and its decline demonstrates that the limits of the interventionist state have, yet again, been reached.

For both of these reasons a state solution appears less and less probable; such that, as ecological and humanitarian crises mount atop financial ones, the historical moment feels like one in which a real shakeout will occur, resulting in either the deep transformation of capitalism as an economic system or an awful remix of the destruction of communities, matériel, and life found in the global Great Depression and Second World War. This is not to make any predictions about the future, but rather only to attempt to account for a shift in the tonality of the historical present which has occurred during the writing of this project: a tonality which is marked by the decreasing faith of large swaths of the global population in states' or capitalists' ability to resolve the crisis. On the back of the recognition of the limited range of action of both state and capital, and of the involvement of each in exploitation and repression, ride many different specters of fascism, nationalism, and supremacist projects. These far right political projects have begun to seize power and legitimacy using the creeping recognition that attempts to alleviate the crisis through the current configuration of the state and market have not been successful.

In the coming years there will be some who, despite the failure of the neostructuralist policies of the marea rosada, will argue, perhaps out of conviction, perhaps out of pragmatism, that we cannot give up on the state as a redistributive apparatus. There will be others who, perhaps taking seriously the above analysis, will link it with literatures on new developmentalism and argue for a return to manufacturing, class alliances, and the like; while others will continue with claims that there is no alternative to capitalism and will shrug their shoulders at the idea of anything other than austere reform. For those who find such options unappealing, the question will be how to construct—as a storm of the far right builds across the globe—a different political option, one not guided by the hope that the state and capital might solve these paradoxes for us but rather one that builds on and extends the long-standing experiments with autonomy seen in many parts of the world and in particular in Mexico. To pry open an exit from this labyrinth built out of the twin dynamics of surplus capital and population before a full hard right turn can only be a difficult project, but it is one which calls us to participate in it, if only because there finally appear to be few other alternatives.

NOTES

Introduction

1. Accumulation is a central concept in Marxist thought with a specific meaning: accumulation is the creation of new value and is what occurs in production via the exploitation of labor. In circulation or finance, because there is no significant production of new surplus value, there can only be profit-taking and thus no actual "accumulation," in the technical sense, can occur. This said, a problem in this book that I faced was the need for a term that would describe from the point of view of actors and states the anticipated outcomes of projects in finance and that would differentiate these projects from ones in production. There was no perfect solution to this problem, and throughout the text I describe financial projects by the term "finance-led" or "finance-primed" accumulation, always with the modifier "attempted" or "failed." See also Cédric Durand, *Fictitious Capital*, who uses the term "profits without accumulation" (Chapter 8).

2. Banco de México, "Exchange Rate Regimes."

3. Oliveri, *Latin American Debt*, 124–25.

4. Marichal, *Century of Debt Crisis*, 4.

5. Drake, "Debt and Democracy," 51, and Griffith-Jones, *International Finance*, 26.

6. Dussel Peters, *Polarizing Mexico*, 10; Roberts, "Revisiting"; Maito, "La transitoriedad histórica," 142.

7. Lissakers, *Banks*, 61–64.

8. Wright, *Foreign Enterprise*, 73–75.

9. A quick overview of this history can be found in Soederberg, *Politics*; Griffith-Jones and Sunkel, *Debt and Development*; and Oliveri, *Latin American Debt*.

10. Roddick, *Dance of the Millions*, 105.

11. Welch, *Capital Markets*, 92–93.

12. Gowan, *Global Gamble*, 25–29.

13. Correa, Vidal, and Marshall, "Financialization," 264.

14. Ffrench-Davis and Devlin, "Diez años," 7.

15. Guttmann, "La crisis," 191, and St. Louis Federal Reserve, "Effective Federal Funds Rate."

16. Skidmore, *Politics*, 254.

17. Bustillo and Velloso, "Bond Markets," 9–10.

18. Green, *Silent Revolution*, 69–71; and Painceira, "Developing Countries," 188–90.

19. Soederberg, *Politics*, 37–47; and Paula, *Financial Liberalization*, 62–63.

20. Morera Camacho, *Capital financiero*, 40; Correa and Vidal, "Financialization," 544–45; and Baer, *Rumo perdido*, 43.

21. Soederberg, *Politics*, 48–50; Palma "How to Create," 43; and Baer, *Brazilian Economy*, 308.

22. Correa, "Changing Constraints," 172.

23. Paulani, "Inserção da economia," 100, and Paulani, "A hegemonia neoliberal," 41.

24. For discussions of derivatives usage in Mexico and Brazil, see Dodd, "Exotic Derivatives"; Kaltenbrunner and Painceira, "Financial Integration"; Mathieson et al., "Emerging Local Securities"; and Soto Esquivel, *Especulación e innovación.*

25. A good example of this is the Mexican *grupo* Cemex, which during the 2000s turned itself into the third largest cement supplier in the world, with operations in over fifty countries using short-term debt financing to effect mergers and acquisitions in other regional markets. As a result, in 2008 after international credit markets froze in the wake of the U.S. financial crisis, Cemex used backing from the Mexican government in order to avoid bankruptcy, even though now it realizes only 16 percent of its sales in Mexico (Mendoza Hernández, "Financiarizacíon," 173, 178). For work on the financialization of nonfinancial corporations in Brazil, see Medialdea, "Brazil."

26. Sartre, *Search for a Method*, 7.

27. In both Mexico and Brazil finance is currently and has been an expansive area of research. Of particular importance for this book since the early stages of writing has been the work of Maria da Conceição Tavares, Juan Pablo Painceira, José Gabriel Palma, and Leda Paulani on Brazil and Carlos Morera Camacho, Eugenia Correa, Alicia Girón, Thomas Marois, and Héctor Guillén Romo on Mexico.

28. Throughout this book I use the term "heterodox Marxism" to name the various lineages of Marxist thought which broke with the political, philosophi-

cal, and political economic precepts of the Second and Third Internationals, the moment in which the position of "orthodox" Marxism (as historical and dialectical materialism) was consolidated. The heterodox tradition includes thinkers such as Georg Lukács, Walter Benjamin, and Rosa Luxemburg, as well as Latin American writers such as José Carlos Mariátegui, Ruy Mauro Marini, and Raquel Gutiérrez Aguilar.

29. Summaries of recent literature on financialization can be found in Lapavitsas, *Profiting without Producing*; van der Zwan, "Making Sense"; and Bonizi, "Financialization."

30. There are, of course, many different flavors of the following positions, and much as this book does, many individual authors draw on and combine ideas from different traditions. One important approach to finance that is not included in this list is that of the French Regulation school. While very influential in Latin American work on finance, particularly in Brazil, it is a body of work whose concepts do not appear with frequency either in popular media or cultural work on finance, so I have left them out of this short summary.

31. For recent accounts that focus on greed and financial crisis, see Tett, *Fool's Gold*; Farrell, *Crash of the Titans*, and Morgenson and Rosner, *Reckless Endangerment*. Important works in the post-Keynesian tradition on finance include: Stockhammer, "Financialisation"; Epstein, *Financialization*; and Palley, *Financialization*. Summaries of some of the relevant post-Keynesian literature can be found in Hein and van Treeck, "'Financialisation'", and Lapavitsas, *Profiting without Producing*. Key post-workerist texts on finance include: Fumagalli and Mezzadra, *Crisis in the Global Economy*, and Marazzi, *Violence of Financial Capitalism*. Accounts which center on a declining rate of profit tendency include: Harman, *Zombie Capitalism*; Roberts, *Great Recession*; Carchedi, *Behind the Crisis*; Chesnais, *Finance Capital Today*; Mattick, *Business as Usual*; Kliman, *Failure of Capitalist Production*; Kliman and Williams, "Why 'Financialisation'"; and Roberts, *Long Depression*. Authors who see the rise of finance and/or the 2007–2008 financial crisis as caused primarily by non–rate of profit factors include: Foster and Magdoff, *Great Financial Crisis*; Harvey, *Enigma of Capital*; McNally, *Global Slump*; Duménil and Lévy, *Crisis of Neoliberalism*; and Lapavitsas, *Profiting without Producing*. It is important to note, as Joseph Choonara does, that sometimes these "two positions cannot be neatly disentangled," and while they do tend to take a position on the causes of crisis, most of the above authors grapple with a number of different factors in their explanations.

32. From Brenner, I take only the rhetorical figure of the long downturn—his work would disagree with parts of the analysis presented here. Work on the rate of profit in both Mexico and Brazil demonstrates a generally declining trend from the 1960s to the 1980s that then never comes close to recuperating its postwar levels. Unlike the debate on the United States which has centered on wheth-

er there was a recuperation of the rate of profit after 1982 through the mid-1990s, the recuperation, in Mexico in the mid-1980s and in Brazil in the early 1990s, was light and in the case of Mexico stagnated thereafter. For estimations of the rate of profit in Mexico, see Mariña and Moseley, "Rate of Profit"; Mateo, "Medidas de la rentabilidad"; Cámara Izquierdo, "La dinámica"; and Sandoval Manzano, "Valor Nuevo." For Brazil, see Marquetti et al., "Profit Rate"; Bruno et al., "Finance-led Growth"; and Gaulard, "Brazillian Deindustrialization." For a computation of a global declining rate of profit across the twentieth century that includes key Latin American countries, see Ezequiel Maito, "La transitoriedad histórica." For a theoretical discussion in a Latin American context that touches on the falling rate of profit, see Carcanholo and Sabadini, "Capital ficticio y ganancias ficticias." It is important to note that the point of discussing declining rates of profit is not that they map one-to-one onto economic crises or explain the totality of a historical moment, but rather that they help to establish the post-1982 period as one in which a full recovery was never achieved and thus enable us to see the intervening years as marked by an unsolved crisis of capital. See also Clover in *Riot. Strike. Riot* who argues for calling this period the "Long Crisis."

33. This would include some of the work on the financialization of everyday life such as Langley, *Everyday Life*, or Martin, *Financialization*, and theoretical works such as LiPuma and Lee, *Financial Derivatives*, and Martin, *Knowledge LTD.* It is also descriptive of some anthropological work on finance such as Zaloom, *Out of the Pits*, chapters 4 and 5.

34. See McClanahan, *Dead Pledges*, 13, and "Investing in the Future"; and Clover, "Autumn of the System" and "*Value | Theory* | Crisis." See as well Gowan, *Global Gamble*, 10–11; Harvey, *Limits to Capital*, chapter 10; and Marx, *Capital*, vol. 3, 599.

35. There has been an explosion of work on finance in English-language literary studies in the last decade, some of which has been in conversation with this heterodox Marxist approach to finance. See Adamson, "End of the Gold Standard"; Haiven, *Cultures*; Kornbluh, *Realizing Capital*; La Berge, *Scandals and Abstraction*; and Poovey, *Genres of the Credit Economy.* In Latin American literary and cultural studies, see Beckman, *Capital Fictions*; Fornazzari, *Speculative Fictions*; Laera, *Ficciones del dinero*; Vilches, *New World Gold*; and Whitfield, *Cuban Currency.*

36. For a sampling of returns and reconsiderations, see Escobar, *Territories of Difference*; Lomnitz, "Time and Dependency"; Smith, *Imperialism*; Sotelo Valencia, *Sub-Imperialism*; and Svampa, *Debates.* For Kay's distinction, see *Latin American Theories*, 126.

37. Svampa, *Debates*, 413–14, also argues for the continuing important of dependency ideas.

38. See Prebisch, *Economic Development*, 12–14, and Marini, *Dialéctica*, 115–20.

39. For early work in Mexico on finance, see José Luis Ceceña, *El capital monopolista* and *El imperio del dolar*, and Héctor Guillén Romo, *Origines de la crisis*. See as well the volume edited by Samuel Lichtenszejn in 1981, *Nueva fase del capital financiero*, which includes two essays by Maria da Conceição Taveres. By the mid-1980s authors associated with *Cuadernos Políticos* had developed an understanding of finance's growing importance in the Mexican economy, as had others associated with *Proceso* and *Nexos*, including Adolfo Gilly.

40. Marini, "Subimperialism," 16–18, and Zibechi, *New Brazil*, 13–33.

41. Boito, *Política neoliberal*, 39–41. See as well Chesnais's helpful distinction between "finance capital" and "financial capital" in *Finance Capital Today*.

42. For more on this contestation, see Rodríguez, *Latin American Subaltern*.

43. In the 1980s and 1990s much academic work on Latin America shifted away from the concepts of authoritarianism and corporatism to focus on democracy and the transition to democracy. There are, however, important currents of thought in Mexico and Brazil that have tracked the continuation and transformation in corporatist and neo-corporatist structures during the democratic transition and opening. See Bensusán and von Bülow, "La reforma"; Boito, "The State"; Chapman, *Struggle*; Gilly, "Nuestra caída"; Hermanson and Garza Toledo, "El corporativismo"; and Power and Doctor, "Another Century." In this book I draw on these currents and on work, such as Wiarda, *Authoritarianism and Corporatism*; Williams, *Mexican Exception*; and Zaverucha, *FHC*, that have examined the legacy of authoritarian forms in the "democratic" present or that trace the ubiquity of forms of sovereign power. My aim is to highlight how Latin American states, in particular Mexico and Brazil, continue to rely on ideas and infrastructures of para-corporatism and governmentality to produce social order, even if these forms are no longer as successful as they once were.

44. My understanding of the term "surplus population" is derived from that of Karl Marx which he elaborated in the first volume of *Capital*. For Marx, relative surplus populations are those individuals who are not (or no longer) necessary to processes of capitalist valorization and which he divided into several categories based on their relationship to the means of production. Marx's work formed the basis for 1960s debates in Latin America over what José Nun would call the "marginal mass" and Aníbal Quijano the "marginal pole" and what others would later call the "informal sector": see Nun, *Marginalidad*; Quijano, *Notas*; and Vekemans, *Marginaliad*. See Svampa, *Debates*, for a summary of marginality debates and their contemporary turns; and Braga, *A política do precariado*; Figueroa Sepúlveda, *Industrial Colonialism*; and Soederberg, *Debtfare*, for recent uses of linked imaginaries in Latin America. While there is a well-developed literature in Latin America on the *potencia* or creativity of in-

formal economies or urban spaces (see Gago, *La razón neoliberal*, and Cocco, *KorpoBraz*), my book focuses rather on surplus populations as a problem for the state and as a reason for increasing state violence.

In the last decade, there have been a number of discussions and redefinitions of Marx's surplus population. While these discussions form part of the background for this book, I will not discuss them in detail, and throughout I will use the term "surplus population" to merely indicate individuals who are precariously integrated into circuits of capitalist production. I will often use figures for "informal employment" as evidence for the existence and growth over time of this population. These two terms are not equivalent, but because I need only establish that there is a significant group of individuals on the edges of the productive system, I have decided not to push harder here. My thinking on how race interacts with surplus population draws heavily on Chris Chen, "The Limit Point." Other important recent work on surplus population or related ideas include: Clover, *Riot. Strike. Riot*; Davis, *Planet of Slums*; Denning, "Wageless Life"; Fernández-Kelly and Shefner, *Out of the Shadows*; Gilmore, *Golden Gulag*; "The Holding Pattern"; Hong, "Existentially Surplus"; Toscano, "Uses of the Useless"; and Wacquant, *Punishing the Poor.*

45. INEGI, "Encuesta Nacional de Ocupación."

46. International Labor Organization, "Statistical Update."

47. Bensusán and von Bülow, "La reforma institucional," 186.

48. Collier and Collier, "Who Does What," 492–93. Moreover, it could be argued that part of the political form of para-corporativism is its contradictory lack of representation within an ostensibly democratic social framework (which can lead to demand-making outside the channels of representative democracy).

49. This book focuses narrowly on surplus populations across this historical period—as such it doesn't aim to offer a more totalizing or broad theorization of state-society relations or the relationship between state logics and practices. For one account that does so in the context of Mexico, see Pansters, *Violence, Coercion, and State-Making.*

50. My use of "infrastructure" throughout this book constellates it in certain ways with ideas of corporatism and Foucault's work on apparatuses. I use the term "infrastructure" because of its association with the material (as opposed to the slightly more epistemically inflected term "apparatus") and also because of its proximity to discussions on the production of race and "groupness." (Thanks to Daniel Nemser for suggesting this way of distinguishing infrastructure and apparatus.) I constellate it with discourses on corporatism in order to bring it into the proximity of the optics of capital and labor and histories of the state. However, I use "infrastructure" less in a predominantly spatial register or as what enables the circulation of people and objects, but rather as a kind of "heterogeneous ensemble" (Foucault, "Confession," 194) for producing groups, col-

lectivities, and organizing interfaces between state and society. As will become clear toward the end of this book, I am interested in "groupness" as a site of political dehiscence and possibility.

51. Nemser, *Infrastructures*, 17.

52. Gilmore, *Golden Gulag*, 28.

53. See, for example, Orloff and Morgan, *Many Hands of the State*. This book also represents a conversation with a long line of other cultural studies works that have attempted to think about the unique specificity, genealogies, and possible definitions of violence in Latin America, including Franco, *Cruel Modernity*; Herlinghaus, *Violence without Guilt*; Rodríguez, *Liberalism at Its Limits*; as well as the works already mentioned in this introduction.

54. Kilanski and Auyero, "Introduction," 7.

55. There are, of course, long-standing debates in cultural studies about the role, positioning, and meaning of the economic. My work draws on those authors in the English-language literature, such as Marjorie Ferguson, Peter Golding, Lawrence Grossberg, Stuart Hall, and Douglas Kellner, for whom political economy does not mean only a discussion of the cultural industries. My framing of these issues also draws on Latin American cultural studies, *estudios culturales*, and earlier works (such as those by Ángel Rama or Antonio Candido) which have frequently had an open dialogue with if not political economy, then most certainly with social theory. See, for example, Cevasco, *Dez lições*; Richard, *En torno*; Del Sarto, Ríos, and Trigo, *Latin American Cultural Studies*; Trigo, *Crisis y transfiguración*; Valenzuela Arce, *Los estudios culturales*; and Walsh, *Estudios culturales.*

56. As has often been noted, the metaphor of base-superstructure does not play an important role in Marx's work. See Williams, *Marxism*, 78: "It is then ironic to remember that the force of Marx's original criticism had been mainly directed at the *separation* of 'areas' of thought and activity." Base-superstructure was primarily an invention of Engels which was then codified by authors such as Kautsky and Plekhanov as part of the mechanical determinism underpinning the thought of the Second International. In the climate that prevailed after 1956, that is, in New Left, May 68, and other anti-Stalinist political formulations, attacking, remaking, or disproving the base-superstructure metaphor was a central theoretical task and drew the attention of thinkers as diverse as Louis Althusser, Jean Baudrillard, Giles Deleuze and Félix Guattari, Stuart Hall, Fredric Jameson, and Raymond Williams. This was also the case in Latin America, where non-vulgar versions of the distinction have been influential; see for example Harnecker's *Los conceptos elementales*; Aricó's *La cola del diablo*; and Portantiero's *Los usos de Gramsci*. However, even in works from the New Left and May 68 movements that argue for its obsolescence or overturning, such as Deleuze and Guattari's *Anti-Oedipus* or Baudrillard's *The Mirror of Production*,

the base-superstructure metaphor is still what motivates the argument. While certainly in the pre- and post-1968 generation it served as a spur to very creative, important work, I think forcing ourselves to continually reference a distinction—that most agree is theoretically unhelpful, serves as one of the great dogmatic bugbears of those "radicals" who like to punch left, and forms a part of a left social formation that is no longer hegemonic—is no longer a gesture that we need to make.

57. Williams, *Marxism*, 81, and Stoler, *Duress*, 19.

Chapter 1: The *Saltos* of Finance

1. In Claudio Lomnitz's work on the 1982 financial crisis, which I will discuss shortly, one can see that financial crisis (which returned in different forms in 1987 and 1994) predated what are normally considered to be the historical markers of neoliberalism (the passage of NAFTA, the full liberalization of capital markets—processes which got under way only in the late 1980s and were completed only in the early 1990s). What this means is that neoliberalism, when used to mark either a process of state transformation or a process of transformation of both the state and the economy, is by itself insufficient for thinking about the historical moment. I want to suggest in this chapter that we think about this period within a dual horizon derived from Lomnitz: the 1980s and 1990s as the moment of national popular breakdown (the shift to the neoliberal state form implied by liberalization), but also as an ongoing financial crisis in the context of new global forms of finance-led accumulation.

2. Pellizzoni, *Ontological Politics*, contains a summary of different versions of current "ontological turns" in social theory.

3. Karatani, *Transcritique*, 8. I owe this insight into and usage of Karatani to the work of Annie McClanahan in her doctoral dissertation, "Salto Mortale." It is important to note that the perspective that I develop here about finance is very different from that of Karatani, in that Karatani seems to argue that surplus value can be produced by exchange. In the work I use to frame my understanding of finance, surplus value is created only through the exploitation of labor, while exchange is where surplus value is either realized or not. Despite this difference, I find Karatani's presentation of credit as salto useful and believe it can be extracted from his other arguments.

4. Lomnitz, "Times of Crisis," 133.

5. Soederberg, *Politics*, 53.

6. Allaz, "Salinas: El caos," 50; "Se presentan como otros tantos síntomas de la honda descomposición de nuestra sociedad a lo largo de los doce años de salinismo. Al gobernante tan imbuido de su poder personal absoluto y sin límite, le quedará para la historia la responsibilidad de haber instalado a la nación en el caos."

7. Alonso, "Novel without Literature," 3.

8. See Pera, "¿Nación?"; Corral, "Qué queda"; Santos, "El Cosmopolitismo"; and Sánchez Prado, *Strategic Occidentalism*.

9. Volpi, *In Search of Klingsor*, 6.

10. Volpi, *In Search of Klingsor*, 6 (trans. mod.).

11. Volpi, *In Search of Klingsor*, 6. (trans. mod.).

12. Volpi, *In Search of Klingsor*, 72, 94.

13. Volpi, *In Search of Klingsor*, 314.

14. Volpi, *In Search of Klingsor*, 313.

15. Volpi, *In Search of Klingsor*, 245.

16. Monsiváis, *Rituales*, 15; "Las formas enredadas—solemnes, divertidas o grotescas—de la vida en sociedad se identifican ante sí mismas de modo más bien típico: multitudes que se hacen y rehacen cada minuto, carnavales previstos e imprevistos, capacidades adquisitivas, placer por extraviarse en los laberintos de la energía o de la inercia. Aquí la avidez todo lo devora, la resignación todo lo santifica, el relajo todo lo conoce y desconoce a la vez. Visto desde fuera, el caos al que aluden estas crónicas (en su acepción tradicional, precientífica) se vincula, básicamente, a una de las caracterizaciones más constantes de la vida mexicana, la que señala su "feroz desorden." Si ésto alguna vez fue cierto ya ha dejado de serlo. Según creo, la descripción más justa de lo que ocurre equilibra la falta aparente de sentido con la imposición altanera de límites. Y en el caos se inicia el perfeccionamiento del orden."

17. Williams, *Other Side*, 36.

18. Palou et al., *Crack Manifesto*, 1; "Las palabras más certeras sobre los retos que se le plantean a las novelas del Crack las iba a pronunciar, creo, Italo Calvino en *Seis propuestas para el próximo milenio*. En esas páginas, Calvino proponía una reflexión necesaria hoy, cuando la literatura y, sobre todo, la narrativa ven desplazado a su lector potencial por las tecnologías del entretenimiento: los juegos de vídeo, los medios masivos y, recientemente, para quien pueda solventarlos, los juegos de realidad virtual / en los cuales / oh, paradojas / el desarrollo / un individuo provisto de un modernísimo casco y un anatómico guante puede ver, oír e incluso palpar las aventuras que un disco compacto le proporcione."

19. Palou et al., *Crack Manifesto*, 1–2; "Hoy, es ocioso apuntarlo, la propia realidad se nos arroja múltiple, se nos revela multifacética, eterna. Se necesitan libros en los cuales un mundo total se abra ante el lector, y lo atrape. En nuestros anterior apartado usábamos este mismo verbo, pero aquí la estrategia es distinta. No es de vértigo, sino de superposición de mundos de lo que se trata. Usar todo el potencial metafórico del texto literario para decirnos nuevamente: 'Aquí están ustedes, encuéntrense.'"

20. Quoted in Cohn, *Latin American Literary*, 5.

21. Solidifying this critique and extending it into the moment of the *marea*

rosada (Pink Tide) is one subject of Volpi's *El insomnio de Bolívar* (2009). No story in the book is more indicative of this complicated relationship than Volpi's narration of the reception of *Klingsor* after his changing the nationality of the main character:

> A fines de 1998 comprendí que había algo ridículo en que un mexicano, y para colmo físico, se dedicase a cazar nazis en Alemania. Sólo entonces decidí, por una simple cuestión de verosimilitud, cambiar la nacionalidad de mi personaje, que se tornó estadounidense y pasó a llamarse Francis Bacon, como el filósofo isabelino. En abril de 1999 ese libro, ya rebautizado por Guillermo Cabrera Infante como *En busca de Klingsor*, obtuvo el Premio Biblioteca Breve, que en su primera etapa había sido un emblemático punto de unión entre las dos orillas del Atlántico, y la prensa se apresuró a señalar que se trataba del libro de un mexicano que no parecía mexicano, de un latinoamericano que—rara cosa—no escribía sobre América Latina. Aquella decisión pragmática de transformar a un mexicano en gringo se convirtió en un inesperado manifiesto. (24)

22. Volpi, "Cuando."

23. González Casanova and Aguilar Camín, *México ante la crisis*, 13; "Se habla de la crisis como . . . en el lenguaje anglosajón que se ha apoderado en gran parte de las ciencias económicas el *crack*."

24. Carpentier, "On the Marvelous Real," 88.

25. See Lund, *Mestizo State*, "Introduction." Christina A. Sue in her *Land of the Cosmic Race* argues that the post-Revolutionary racial ideology in Mexico has been defined by three "pillars": mestizaje, nonracism, and nonblackness. In my characterization of Mexican racial theories as defined by mestizaje/antiblackness, I am following Sue's work and folding her first two pillars into the category of mestizaje, while preferring the language of antiblackness to nonblackness.

26. Key works on this period in Mexico include Overmyer-Velázquez, *Folkloric Poverty*; Chorba, *Mexico*; Miller, *Rise and Fall*; and Mora, *Kuxlejal Politics*. For an influential theorization of neoliberal multiculturalism which many others have drawn on, see Hale, *Más Que un Indio*. My approach is not an attempt to invalidate these works; rather I aim to account for a second response to state crisis (both financial and representational) in the form of a re-elaboration of categories and discourses that do the work of race and sustain racism.

27. Foucault, *Security, Territory, Population*, 4–6.

28. This is not to try to argue, of course, that racial formations and discourses of indigeneity or antiblackness disappear, nor to elide the lives and experiences of indigenous and Afro-descendent communities that continue to live under them, nor the important work that is being done tracking shifting relations and

the production of difference between indigenous and nonindigenous communities in Mexico. See for example Saldívar "'It's Not Race.'"

29. For an account of this, see Acosta Córdova, "La transformación": "Antes de la crisis económica, los guerrilleros zapatistas eran, para Zedillo, no 'profesionales de la violencia' ni 'grupo armado infiltrado por extranjero'—como lo calificó inicialmente su antecesor, Carlos Salinas de Gortari—, sino 'inconformes' que se rebelaron por la violencia cotidiana en Chiapas . . . Después pasada la turbulencia financiera causada por la devaluación, su opinión es otra" (7–8). See also Montemayor, "Chiapas, otra vez"; Fuentes, "La cuestión chiapaneca"; and Schwarz, *Crónica*, 25–27.

30. This was the march that made (in)famous the slogan "Haz patria, mata un delincuente" (Be a patriot, kill a delinquent), which now forms part of far-right inflected Twitter and Internet commentary discourses; see Hernandez, "The War on Crime."

31. I am overdrawing the distinction between biological and cultural definitions of race here only to try to bring out the difference of delincuente as a category. As María Elena Martínez has demonstrated in *Genealogical Fictions*, racial discourses are extremely flexible invoking biology in one moment and culture in the next (11).

32. There is a much longer history of the association between the lower class/indigenous communities and criminality that for reasons of space and focus I have had to leave out of this discussion. This history stretches back to the early colonial period and the elaboration of the distinction between *gente de razón* and *gente sin razón* which, as Gabriel Haslip-Viera has shown, became inserted into criminological discourse by the late colonial period. It can be seen as well in the liberal period in Mariano Otero's writing which distinguishes between gente de razón and *leperos*. As Robert Buffington writes: "Otero suggested that all leperos were potential recidivists, thus stigmatizing them as a 'class' in advance of any actual criminal act" (*Criminal and Citizen*, 21). This "potentiality" is certainly a forerunner of the mobile nature of the present usage of "delincuente." Finally, the category "delincuente" itself has important antecedents in both nineteenth-century criminology but also in 1950s, 1960s, and 1970s government campaigns against guerrillas in southern Mexico. Here "delincuente" was the term government officials used: 1) to argue that guerrillas did not exist in Mexico (they were/are just delincuentes or bands of criminals) and 2) to undercut the guerrillas' moral critique of the state's own violence and corruption (e.g., we [the state] are not violent/criminal; it is the guerrillas/delincuentes who are because they kidnap, shoot at police, etc.). One can find more on this use of "delincuente" as state discourse in the context of guerrilla struggles in Padilla, *Rural Resistance*, and Aviña, *Specters of Revolution*.

33. Reforms concerning indigenous self-governance were left by the federal government to individual states. Reforms were passed by twenty-two states; Oaxaca passed legislation allowing for governance by *usos y costumbres* (uses and customs) in 1995. See Eisenstadt, *Politics*, 47–48.

34. Howard Winant has argued that after the Second World War, the United States passed through a "racial break" where forms of white supremacy were supplanted by forms of racial liberalism. Winant generally sees forms of white supremacy and racial liberalism as coexisting after the racial break, but with racial liberalism as having the upper hand. Jodi Melamed's *Represent and Destroy* has advanced two corrections of this argument: first, that racial liberalism became a new hegemonic perspective that was then attacked by more radical forms of antiracism and resurgent forms of white supremacy and, second, that racial liberalisms were globally exported by the United States as part of its role as global hegemon in the postwar period. What we can see in our brief account of race in Mexico is how Mexico complicates this understanding both of the birth of racial liberalisms and the timeline of their "implantation" in non-U.S. spheres. Mestizaje, while not a form of racial liberalism, is something other than a crude theory of white supremacy—but one which, à la Winant, operates alongside and serves as a cover for the most vulgar and defamatory understandings of racial others, particularly as directed at indigenous and Afro-Mexican communities. Having said this, however, the arrival of neoliberal multiculturalist discourses, as traced by Charles Hale in Guatemala and other authors in Mexico, is indeed a significant event, and it is clear that the language used to articulate a state response to indigenous mobilizations in the 1980s and 1990s, while translated into the Mexican racial formation, is marked by and in conversation with sites of neoliberal multicultural discursive production in the United States (so ably traced by Melamed). This represents a partial convergence between the idea of a global, U.S.-led racial formation and the Mexican experience, and we could perhaps read the subsequent rearticulation of racial discourses around an ontological divide, discussed in this chapter, also following Melamed, as a resurgent racialization project that emerges alongside the circulation of pluricultural racial neoliberalism in Mexico.

35. In the current literatures on race and finance, common lines of research examine the racialization of debt/credit, housing markets, and/or predatory lending practices, and with respect to financial crisis, how people of color are turned in mainstream accounts from being the victims of predation to being the "cause" of a given financial crisis. See for example Chakravartty and Ferreira da Silva, "Accumulation, Dispossession, and Debt," and Wyly et al., "New Racial Meanings." The specificity of the race-finance relation in Mexico is how racialization responds to and moves in sync with the destabilizations caused by financial crisis.

36. Palou et al., *Crack Manifesto*, 8.

37. Benjamin, *Arcades*, 473, trans. mod. See Dove, *Catastrophe of Modernity*, for a more expansive approach to the relation between the literary and societal catastrophe.

38. There is a body of work in critical security studies, including Aradau and van Munster's *Politics of Catastrophe*, that also examines the emergence of the figure of catastrophe. In their work Aradau and van Munster defend a break between discourses of risk and uncertainty and those of catastrophe, associating catastrophe with the "non-calculable." Here I frame the idea of catastrophe or disaster in a global North context as related to the near future, or as a part of attempts to make the "non-calculable" calculable—an endeavor that is inherently uncertain. It functions as a critique of the use of "catastrophe" in pop and right social "theorizing," such as Posner, *Catastrophe*.

39. Christopher Nealon makes a similar point in his excellent *PMLA* essay "Value | *Theory* | *Crisis*," 102–3.

40. Sales-Sarrapy, Solis-Soberon, and Villagomez-Amezcua, *Pension System Reform*, 135.

41. Ilyina, "Role of Derivatives," 68.

42. The opening scene of the preface is not included in some English translations of the novel. The following citations from the Spanish original will be given in my own translation.

43. Volpi, *En busca de Klingsor*, 12; "Con el entusiasmo de un niño que escucha de nuevo su historia favorita, Hitler saborea por enésima vez el espectáculo."

44. Volpi, *En busca de Klingsor*, 12; "La sucesión de causas y efectos inicia su ciclo ritual, celebrado una y otra vez según el estado de ánimo que le provocan las noticias que llegan del frente."

45. Volpi, *En busca de Klingsor*, 13; "Un mínimo error de cálculo—una nimiedad: una de las bombas no pudo ser activdada o acaso el maletín quedó desmasiado lejos del lugar donde se sentaba Hitler—hizo que el plan se viniese abajo."

46. Volpi, *In Search of Klingsor*, 6 (trans. mod.).

47. Volpi, *In Search of Klingsor*, 6 (trans. mod.).

48. Volpi, *In Search of Klingsor*, 6 (trans. mod.).

49. Alejandro Álvarez and Gabriel Mendoza, writing in *Cuadernos Políticos* in 1988, offer a different perspective: "No es el fantasma de los cuatro jinetes del apocalipsis el que se pasea por el territorio nacional, es más bien la dinámica compleja de un proceso de transnacionalización que vive la economía mexicana bajo la política gubernamental de promover los intereses del gran capital nacional e internacional" (43).

50. Wingrove, "Ontology," 91.

51. Joshua Clover's "Retcon" discusses two forms of causality linked to

post-1973 cultural production: "Hysteron proteron," or the inversion of cause and effect, and "retroactive continuity" (retcon), which involves an "annealing of logical fissures in a given backstory after they have cracked open into system threatening incoherence in the present" (14). In Volpi we might see a third, subaltern form, the cancellation of causality itself.

52. Bartra, *Blood, Ink, and Culture*, 9. The essay this quote is taken from, "The Mexican Office," was written in 1990. In it Bartra develops an account of these shocks as contributing to the end of the state's control over national culture and the formation of Mexican nationalism. See also Sánchez Prado's discussion of Bartra and Volpi in *Strategic Occidentalism*, 100-101.

53. They have filtered forward in the works of Volpi as well. His *Memorial del engaño* (2014) deals with the financial crisis of 2008 and continues some of the main themes of *Klingsor*, but with key differences. First, *Memorial* takes the form of the autobiography of a fictitious New York financier named J. Volpi and is built around a series of literary tricks and shifting frames that destabilize the reader's ability to interpret the events of the novel. In a way similar to *Klingsor*, *Memorial* turns around indeterminacy, but it feels less concerned with causality. *Memorial* also shares with *Klingsor* a certain moralism; however *Memorial* is driven more by a sense of moral outrage at the depredations of politicians and Wall Street types in producing the 2008 financial crisis. The issue with this work is that it conceives of the financial crisis as the result of individual behavior and is unable to see how it was the result of ongoing crises in production, a situation that will not be solved by re-regulating the financial sector, restoring production's rightful primacy, or castigating poorly behaved financiers and politicians.

54. González Rodríguez, *Mal de origen*, 21–22; "En otras palabras, el lastre diario de la catástrofe, ese cortocircuito de los vínculos entre lo humano y lo inhumano que describe Annie Le Brun: en el fondo de cada persona, reside un sentimiento obsesivo de la catástrofe, como un eco lejano de pulsiones de largo alcance, cuya amplitud a veces percibimos 'con estupor pero cuyo origen se nos escapa.' ¿Qué hacer?"

55. Yépez, *Empire of Neomemory*, 251; "El mundo es un archipiélago en el tiempo. Cada universo es una macroisla que ya dentro de su propia continencia, parpadea. Pero el espacio-tiempo muta, y su información se extravía para siempre y donde anteriormente estaba su cuerpo ahora hay otro diferente, obediente a leyes otras, y entre universo y universo, la ilusión de la fijeza. Si sincrónicamente hay universos paralelos—cada uno regido por sus propias leyes—también diacrónicamente desaparecen y aparecen caosmos heteróclitos; separados uno del otro por un abismo insalvable, por una palpitación irregular, querer hacer ciencia es absurdo, si desconoce que los principios que se descubrirán sólo valen para un periodo indeterminado de espacio-tiempo mortal, porque la vida es una vida siempre dentro de otra muerte. Toda memoria es temporal.

Toda ley perecerá. Toda historia tiene límites. Todo tejido, extravía su trama" (270).

56. Hacking, *Emergence of Probability*, xx.

57. Wennerlind, *Casualties of Credit*, 3.

58. Wennerlind, *Casualties of Credit*, 3.

59. Wennerlind, *Casualties of Credit*, 10.

60. Laclau and Mouffe, *Hegemony*, x.

61. Laclau and Mouffe, *Hegemony*, xii.

62. Laclau and Mouffe, *Hegemony*, xi.

63. Strathausen, "Critique."

64. In the Mexican context, the work of the Spanish exile and Mexican philosopher Adolfo Sánchez Vázquez registered this problematic in an interesting, perhaps alternative, fashion. In a summary of his position ("La filosofía de la praxis como nueva práctica de la filosofía") written for *Cuadernos Políticos* in 1977, Sánchez Vázquez argues that a philosophy of praxis has to reject three interpretations of Marxism: "ontologizante (según la cual el problema filosófico fundamental es el de las relaciones entre el espíritu y la materia)," "epistemológica (según la cual el marxismo se reduce a una nueva práctica teórica)," and "antropológico-humanista (según la cual el marxismo como proyecto de emancipación se enraíza en un concepto abstracto de hombre)." What Sánchez Vázquez aims to put in their place is a philosophy of praxis, which is a way of thinking that both recognizes its limits as thought (what is thought cannot be completed in thought itself) and, second, thinks itself as not a reflection on but rather as an insertion into a particular world.

Chapter 2: The Failures of Finance

1. Skidmore, *Politics of Military Rule*, 30, 32, 35.

2. Moreira Alves, *State and Opposition*, 3, 27, and Skidmore, *Politics of Military Rule*, 62.

3. Payer, *Debt Trap*, 149–50; Vidal Luna and Klein, *Economic and Social History*, 164, 198–201; Skidmore, *Politics of Military Rule*, 59–62.

4. Skidmore, *Politics of Military Rule*, 234–36, and Moreira Alves, *State and Opposition*, 148–52, 194–99.

5. Coes, *Macroeconomic Crises*, 21.

6. Skidmore, *Politics of Military Rule*, 231.

7. Moreira Alves, *State and Opposition*, 8. It is important to note, as both R. S. Rose and Christen A. Smith have, that death squads and violent policing practices existed before the dictatorship and have always had an antiblack racial component.

8. "A Marca," 17.

9. The movement from the motto "Ordem e Progresso" (Order and Prog-

ress) to "Brasil, ame-o ou deixe-o" (Brazil, Love It or Leave It) marks this partial shift from national culture to state violence (Dunn, *Contracultura*, 24). However, throughout this period "national culture" remained a contested terrain between the dictatorship and left cultural formations. National popular cultural arguments were made by left artists throughout the dictatorship from Glauber Rocha to Carlos Diegues and came to structure many of the key critical debates of the period, including that over Tropicália and MPB (Música popular brasileira) (Dunn, *Brutality Garden*, 40–45, 73–74).

10. Zaverucha, *FHC*, 15; "Certamente, ele se esqueceu que a Lei de Segurança Nacional, os Códigos Penal e Processual Militar, o Decreto estipulando que os serviços reservados das Polícias Militares façam parte do sistema de informação do Exército, a Lei de Imprensa, o Estatuto dos Estrangeiros e o Decreto que dispõe sobre a salvaguarda de dados, informaçoes, documentos e materiais sigilosos de interesse da segurança da sociedade e do Estado, no âmbito da Administração Pública etc. continuam em vigor. E que se não houve prontidão militar, deveu-se ao fato de os civis cederem às pressões militares quando estas ameaçam acionar os dispositivos de uma prontidão militar."

The police force in Brazil is divided into two branches. The Military Police is responsible for the day-to-day patrolling, interventions into neighborhoods, and policing of the city. The Civil Police, who are plainclothes officers, investigate and report on crimes.

11. Caldeira, *City of Walls*, 159.

12. Zaverucha, *FHC*, 128–29. For a sampling of parallel arguments in different fields and moments, see Salla, "Os impasses"; Amar, *Security Archipelago*; Telles, "Entrevista"; and Pinheiro, *Escritos indignados*.

13. "Negros dias," 27.

14. "Septembro quente," 38. Some academic work does exist on the transportation riots in the 1970s: see Moisés et al., *Contradições urbanas e movimentos sociais* (1977) and *Cidade, povo e poder* (1981). The saques of the 1980s and before have received notice primarily in the periodical literature (and occasionally in the novelistic, such as Ignácio de Loyola Brandão's *Zero*, which serves as the epigraph to this chapter). Although more research is necessary to confirm this, it appears that saques were a lower-class survival tactic during the period of hyperinflation (see Gabeira, "Morte e vida"). One academic study of media representations of saques from 1983 can be found in Buso Ferreira, "Representações de intolerância."

15. Although the indexing of wages was maintained until 1986 (Skidmore, *Politics of Military Rule*, 278–80), indexation was attacked in a variety of indirect and not-so-indirect ways. Food prices were allowed to rise, subsidies were cancelled, and export crops put additional pressure on basic commodity prices. Inflation and the socialization of crisis led to scenes like this: in July 1987, after

an order indicating a 49 percent rise in the price of bus tickets in Rio de Janeiro, the city center was taken by a multitude of thirty thousand people who in a daylong confrontation with police burned sixty buses and damaged hundreds of others ("Um duro aviso," 18). The memories of the saques of 1983 were clearly still fresh: "As cenas de violência do Rio de Janeiro trouxeram de volta o pesadelo de recessão de 1983, quando ocorreram saques e depredações na maioria das capitais brasileiras" (18).

16. Chevigny, *Edge of the Knife*, 147.

17. Pereira, "Review," 169.

18. Rose, *Unpast*, 272.

19. Rose, *Unpast*, 277, and Amparo Alves, *Anti-Black City*.

20. For example, Caldeira reports that between 1982 and 2002 the São Paulo police killed 11,692 people (Caldeira, "Paradox," 236). See also Chevigny, *Edge of the Knife* (chapter 5).

21. Roddick, *Dance*, 142–43.

22. Saad-Filho, "Political Economy," 226.

23. Romão cited in Faria, "Current Social Situation," 7.

24. Marois, *States, Banks and Crisis*, 34.

25. Baer, *Economia brasileira*, 118.

26. Baer, *Economia brasileira*, 141–47, 151–53; Bin, "Politics of Financialization," 114–15.

27. Debates on the etiology of inflation in (or caused by) Latin America date back to the work of the School of Salamanca's attempts to understand why the possession of more silver was not making Spain "richer" but rather causing price increases—thus discussions of inflation are intertwined with the very beginning of colonial history in Latin America. This specific period in Brazil receives treatments in Bresser Pereira, *Desenvolvimento e crise*, and Baer, *Economia brasileira* (see the extended discussion of inflation in chapter 7). The best register of the popular concern with hyperinflation, beyond the numerous articles in the popular press on strategies for dealing with inflation, is that in 1986 as part of his Plano Cruzado—an attempt to deal with hyperinflation—President Sarney asked all citizens to become *as fiscais do Sarney* (Sarney's price police) to enforce the price freeze in supermarkets and other stores that this plan called for. Thousands of homemakers and ordinary people across Brazil signed up to do their part against hyperinflation by policing prices in their local stores (this story is told in the context of Minas Gerais in Mauro Amado's dissertation "As Fiscais do Sarney").

28. Rohter, *Brazil on the Rise*, 142.

29. "Até quarenta," 88.

30. As Marx writes of this duopoly: "The bourgeois, drunk with prosperity and arrogantly certain of himself, has just declared that money is a purely imag-

inary creation. 'Commodities alone are money,' he said. But now the opposite cry resounds over the markets of the world: only money is a commodity. As the hart pants after fresh water, so pants his soul after money, the only wealth." *Capital*, vol. 1, 236.

31. Baer, *Economia brasileira*, 221–24.

32. Belluzzo and Almeida, *Depois da queda*, 388–90.

33. Alba Zaluar, the anthropologist Lins would work for doing ethnographic research, wrote one of the few pieces I have been able to find on the connection between violence and hyperinflation. Zaluar's "Hiperinflação e (é) violência" in *Condomínio do diabo* notes that inflation is an issue but argues that there has also been a revolution in patterns of consumption. She argues that this has led young people to fall into the pursuit of "dinheiro facil," that is, the drug trade. Interestingly, Zaluar also notes that the inflation saques of 1983 brought "bandidos" and "trabalhadores" together in the streets: "Durante os saques da época, ouvi de trabalhadores respeitáveis: 'agora somos todos uma coisa só,' 'roubamos quem nos rouba'" (120).

34. Zaluar and Alvito, *Um século*, 8, 12.

35. Valladares, *Invenção*, 143, 148–51.

36. Ventura, *Cidade partida*, 13:

> Na verdade, durante este século, desde a reforma de Pereira Passos e passando pelos planos Agache e Doxiadis, a opção foi sempre pela separação, senão pela simples segregação. A cidade civilizou-se e modernizou-se expulsando para os morros e periferia seus cidadãos de segunda classe.
>
> O resultado dessa política foi uma cidade partida. Juntála talvez seja tarefa para o próximo século, mas será preciso começar já—até porque a política de exclusão foi um desastre. Não apenas moral e humanitário, mas também do ponto de vista de eficácia. O seu principal produto, o apartheid social, corre o risco de ter o destino que teve o apartheid racial em outros lugares.
>
> A fantasia da solução final—a remoção e o extermínio—revelou-se igualmente desatrosa, por iníqua e impraticável. No fim do século passado havia no Rio uma só favela; no fim deste século elas são mais de quinhentas."

Zuenir Ventura's *Cidade partida* is often translated as "broken city" but due to the nature of Ventura's argument stressing a spatial separation in the urban, it is also rendered as "divided city." When referencing the book's ideas in this section I will usually note both usages in the translation of "cidade partida."

37. Arias, *Drugs and Democracy*, 3.

38. Arias, *Drugs and Democracy*, 4.

39. Arias, *Drugs and Democracy*, 3.

40. Arias, *Drugs and Democracy*, 4.

41. The piece I discuss here was a follow-up to his original critique of Ventura's divided/broken city, "Adeus 'Cidade partida.'" For other discussions of the

limitations of the "divided city," see Perlman, *Favela*, and Novaes, "Favelas and the Divided City." Critiques of formal-informal dualism and the reification of separation can be found in Cavalcanti, "Politics of Concrete and Cocaine" and "Do barraco à casa"; Nun, *Marginalidad y exclusión social*; and Mezzadra and Nielson, "Fronteras de inclusión diferencial." In the cultural realm Allen's "Shifting Perspectives" and her other work on the movement for *inclusão visual* (visual inclusion) are sensitive to the need to avoid "the dualistic mode of thought that constructs for the favelas the role of urban anomaly" (81). In the field of literary and cultural studies, see Lehnen's reading of *Guia afetivo da periferia* (in *Citizenship and Crisis*), Jaguaribe's *Rio de Janeiro* (chapter 6), and Larkins, *Spectacular Favela* (chapter 3) for important thinking on the circulation and reinscription of the favela in the 1990s and in later years. Within the larger field of urban studies the dichotomy of formal and informal as a means of understanding contemporary urban processes has received many critiques; see for example Roy and AlSayyad, *Informality*.

42. Souza e Silva, "Carta," 20–21:

> Nesse caso, a cidade é atravessada por um conjunto de práticas de circulação que faz com que ela não seja "partida" para os pobres, pelo menos não na dimensão da inserção no território, de forma global. Eles buscam viver na cidade de forma plena.
>
> Acho que talvez fosse mais adequado falar que o "Estado é partido," pois ele, dominado pelo interesse em servir apenas a grupos sociais específicos, não cumpre o seu pretenso "papel universal." Da mesma forma, temos um "Mercado partido," pois, dominado por preconceitos e visões restritas das relações de custo x benefício, nunca reconheceu o conjunto de moradores da cidade como cidadãos plenos de direitos.

43. Ribeiro, "Cidade desigual," 95. As Ribeiro also notes, politically, the divided city or exclusion perspective serves to justify technocratic solutions and to sideline discussions of distribution and redistribution (94).

44. Alberto, *Terms of Inclusion*, 10–12; Heise, *Remaking Brazil*, 35–37; Paschel, *Becoming Black*, 38–39; Telles, *Race in Another America*, 36–37.

45. Alberto, *Terms of Inclusion*, 17.

46. Reiter and Mitchell, *Brazil's New Racial*, 7; Paschel, *Becoming Black*, 117–20; Hanchard, *Orpheus*, 109–29.

47. While Rio's favelas number in the hundreds and as such are heterogeneous spaces, Ribeiro and Telles, "Rio de Janeiro," reported that in 1991, 70 percent of favela residents identified as a black or brown. Favelas house a disproportionate percentage of the city's black population and that population is disproportionately exposed to the criminal justice system and death at the hands of the police.

48. There has been a great deal of sustained attention given to abstraction

in cultural work, of which Fredric Jameson's "Culture and Finance Capital" and "The Brick and the Balloon" might be the most well-known contemporary examples. See however Leigh Claire La Berge's excellent critique of how humanities discourses mishandle the "abstraction" of finance, "Rules of Abstraction." For a critique of Jameson's understanding of finance see McClanahan, "Investing in the Future," 89–90.

49. Virno, *Grammar*, 64.

50. Toscano, "Open Secret," 273.

51. Sohn-Rethel's take on real abstractions locates them in the process of exchange. Some Marxist theorists prefer an explanation that bases real abstraction in abstract labor, see Anslem Jappe, "Sohn-Rethel." Sohn-Rethel's work, while perhaps little known today outside specialist circles, was an important influence on Adorno as well as Žižek's *Sublime Object of Ideology.*

52. Sianne Ngai, "Visceral Abstractions," has nicely brought out this side of Sohn Rethel's work:

> In societies where producers do not explicitly coordinate their acts of production, this mediation happens only when their products are exchanged. But although the mediations of exchange have the "formal ability to weave a web of social coherence among the mass of private individuals all acting independently of another," as Alfred Sohn-Rethel notes, the socializing effects of their activities *also come to appear to them as an independent force not of their own making*, one that oppositionally confronts them as a "second nature." As Marx puts it, referring to the rise of the world market, what appears is not just the "connection of the individual with all, but at the same time also the independence of this connection from the individual." (39)

53. Indeed, capturing the particularity of formal-adjacent urban areas in their relationality without collapsing their internal class differentiation has been the project of the best critical urban commentary ever since Machado da Silva's foundational 1967 essay "A política na favela."

54. This point has been widely made: see Observatorio de Favelas, *O que é a favela, afinal?*; Valladares, *Invenção*; and McCann's historicization of the favela construct (*Hard Times*, 21–33).

55. Mbembe, *Critique*, 54. It is important to reiterate here that my argument is not that "race" somehow disappears in this moment. Rather what I am arguing is that, due to push back by black and nonwhite intellectuals, activists, and everyday people and a shift from corporativist infrastructures to police violence (a process which began during the dictatorship), the ideology of "racial democracy" becomes supplemented in this moment by a spatialized distinction between the "favela" and the formal city. I am also arguing that this distinction becomes something more than discursive, in its popular sense: it becomes a

structuring "force"—which is what becoming a substitute for real abstraction means.

56. The importance of Lins's work, in terms of opening a new space and set of aesthetic possibilities in Brazilian literary writing, has been widely discussed—so my approach here takes those discussions and achievements as a given. It is also critical to note that Lins does not serve as a stand-in here for the vast world of cultural production (in particular musical) that has been generated in the last three decades from peripheral urban areas and which has been incredibly important in providing cultural visibility to individuals and groups who often have had to fight for it. An evaluation of this larger body of work would require a much different project and framing. My aim here is rather much narrower: to try to pull out the thread of the divided city imaginary's influence on this period's cultural work and to thus attempt to pose its production and structuring as a problem for thought.

57. Lins, *City*, 324.

58. Lins, *City*, 328.

59. Lins, *City*, 392.

60. Roberto Schwarz, in his early and influential review of the novel, "City of God," also seized on the tension between these aspects: "The action takes place within the closed world of the City of God, with only a few forays outside—mainly to prisons, following characters' destinies. Events are portrayed on a grand scale but the space in which they unfold is far more limited than the social premises on which they rest. . . . This limited compass functions as a strength in literary terms, dramatizing the blindness and segmentation of the social process" (107).

61. Approaching the question of transformations in the representation of nonelite urban spaces from the perspective of race and state violence necessarily must bridge several different literatures. Works that attempt to consider the relation between race, state violence and/or public security, and urban transformations are fewer in number than one might first suppose, but among these the works of Paul Amar, Jaime Amparo Alves, João Costa Vargas, Denise Ferreira da Silva, and Christen Smith stand out. The approach I have taken here—examining how the rearticulation of the favela as part of a "divided city" shores up failing forms of social synthesis and racial domination—is meant as a contribution to and extension of this growing body of literature that attempts to put critical race studies, urban studies, and histories of state violence into conversation.

62. Gilmore, *Golden Gulag*, 28.

63. For an example of the continued mobilization of divided city discourses by various governmental agencies in the recent past (and with link to finance), see Alexandre F. Mendes, "Between Shocks and Finance."

64. Hallward, *Absolutely Postcolonial*, xiv.

65. See Resende, *Contemporâneos*, and Schøllhammer, *Ficção brasileira*, as well as the work of Jaguaribe cited below, for readings of contemporary Brazilian literature and its relationship to realism.

66. Jaguaribe, "Beyond Reality," 261.

67. Schøllhammer, *Ficção brasileira*, 100–101; "Percebe-se, então, uma linguagem em texto e imagem que incorpora a crueza da realidade periférica, numa representação midiática pasteurizada que dilui qualquer problema de conteúdo e do 'como' dar visibilidade a esse tipo de questao. . . . Aqui, fica claro que já não é mais possível avaliar o engajamento ou o compromisso com a realidade pela opção temática e nem pelos conteúdos escolhidos, uma vez que a realidade marginal e periférica foi há muito incorporada pelo desejo espetacular." The interventions and debates on this point are numerous; an example that cuts quickly to the chase is the exchange between Paulo Lins and MV Bill described in Hart, *Companion*, 263.

68. For a summary of these debates, see Gugelberger, *Real Thing*.

69. For an early version of this matrix which situates its emergence from class-based Marxism, see Harding, *Whose Science?*, 175–78.

70. The domain of work related to either contemporary or historical versions of value-form theory is now very large and defies easy summary. For introductions, see Elbe, "Between Marxism," and "Communisation and Value-Form Theory." My approach here focuses on a specific variant of it, Neue Marx-Lektüre, and the work of Moishe Postone, who shares some but not all of their ideas. In Brazil some of these ideas have circulated through the work of Robert Kurz. Kurz's *O colapso da modernização* became an important and influential book, in part after being reviewed by Roberto Schwarz, and in subsequent years Kurz was well known enough to have a column that was regularly published in *Folha de São Paulo*. See Cevasco, "São Paulo Fraction"; Schwarz, "An Audacious Book"; and "Três resenhas."

71. Bonefeld, *Critical Theory*, 3–8.

72. Backhaus, "On the Dialectics of the Value-Form," 99.

73. Backhaus, "On the Dialectics of the Value-Form," 103.

74. This brief summary does not begin to do justice to Backhaus's work. For a more detailed account, see Bellofiore and Redolfi Riva, "*Neue Marx-Lektüre*."

75. This was Georg Lukács's assessment in the 1962 preface to *Theory of the Novel*: "A considerable part of the leading German intelligentsia, including Adorno, have taken up residence in the 'Grand Hotel Abyss' . . . a beautiful hotel, equipped with every comfort, on the edge of an abyss, of nothingness, of absurdity. And the daily contemplation of the abyss, between excellent meals or artistic entertainments, can only heighten the enjoyment of the subtle comforts offered" (22).

76. For one version of this argument see the introduction to Koonings and Kruijt, *Armed Actors*. More recently, there have been attempts to think democracy and proliferating violence not merely as paradoxical, but rather as co-constitutive; see for example Arias and Goldstein, *Violent Democracies*. While there have been many useful attempts to break with the Weberian paradigm, such as Comaroff and Comaroff's influential *Law and Disorder*, it continues to reappear in academic circles and to dominate journalistic accounts.

77. Fausto and Fausto, *Concise History*, 285.

Chapter 3: Anti-Subjects of Credit

Epigraph: Interview conducted in 1979, republished in Gaspari, Hollanda, and Ventura, *70/80 cultura em trânsito*, 182.

> E: And to conclude, what do you think about the possibility of socialism today in Brazil?
>
> F.G.: Very distant. . . . Very distant . . .
>
> E: And with interest! [A play on words: *prazo* means a period of time, but also the period of a loan.]
>
> F.G.: And with interest!

1. For an early account of the emergence of this matrix see Morais and Saad-Filho, "Lula," 20–22. While Svampa and Viale in *Maldesarrollo* argue, primarily in the context of Argentina, for a complicated transition between a period of financial valorization (the Washington Consensus) to one of resource extraction (the Commodity Consensus), in Brazil many authors see financial valorization persisting as an important social dynamic throughout this period (see Paulani, "A experiência brasileira" for example).

2. Filgueiras and Gonçalves, *A economia política*, 61–64; Paulani, *Brasil Delivery*, 46–49; Anderson, "Lula's Brazil." Some authors, including José Gabriel Palma (see "How the Full Opening," 5), have argued that much of this period's commodity boom was driven in fact by financialized speculation.

3. Paulani, "A inserção," 93–98; Morais and Saad-Filho, "Neo-developmentalism," 792–94; and Gonçalves, "Novo desenvolvimentismo," 16–19.

4. Kaltenbrunner and Painceira, "Subordinated Financial Integration," 7–8.

5. On the role of the state in Brazil, see Paulani, "A inserção," and Lavinas, *Takeover*; on the state in credit provision more generally, see Soederberg, *Debtfare States*. See as well Müller, "Negotiating Debts."

6. Lavinas, *Takeover*, 35.

7. See Lavinas, *Takeover*, chapter 3, and Soederberg, *Debtfare States*, 161–91, for critiques of financial inclusion discourses.

8. Paulani, "A inserção da economia," 100, and Paulani, "A hegemonia neoliberal," 41.

9. The legal framework for payroll lending had existed since the 1930s, and

BMG had been making consignado loans to governmental employees since the late 1990s; see Ferreira, "Crédito consignado," 8.

10. Moreira, "BMG é o pioneiro," A4.

11. Salomon, "Procuradoria"; Gigliucci, *Crédito consignado*; Rodrigues, "Bancos devem."

12. Anderson, "Lula's Brazil," and Watts, "Brazil's *Bolsa Familia.*" As Anderson notes, "Social transfers have doubled since the 1980s, but payments on the public debt trebled. Outlays on the Bolsa Família totaled a mere 0.5 per cent of GDP. Rentier incomes from the public debt took a massive 6–7 per cent."

13. Banco Central do Brasil, "Séries Temporais: 20624."

14. See Bensusán and von Bülow, "La reforma institucional"; Boito, *Política neoliberal*; and Oliveira, "Lula."

15. I am bracketing here a larger debate about the definition of class in these works on the nova classe média, in particular the Bourdieusian and Marxist critiques they have received. For example, Brazilian sociologist Jessé Souza in *Os Batalhadores* argues, from a position informed by Bourdieu, that definitions of the nova classe média that focus on the power of consumption are economistic and as such miss the crucial spectrum of symbolic and cultural capital. Philosopher Marilena Chauí, "10 anos de governos," has argued in a series of talks that circulated widely in the Brazilian blogosphere for a more traditionally Marxist definition of the middle class as defined by a position in the relations of production. My argument with the Bourdieusian and classical Marxist positions is that they also push into the background the credit expansion. (See Pochmann's *O mito*, however, for some discussion of credit expansion.) The Brazilian works cited in this chapter were produced in the midst of a set of global and regional debates about the potential existence (and possible meaning) of "new middle classes." A good starting point for these global and regional discussions is Ricardo López and Weinstein, *Making of the Middle Class*. Region-specific approaches can be found in Melber, *Rise of Africa's Middle Class*; Pellegrini Calderón, *Beyond Indigeneity*; and Tsang, *New Middle Class in China*. The most uncritical versions of these new middle-class discourses intersected with, and in some cases built upon, a body of work which positioned the poor as a new source of capitalist profits and corporations as a mechanism for poverty alleviation: see Prahalad, *Fortune at the Bottom*.

16. Associação Brasileira de Empresas de Pesquisa, personal communication.

17. Associação Brasileira de Empresas de Pesquisa, "Critério." The original reads: "a pretensão de classificar a população em termos de 'classes sociais.'"

18. Associação Brasileira de Empresas de Pesquisa, personal communication.

19. Neri, *A nova classe*, 12–13, 7, 24–25.

20. See the excellent discussion of the reception of Neri in Yaccoub, "A chamada."

21. Neri, *A nova classe*, 29; "é a imagem mais próxima da sociedade brasileira."

22. Alberto, *Terms of Inclusion*, 10–12; Heise, *Remaking Brazil*, 35–37.

23. Alberto, *Terms of Inclusion*, 17.

24. This is part of a larger recalibration of the state's approach to race in this period; see Reiter and Mitchell, *Brazil's New Racial*, for a window into this new environment, which is shaped by new forms of black and nonwhite political organizing; and Joseph, "How Does Racial Democracy," for a summary of the different positions in current debates on racial democracy.

25. Gomes de Moura, "De empregada"; Grijó, "De voyeur," 193; and Mauro and Trindade, "Telenovela e discurso," 171–72.

26. In one episode (no. 79) Penha buys a new car (a Volkswagen) and cooks dinner using her new kitchen while Cida dines in the same restaurant as her former employers, much to their disgust.

27. Interested readers can see the song and video at: https://globoplay.globo.com/v/1953958/.

28. Suspicion is an affective category that seems to accompany finance: this was the case with the introduction of paper money in Great Britain in the seventeenth and eighteenth centuries (Poovey, *Genres of the Credit Economy*, 6) and with early forms of credit instruments (Wennerlind, *Casualties of Credit*, 242–43).

29. This is not to ignore the real gains in this period made by domestic workers in securing additional formal legal protections; see Costa, Hollanda Barbosa, and Hirata, "Efeitos da ampliação."

30. In this piece, Oliveira uses the metaphor of a duckbilled platypus (that is, of a creature who appears to blend elements which should not or traditionally do not belong together, i.e., the fur of a mammal with the bill of a duck) as an ironic description of contemporary Brazil which, he argues, has joined classic forms of dependency with the most contemporary forms of "casualized" labor.

31. Oliveira, "Duckbilled Platypus," 54–55.

32. Oliveira, "Duckbilled Platypus," 55–56.

33. Affect, feeling, and emotion emerged as important topics of critical discussion in the early to mid-1990s, and since then there has been a sustained debate over the question whether current forms of "affect theory" make too deep a scission between preconscious forms of "affect" and conscious processes of cognition and judgment (see Leys, "Turn to Affect," and Zerilli, "Turn to Affect"). My approach to emotion or feeling draws primarily on Williams's structure of feeling because it allows me to avoid the noncognitivist implications of some affect theory. This is important because the structure of financial "projection" combines feeling and mental habit in unique ways and thus is neither wholly

preconscious nor entirely a rational cognitive act. A key part of this structure is that it moves loosely around and through all these distinctions, manifesting on both sides of this heuristically drawn line.

34. Flatley, *Affective Mapping*, 25.

35. Love, *Feeling Backward*, 12.

36. Williams, *Marxism and Literature*, 133.

37. Williams, *Marxism and Literature*, 129.

38. McClanahan, *Dead Pledges*, 13; McClanahan, "Investing in the Future," 90; and Clover, "*Value* | *Theory* | Crisis," 110.

39. The literature is rich with ethnographic accounts of travesti life and more recently accounts of political discussions and conflicts between travestis and transgender individuals; see Kulíck, *Travesti*; Pelúcio, *Abjeção e desejo*; and Silva, *Travesti*. For political debates, see Silva and Ornat, "Transfeminism."

40. Pelúcio, "Sexualidade."

41. Pelúcio, "Sexualidade"; "Beijos e clima de namoro não são incomuns nos encontros, mas segundo o código de conduta implícito do encontro de t-lovers paulistas, não se pode fazer sexo, nem causar constrangimentos às travestis com assédios insistentes ou atitudes invasivas como passar as mãos no corpo delas. Atitudes desse tipo já geraram expulsão de alguns membros."

42. An "initial public offering" refers to the first time a company sells shares in itself on a stock exchange. This process is also known as "going public" or opening a company to outside investors. See Spinetto and Levin, "Brazil Fire Sale."

43. "Brazilian Equity Market."

44. It is common in the Brazilian press to refer to Batista by his first name and this naming convention is followed here.

45. Batista, *O X da questão*, 121–22.

46. Batista, *O X da questão*, 121.

47. Gaspar, *Tudo ou nada*, 255.

48. Leitão, "A questão do X."

49. Batista, *O X da questão*, 121; "A constatação de que a atividade de exploração e produção no Brasil ostenta taxa de êxito de 50%, enquanto a média mundial não ultrapasa 18%, me chamou atenção para as possibilidades de empreender em território nacional. Ou seja, eu teria três vezes mais chances de encontrar petróleo por aqui do que teve meu colega americano um século atrás. Se o negócio já era fantástico com apenas 18% de possibilidade, ele certamente seria espetacular com 50%."

50. It was in June 2012 that OGX released their first statement lowering the projected production at their highly valued Tubarão Azul (Waimea) site, from twenty thousand to five thousand barrels per day. When this was announced on June 26, OGX's stock price fell 25.32 percent ("Antes presença").

51. Jardim, "A construção," 172.

52. Jardim, "A construção," 174.

53. Cavalcanti, "Waiting in the Ruins," 110.

54. Monteagudo, "Sete anos," and P. Oliveira, "Dilma é."

55. In June and October 2013 millions of Brazilians took to the streets in hundreds of cities across Brazil. The demonstrations were sparked by a series of protests in São Paulo against the hiking of the transit fare, protests which had been brutally and very visibly repressed by security forces. The nationwide marches that built from the São Paulo transit fare movement quickly articulated a much wider range of concerns.

56. For a version of the second position, see Chauí, "O inferno." For the first, André Singer argues for reading the sequence as composed of two main actors, a traditional middle class and then a "new proletariat." His reading charts the tension between them but also how a center position came to dominate, one which he calls "post-materialist": "in the sense used by Ronald Inglehart: as societies gradually resolve their material problems, values change, shifting from an emphasis on 'economic and physical security' to one on 'self-expression and quality of life.' This is a trans-generational process that takes place as those already socialized in a middle-class milieu, free from the material burdens of previous generations, become the majority, producing a sea-change in their manner of political engagement" ("Rebellion," 34). Other important interventions can be found in Cava and Cocco, *Amanhã vai ser maior*; Cava, *A multidão foi ao deserto*; and Arantes, *O novo tempo do mundo.*

57. In his article on the 2013 movements, Singer lists the following: "Copa do Mundo eu abro mão, quero dinheiro pra saúde e educação," "Queremos hospitais padrão Fifa," "O gigante acordou," "Ia ixcrever augu legal, maix fautô edukssão," "Não é mole, não. Tem dinheiro pra estádio e cadê a educação," "Era um país muito engraçado, não tinha escola, só tinha estádio," "Todos contra a corrupção," "Fora Dilma! Fora Cabral! PT = Pilantragem e traição," "Fora Alckmin," "Zé Dirceu, pode esperar, tua hora vai chegar" ("Brasil," 25).

58. Oliveira, "Lula in the Labyrinth," 5.

59. Oliveira, "Lula in the Labyrinth," 10.

60. Foucault, *Discipline and Punish*, 23.

61. In this chapter and in Chapter 4 where I discuss it again, my understanding of the subject will be drawn from the work of Foucault. As Robert Strozier notes, in Foucault "the subject produced is a subject of knowledge: self-inquiry and confession in the modern era always led to knowledge, both in the local, individualizing form and larger institutional forms" (151). In his later work, such as *History of Sexuality*, vol. 1, Foucault tracks how the Christian device of confession is secularized by the modern state and human sciences to produce a modern subject open to regulation by the state and these sciences. This under-

standing of the subject is present throughout much of Foucault's work, and for Foucault this soul or "interiority" is both "real" and ideological. As he writes in *Discipline and Punish*:

> It would be wrong to say that the soul is an illusion, or an ideological effect. On the contrary, it exists, it has a reality, it is produced permanently around, on, within the body by the functioning of a power that is exercised on those punished—and, in a more general way, on those one supervises, trains and corrects. . . . This is the historical reality of this soul, which, unlike the soul represented by Christian theology, is not born in sin and subject to punishment, but is born rather out of methods of punishment, supervision and constraint. (29)

I deploy this understanding of the subject as a produced interiority here in order to highlight how this technique of control begins to fade with the expansion of credit in Brazil. What I am particularly interested in is how states in moments of finance and circulation appear less interested in tracking, policing, regulating, and cataloging the interior states of their "subjects." I will use, here and again in Chapter 4, the phrase "hollows out" to refer to the de-emphasizing of secularized confessional modes of control in the financialized present.

62. Foucault, "The Subject," 781.

63. Lazzarato, *Making*, 33.

64. Lazzarato, *Making*, 30–31, 77–79. Another important approach has been through Deleuze's concept of the "dividual" (briefly elaborated in his "Postscript on the Societies of Control")—see, in addition to Lazzarato, Appadurai, *Banking on Words*. While certainly finance, algorithmic, and other security processes have broken down the modern concept of the individual, I am most interested not in the "dividual" level per se but rather in what happens to and with the interiority of the subject. My aim here is not to argue that the entirety of the disciplinary formation identified by Foucault has been overthrown by this one instance, nor that there is only one or even a dominant subject "position" in a given historical moment; rather I see "hollowing out" as a crack within the disciplinary structure, one perhaps which could be mapped in a future moment alongside other ongoing transformations of disciplinary institutions.

65. Costa and De Mello, "Judicial Risk," 2.

66. Ferreira, "Crédito consignado," 13. See also Assunção, Benmelech, and Silva, "Repossession"; De Mello and Garcia, "Bye, Bye Financial Repression"; and Araujo, Ferreira, and Funchal, "Brazilian Bankruptcy."

67. Assunção, Benmelech, and Silva, "Repossession," 1–2.

68. For a brief recounting of some of the history behind the ISA essay, see Etienne Balibar's foreword to *On the Reproduction of Capitalism*.

69. While it is true that part of Foucault's aim was to move beyond the violence/ideology distinction so prevalent in Marxist thought, I would hold

both that his work evidences an attentiveness to forms of physical violence and that the present demands more expansive means for accounting for state violence and its effects on the subject.

70. It is important to note that as of 2017 Brazil did not have a system of what are called "positive bureaus" or credit reporting agencies that track individuals' credit history. Only in 2016 did the government lift the prohibition on collecting sustained credit information on individuals without their prior consent. Brazil does have what are known as "negative lists" or lists of *nomes sujos* that record people currently in default, but names are removed from those lists after the debt is paid or a certain period has expired. See Parra-Bernal, "Brazil Partially."

71. In a section in *Crowds and Power* entitled "Inflation and the Crowd," Canetti describes the relationship between individuals and an inflationary financial crisis: "An inflation can be called a witches' sabbath of devaluation where men and the units of their money have the strangest effects on each other. The one stands for the other, men feeling themselves as 'bad' as their money; and this becomes worse and worse. Together they are all at its mercy and all feel equally worthless" (186). A credit crisis featuring seizure of assets and income has a different effect upon the subject: the subject is now without a face and becomes blank. Not the internal masculine pathos of "devaluation" but a cipher, a Sphinx, an unreadable mask.

72. On transformations in militarized public security see also Amar, *Security Archipelago.*

73. Serasa, "Mapa."

74. "Há espaço"; "48% disseram ter usado o cartão de crédito emprestado de parentes ou amigos." Instituto GEOC, "41,16% dos brasileiros."

75. Serasa, "Inadimplência atinge 60 milhões." A common way in Brazil of discussing income is to break earners into categories based upon multiples of the minimum wage. Thus it is a common shorthand to discuss individuals who earn up to two times the minimum wage, between one and two, and under one. Also it should be noted that in these numbers utility bills are counted as an "account."

Chapter 4: Voided Collectivities

1. Moreno-Brid and Ros, *Development*, 186–87, and Cypher and Delgado Wise, *Mexico's Economic Dilemma*, 80.

2. Dussel Peters, *Polarizing Mexico*, 55–56; Moreno-Brid and Ros, *Development*, 158, 187–90; and Banco de Mexico, "Cuenta corriente."

3. Dussel Peters, *Polarizing Mexico*, 98–99; Cypher and Delgado Wise, *Mexico's Economic Dilemma*, 99–100; and Moreno-Brid and Ros, *Development*, 189–90. A perennial issue of the Mexican economy in the export-oriented era, in particular after the 1994 crash and throughout the late 1990s, has been how

to balance the current account and how to cheaply acquire foreign, namely U.S., currency.

4. Consejo Nacional de Inclusión Financiera, "Política nacional," 8, 12. This is something that Peña Nieto's 2014 financial reform law attempted to change. After 2008, and in particular after 2015, there has been an important expansion of consumer credit, but I do not deal with this most recent period in this chapter.

5. Banco de México, "Deuda neta." The unfolding debt problems in states like Puebla, Tabasco, Michoacán, and others is another marker of this process. See Centro de Estudios Espinosa Yglesias, "Deuda estatal."

6. Dussel Peters, *Polarizing Mexico*, 110.

7. Marx, *Capital*, vol. 1, 247.

8. In reading the contemporary period through the production-circulation distinction, I am drawing on a great deal of prior work. One way finance has been thought is through the category of circulation; see Christopher Arthur and Geert Reuten's edited *The Circulation of Capital* and David Harvey's earlier *Limits to Capital.* Joshua Clover's "The Time of Crisis" represents a sophisticated use of circulation to link globalization and financialization into a common framework; his more recent *Riot. Strike. Riot* also makes a circulation argument. LiPuma and Lee's *Financial Derivatives* also used circulation to discuss contemporary finance, although in a different way than pursued here. In literary and cultural studies circulation has been discussed as a critical concept but never quite taken as central to cultural life. See, for example, Gagnier's "Global Circulation" and Whitfield's *Cuban Currency*, both of which employ a notion of circulation.

9. The size of the drug trade is notoriously difficult to estimate: figures of US$30–35 billion for the cocaine market are common, with perhaps US$5–6 billion of that staying or returning to Mexico. Remittances from workers are now the single largest source of foreign exchange, totaling US$24.8 billion in 2015, and in the first quarter 2016 they doubled the long-standing number-one source, crude oil exports (see Estevez, "Remittances Supersede Oil"). Concerning immigration, the PEW Research Center reports: "In 1970, fewer than 1 million Mexican immigrants lived in the U.S. By 2000, that number had grown to 9.8 million, and by 2007 it reached a peak of 12.5 million" ("Demographic Portrait"). Since the 2007–2008 crisis, the total number of undocumented Mexican and Central American immigrants has held steady; at some moments for Mexico the overall figure has been negative.

10. INEGI, "Encuesta Nacional." It is important to note that informality is unevenly distributed across the national space. For example, using 2000 numbers, Oaxaca had the highest percentage of economically active residents in the informal economy at 76.73 percent, with Chiapas at 69.23 percent, Guerrero at 69.49 percent, and Michoacán at 69.67 percent (Flores Curiel and Valero Gil,

"Tamaño"). Throughout this chapter I will use the term "unfree" labor to refer to forms of labor that fall to some extent outside classical forms of state mediation of the capital-labor relationship. Of course, no labor is "free." My use of "unfree" is only an attempt to mark a slow historical turn from one labor regime to another, in which certain contemporary forms of labor in Mexico are marked by new, more intensive forms of exploitation, self-exploitation, danger, and death.

11. Paley, *Drug War Capitalism*, 87 (citing a RAND Corporation report).

12. Moloeznik and Suárez de Garay, "El proceso," 123.

13. Sabet, *Police Reform*, 16.

14. Molloy, "Colombia."

15. As Foucault writes in "The Subject and Power," 782: "But I'd like to underline the fact that the state's power (and that's one of the reasons for its strength) is both an individualizing and a totalizing form of power. Never, I think, in the history of human societies . . . has there been such a tricky combination in the same political structures of individualization techniques and of totalization procedures." These weak collectivities have always carried with them the possibility for their politicization. Thus the large corporativist unions were exposed to (and had to be protected from) a far-left radicalization (think of the Revueltas-Lombardo antagonism in Mexico, for example), and in most revolutionary theory of the twentieth century developing a split within (or politicizing the collectivity of) the army was seen as a key to seizing state power. A number of recent works have pursued readings of Marx and Foucault: Bidet, *Foucault with Marx*; Chitty, "Reassessing Foucault" and "Towards a Socialist Art"; and Laval, Paltrinieri and Taylan, *Marx et Foucault*.

16. The "drug war" is a generally unhelpful term, particularly in Mexico, as it evokes the idea of two clearly defined sides, both represented by a state or with a desire for state power (see Paley, *Drug War Capitalism*, 29–30, and Boullosa and Wallace, *Narco History*, 179; as well Zavala's excellent *Los cárteles* which appeared as this book was going to press). The best work on what I call here "drug logistics," from Luis Astorga to Dawn Paley, has demonstrated that narratives of the state being "corrupted" by traffickers are misleading at best—rather the state itself has produced, in large part, the space, figures, and means for drug logistics since the 1970s. Thus, the term "drug war" is inherently misleading. However, I continue to use it here as a shorthand for a historical period in Mexico, since moving to a different formulation would likely unnecessarily confuse many readers.

17. There are, of course, any number of cultural works which continue to repeat the classical dictums of the collectivizing structure of labor. One example is the 2013 film *Nosotros los nobles* (the title being a play on the classic Golden Age film *Nosotros los pobres*) in which a group of ultra-wealthy *niños bien* are forced into employment by their father after he lies to them that they are bankrupt.

18. These figures are difficult to estimate. The 2008 UN *World Drug Report* noted that in 2006, 705 tons of cocaine had been seized worldwide (8). Some estimate that world production (of cut, not pure cocaine) is perhaps double that figure.

19. Gootenberg, "Cocaine," 171–74. Occasionally one will see a citation that since 2007 marijuana has overtaken cocaine as the largest contributor to drug profits. See Kilmer, "Debunking," for a discussion of these numbers, and Hope, "*Plus Ça Change*" for a thorough summary of the most recent debates.

20. Wainwright, *Narconomics*, 16–17, makes a similar point toward a slightly different end.

21. Bernes, "Logistics."

22. Keefe, "Cocaine Incorporated." Part of what has happened in the last few years is the fragmentation of larger groups, which has meant some have lost access to the cocaine supply and have turned to kidnapping, extortion, etc. for income.

23. Dawn Paley notes that the lion's share of the profits stay in the United States: "According to a 2010 report by the UN Office on Drugs and Crime, 85 percent of gross proceeds in the $35 billion cocaine market stayed in the United States. Of that amount, 15 percent went to US wholesalers and mid-level dealers, and 70 percent went to street-level dealers who sold to US consumers. Compare this to the $4.6 billion (13 percent) that stayed with traffickers moving the product between the Andean region and the US, or with the mere 1 percent that stayed with Andean producers" (*Drug War Capitalism*, 88). Nonetheless the relative supremacy of logistics versus cocaine production profits is significant.

24. Astorga, *Seguridad*, 33–34, indicates that the imbrication between state-linked groups and drug logistics groups has a long history.

25. By making El Sargento and El Sardo the only visibly indigenous figures in the film, what perhaps was intended as a critique of the military secures the ground of that critique only by associating indigeneity with the capacity for unchecked cruelty—a racializing trope with a long history in Mexico and elsewhere.

26. Dolores Dorantes, blog, September 2012, http://doloresdorantes.blogspot.com/2012/09/.

27. Lomnitz, *Death*, 27.

28. Lomnitz, *Death*, 445–46.

29. One of the exemplary figures in the use of the skull as critique was the artist with whom I began this book, Naranjo.

30. Dorantes, *Querida fábrica*, 12–13.

31. Dorantes, *Querida fábrica*, 12–13.

32. Dorantes, *Querida fábrica*, 12–13.

33. La Berge, "Rules of Abstraction," 98–99.

34. McClanahan, "Investing in the Future," 89–90.

35. Lomnitz, *Death*, 25.

36. Carroll, "*Muerte sin fin*," 115.

37. Mendoza Hernández, "Financiarización," 173, 178.

38. Lapavitsas, *Profiting*, 224.

39. For more on these changes generally, see Lapavitsas, *Profiting*. In Mexico, see Soto Esquivel, *Especulación*.

40. This is the notational amount, meaning the face value of all transactions. Since the majority of derivatives come into and pass out of being without being acted upon, the actual amount of money changing hands is much less. See Bank for International Settlements, "OTC."

41. The historical origin point of modern-day derivatives is the commodity futures contract, which is an agreement to buy or sell a certain quantity of a certain commodity at a fixed price at a future date. A helpful introduction to derivatives is Chisholm, *Derivatives Demystified*. There is in the critical literature an ongoing debate between Bryan and Rafferty on derivatives as money, *Capitalism with Derivatives*, and Norfield, "Derivatives." Bryan and Rafferty respond to Norfield's critique in "Why We Need."

42. Another popular derivative, particularly with Mexican corporations, is an interest rate swap. In an interest rate swap, two parties agree to exchange interest payments on an underlying notional amount. A hypothetical transaction would be set up like this: party A agrees to pay a fixed interest rate, say 7.5 percent, and party B agrees to pay a floating interest rate, based on LIBOR or some other market rate plus some amount of basis points, at given intervals on an underlying amount.

In theory, one use of interest rate swaps are as a hedge (that is, as protection) for corporations who have exposure to interest rate fluctuations. For example, let's say party A is Cemex and they have exposure to a change in U.S. interest rates. Cemex thinks that interest rates in the United States are going to rise over the course of the next year. Cemex might engage in an interest rate swap where they agree to pay out a fixed rate (7.5%) while receiving a floating rate (which, if Cemex is right and interest rates do rise in the United States, would mean they would receive a payment higher than 7.5%). In a perfect theoretical world Cemex would engage in this swap with a counterparty that has the exact opposite form of risk (in this hypothetical case, an exposure to interest rates going down). In this perfect world both parties would offset their risk or exposure to interest rate fluctuations by, in a sense, exchanging them, via an interest rate swap.

This is a world of perfect equilibrium that exists only in economics textbooks. The reality of interest rate swaps (and other derivatives) is that their actual and speculative purposes cannot be untangled, and for two reasons. First, banks are the derivatives market makers—meaning that it is rare for two counterparties to directly swap offsetting risks. What is much more common is that corporations engage in a swap directly with a bank as the counterparty. Second, this means that each side is not necessarily offsetting their risk but (potentially) betting against the other. In our above example party A is betting interest rates will go up (meaning that the payment they receive from B will be greater than 7.5%), while party B is betting interest rates will go down (meaning the payment they receive from A will be greater than the floating rate they are paying out).

43. The difference here from Jameson's notion of "second order abstraction" is that the reading of the derivative that I am advancing is predicated on its *tie* to the underlying element. The specificity of the derivative is that it produces a middle zone, a blurred zone of new relations between the material and immaterial, between the underlying and its possible futures. Jameson's notion of "second order" is predicated on the cutting of all ties, on the becoming "abstract" of the concrete. Riffing on Arrighi in "Culture and Finance Capital," Jameson writes: "Capital itself becomes free-floating. It separates from the concrete context of its productive geography. Money becomes in a second sense and to a second degree abstract (it always was abstract in the first and basic sense), as though somehow in the national moment money still had a content. It was cotton money, or wheat money, textile money, railroad money, and the like. Now, like the butterfly stirring within the chrysalis, it separates itself from that concrete breeding ground and prepares to take flight" (251). See also Shonkwiler, *Financial Imaginary*, who argues that "finance must be understood as a process of abstractifiation and concretization" (xxiii).

44. Dorantes, *Querida fábrica*, 50.

45. Franco, "Journey," 442, 444. See also Gareth Williams's discussion of *Páramo* and Jean Franco in *Mexican Exception.*

46. Lomnitz, *Death*, 491.

47. Dorantes, *Querida fábrica*, 20.

48. Lomnitz, *Death*, 447.

49. Dorantes, *Querida fábrica*, 20.

50. Dorantes, *Querida fábrica*, 22;

51. This is in contrast with some work emerging from the social sciences which has focused on the construction of transnational linkages (mediated by the state, Church, or hometown associations). See for example, Iskander, *Creative State*; Lattanzi Shutika, *Beyond the Borderlands*; and Fitzgerald, *Nation of Emigrants.*

52. This is not to say that individual migrants have ceased to have feelings and emotions or significant interior lives; rather I am referring only to how cultural works dramatize and figure these subjects in a representational universe.

53. Foucault, "Subject and Power," 783.

54. See for instance David Fitzgerald, "Inside the Sending State" and "The

Church's Eye on Its Flock" in *Nation of Emigrants.* The U.S. government is investing in tracking programs and technology in Mexico as well, but at the time of writing the scope and outcomes are not yet clear.

55. Foucault, *Discipline and Punish*, 59–62, 83–84.

56. Foucault also notes how later political projects—after the emergence of disciplinary formations—aimed at the reestablishment of these popular illegalities: "The lessons of *La Phalange* were not quite wasted. They found an echo when, in the second half of the nineteenth century, taking the penal apparatus as their point of attack, the anarchists posed the political problem of delinquency; when they thought to recognize in it the most militant rejection of the law; when they tried not so much to heroize the revolt of the delinquents as to disentangle delinquency from the bourgeois legality and illegality that had colonized it; when they wished to re-establish or constitute the political unity of popular illegalities" (*Discipline and Punish*, 292).

57. See Angela Mitropoulos's work on the contract in *Contract and Contagion.*

58. The exportation and cultivation of counterinsurgency and low-intensity combat (LIC) practices by the United States in the region produced two important changes in the forms of state and military violence. First, LIC shifted the role of states from actors (in war and in state terrorism) to being creators of the possibility for violence. States' roles shifted from planning and carrying out attacks on enemies (external or internal) to a productive relationship to the conditions that would allow decentralized groups, either linked directly or not to the state, to carry out attacks (Molloy, *Rolling Back*, 15). Violence became increasingly "authorless," and as it became more difficult to connect to a specific actor or group, it became more terrifying; it seemed like none of the prior rules governing warfare applied. The second major change effected by LIC is tied to notions of trauma and terror, as the point of violence ceased being merely the defeat of an enemy. Rather, violence became aimed at social destabilization, at terrifying a populace into submission, and especially as it was applied in Central America, LIC unleashed new, more catastrophic forms of social war. LIC or counterinsurgency practices were spread deeply in the military structures and governmental thinking of Latin American countries through the training of military, police, and paramilitary personnel for U.S. containment strategies. It is important to note that state violence as a tool for disciplining populations has a long history in Latin America, predating LIC, but the current ubiquity of weaponized terror and its normalization is influenced by these counterinsurgency practices. See also Astorga, *Seguridad*, who tracks in various moments the bridging of counterinsurgency and "war on drugs" discourses by U.S. and Mexican politicians; and Dawn Paley, "Guerra en México," who develops an idea of "contrainsurgencia ampliada."

59. For important and detailed discussions of the debates around theories of autonomy and communal governance, see Díaz-Polanco "Siete mitos sobre autonomía" and *La rebelión zapatista*; Maldonado Alvarado, *Autonomía y comunalidad india*; Rendón Monzón, *La comunalidad.* More recently, see Gutiérrez Aguilar, *Horizonte comunitario-popular.*

60. del Valle, "Mexico's Re-colonization."

61. The localized expressions of the state's production and cultivation of these commodity flows and violent practices of enforcement are incredibly complicated and dependent on a host of precise geographical and contextual factors. It is beyond the scope of this current chapter to deal with these histories, their specificities, and their awful contemporary consequences in the detail that they deserve and require—so I will remain instead at this level of generality.

62. On Cherán see the work of Orlando Aragón Andrade, "El derecho en insurrección" and "La construcción."

63. The first usage of the term in cultural writing about Mexico that I have been able to find is in a 2004 Medina essay "SEMEFO: The Morgue." Other important usages include: Marta Lamas "Necropolítica y rehabilitación"; Diego Osorno, *La guerra de los Zetas*; and Sayak Valencia, *Capitalismo gore.* The term has also been adopted into various forms of journalistic or commentary writing, as a quick internet search will demonstrate. See as well an essential piece from Melissa Wright, "Necropolitics."

64. Foucault, *History of Sexuality*, 138.

65. Mbembe, "Necropolitics," 34.

66. Mbembe, "Necropolitics," 12, 14.

67. Mbembe, "Necropolitics," 33.

68. Mbembe, "Necropolitics," 34.

69. Mbembe, *Critique*, 179.

Coda

1. "Grupo Elektra"; Rodríguez Nieto, "Pensiones."

2. IMF, *Global Financial Stability Report*, 21. See also the excellent article by Palma, "How the Full Opening."

3. This is an overly simplified account of what is a very contested, and long-debated, set of relationships and theoretical positions. My aim here is not to give a detailed account of how this process may or may not have played out in a given national space or historical sequence; rather I want only to reverse-engineer an explanation or provide a narrative for readers as to how surplus capital and surplus population could possibly emerge in the same moment.

4. I am far from the first person to center this distinction as critical to the present. See Clover, *Riot. Strike. Riot*, and "Misery and Debt."

BIBLIOGRAPHY

"A Marca do Horror." *Veja*, Jan. 7, 1981, 17–22.

Acosta Córdova, Carlos. "La transformación de Zedillo." *Proceso*, Feb. 1, 1995, 6–10.

Adamson, Morgan. "The End of the Gold Standard: Finance, Crisis, and the Cinema of the New Left, 1967–1974." PhD diss., University of Minneapolis, 2012.

Alazraki, Gary. *Nosotros los nobles*. 2013. Mexico: Umbrella Entertainment, 2013. DVD.

Alberto, Paulina. *Terms of Inclusion: Black Intellectuals in Twentieth-Century Brazil*. Raleigh: University of North Carolina Press, 2011.

Allaz, Tomás Gerardo. "Salinas: El caos," *Proceso*, Nov. 20, 1994, 50.

Allen, Alice. "Shifting Perspectives on Marginal Bodies and Spaces: Relationality, Power, and Social Difference in the Documentary Films Babilônia 2000 and Estamira." *Bulletin of Latin American Research* 32, no. 1 (2013): 78–93.

Alonso, Carlos J. "The Novel without Literature." *Novel. A Forum on Fiction* 44, no. 1 (2011): 3–5.

Althusser, Louis. "Ideology and Ideological State Apparatuses (Notes towards an Investigation)." In *Lenin and Philosophy and Other Essays*. Translated by Ben Brewster. New York: Monthly Review Press, 1971.

Althusser, Louis. *On the Reproduction of Capitalism: Ideology and Ideological State Apparatuses*. Translated by G. M. Goshgarian. London: Verso, 2014.

Álvarez, Alejandro, and Gabriel Mendoza. "México 1988: Un capitalismo depredador en crisis." *Cuadernos Políticos* 53 (Jan.–Apr. 1988): 34–46.

Amado, Mauro. "As Fiscais do Sarney: A participação do Movimento das Donas de Casa e Consumidores de Minas Gerais no Plano Cruzado entre 1986 a 1987." PhD diss., Pontifícia Universidade Católica de Minas Gerais, Instituto de Ciências Humanas, 2012.

Amar, Paul. *The Security Archipelago: Human-Security States, Sexuality, Politics, and the End of Neoliberalism.* Durham, NC: Duke University Press, 2013.

Amparo Alves, Jaime. *The Anti-Black City: Police Terror and Black Urban Life in Brazil.* Minneapolis: University of Minnesota Press, 2018.

Anderson, Perry. "Lula's Brazil." *London Review of Books* 13 (Mar. 2011). https://www.lrb.co.uk/v33/n07/perry-anderson/lulas-brazil.

"Antes presença frequente em Brasília, Eike é decepção agora." *O Globo*, Oct. 31, 2013. http://oglobo.globo.com/economia/antes-presenca-frequente-em-brasilia-eike-decepcao-agora-10611345.

Antunes, Ricardo. "A trajetória (e a tragédia) do PT." *Folha de S.Paulo*, Apr. 11, 2004. http://www1.folha.uol.com.br/fsp/opiniao/fz1104200409.htm.

Appadurai, Arjun. *Banking on Words: The Failure of Language in the Age of Derivative Finance.* Chicago: University of Chicago Press, 2015.

Aradau, Claudia, and Rens van Munster. *Politics of Catastrophe: Genealogies of the Unknown.* Oxford: Routledge, 2011.

Aragón Andrade, Orlando. "La construcción de la diversidad jurídica desde el Estado: El proceso de oficialización de las justicias indígenas en Michoacán." *Relaciones: Estudios de historia y sociedad* 35, no. 137 (2014): 115–47.

Aragón Andrade, Orlando. "El derecho en insurrección: El uso contra-hegemónico del derecho en el movimiento purépecha de Cherán." *Revista de Estudos e Pesquisas sobre as Americas* 7, no. 2 (2013): 37–69.

Arantes, Paulo. *O novo tempo do mundo: E outros estudos sobre a era da emergência.* São Paulo: Boitempo, 2014.

Araujo, Aloisio P., Rafael V. X. Ferreira, and Bruno Funchal. "The Brazilian Bankruptcy Law Experience." *Journal of Corporate Finance* 18, no. 4 (2012): 994–1004.

Arias, Enrique Desmond. *Drugs and Democracy in Rio de Janeiro: Trafficking, Social Networks, and Public Security.* Chapel Hill: University of North Carolina Press, 2009.

Arias, Enrique Desmond, and Daniel M. Goldstein, eds. *Violent Democracies in Latin America.* Durham, NC: Duke University Press, 2010.

Aricó, José. *La cola del diablo: Itinerario de Gramsci en América Latina.* Buenos Aires: Puntosur, 1988.

Arrighi, Giovanni. *The Long Twentieth Century: Money, Power and the Origins of Our Times.* New York: Verso, 1994.

Arthur, Christopher, and Geert Reuten, eds. *The Circulation of Capital: Essays on Volume Two of Marx's Capital.* New York: St. Martin's Press, 1998.

Associação Brasileira de Empresas de Pesquisa. "Critério de Classificação Econômica Brasil (2003)." Accessed July 23, 2015. http://www.abep.org/criterio-brasil.

Assunção, Juliano, Efraim Benmelech, and Fernando S. S. Silva. "Repossession and the Democratization of Credit." *Review of Financial Studies* 27, no. 9 (Sept. 2014): 2661–89.

Astorga, Luis. *Seguridad, traficantes, y militares: El poder y la sombra.* Mexico City: Tusquets Editores, 2007.

"Até quarenta dias." *Veja,* Aug. 31, 1988, 88–89.

Aviña, Alexander. *Specters of Revolution: Peasant Guerrillas in the Cold War Mexican Countryside.* Oxford: Oxford University Press, 2014.

Backhaus, Hans. "On the Dialectics of the Value-Form." *Thesis Eleven* 1, no. 1 (1980): 99–120.

Baer, Monica. *O rumo perdido: A crise fiscal e financeira do estado brasileiro.* São Paulo: Paz e Terra, 1993.

Baer, Werner. *The Brazilian Economy: Growth and Development.* 5th ed. New York: Praeger, 2001.

Baer, Werner. *Economia brasileira.* São Paulo: Noble, 2002.

Banco Central do Brasil. "Séries Temporais, 20624." Credit operations outstanding—Households—% of GDP. Accessed July 19, 2017. http://www4.bcb.gov.br/pec/series/port/aviso.asp.

Banco de México. "Cuenta corriente." Accessed Mar. 3, 2017. http://www.banxico.org.mx/SieInternet/consultarDirectorioInternetAction.do?sector=1&accion=consultarCuadro&idCuadro=CE176&locale=es.

Banco de México. "Deuda neta total del sector público." Accessed Mar. 3, 2017. http://www.banxico.org.mx/SieInternet/consultarDirectorioInternetAction.do?sector=9&accion=consultarCuadro&idCuadro=CG7&locale=es.

Banco de México. "Exchange Rate Regimes since 1954." Accessed Mar. 3, 2017. http://www.banxico.org.mx/sistema-financiero/material-educativo/basico/%7BA363683E-9B8D-C3A9-610C-E2153395E4B8%7D.pdf.

Bank for International Settlements. "OTC Derivatives Statistics at End-June 2017." Accessed Apr. 4, 2018. https://www.bis.org/publ/otc_hy1711.htm.

Barcellos, Caco. *Rota 66: A história da polícia que mata.* 3rd ed. São Paulo: Editora Globo, 1992.

Bartra, Roger. *Blood, Ink, and Culture: Miseries and Splendors of the Post-Mexican Condition.* Translated by Mark A. Healey. Durham, NC: Duke University Press, 2002.

Batista, Eike. *O X da questão.* Rio de Janeiro: Primeira Pessoa, 2011.

Baudrillard, Jean. *The Mirror of Production.* Translated by Mark Poster. St. Louis: Telos Press, 1975.

Beasley-Murray, Jon. *Posthegemony: Political Theory and Latin America.* Minneapolis: Minnesota University Press, 2010.

Beckman, Ericka. *Capital Fictions: The Literature of Latin America's Export Age.* Minneapolis: University of Minnesota Press, 2013.

Bellofiore, Riccardo, and Tommaso Redolfi Riva. "The *Neue Marx-Lektüre*: Putting the Critique of Political Economy Back into the Critique of Society." *Radical Philosophy* 189 (Jan./Feb. 2015): 24–36.

Belluzzo, Luiz Gonzaga de Mello, and Júlio Sérgio Gomes de Almeida. *Depois da queda: A economia brasileira da crise da dívida aos impasses do real.* Rio de Janeiro: Civilização Brasileira, 2002.

Benjamin, Walter. *The Arcades Project.* Translated by Howard Eiland and Kevin McLaughlin. Cambridge, MA: Harvard University Press, 1999.

Bensusán, Graciela, and Marisa von Bülow. "La reforma institucional del corporatismo sindical: Las experiencias de Brasil y México." *Perfiles Latinoamericanos* 11 (1998): 185–229.

Bernes, Jasper. "Logistics, Counterlogistics and the Communist Prospect." *Endnotes 3* (2013). http://endnotes.org.uk/en/jasper-bernes-logistics-counterlogistics-and-the-communist-prospect.

Beverley, John. *Latin Americanism after 9/11.* Durham, NC: Duke University Press, 2011.

Bidet, Jacques. *Foucault with Marx.* Translate by Steven Corcoran. London: Zed Books, 2016.

Bin, Daniel. "The Politics of Financialization in Brazil." *World Review of Political Economy* 7, no. 1 (Spring 2016): 106–26.

Boito, Armando, Jr. *Política neoliberal e sindicalismo no Brasil.* São Paulo: Xamã, 1999.

Boito, Armando, Jr. "The State and Trade Unionism in Brazil." *Latin American Perspectives* 21 (Winter 1994): 7–23.

Bonefeld, Werner. *Critical Theory and the Critique of Political Economy: On Subversion and Negative Reason.* New York: Bloomsbury, 2014.

Bonizzi, Bruno. "Financialization in Developing and Emerging Countries: A Survey." *International Journal of Political Economy* 42, no. 4 (2013): 83–107.

Boullosa, Carmen, and Mike Wallace. *A Narco History: How the United States and Mexico Jointly Created the "Mexican Drug War."* New York: OR Books, 2015.

Braga, Ruy. *A política do precariado: Do populismo à hegemonia lulista.* São Paulo: Boitempo, 2012.

Brandão, Ignácio de Loyola. *Zero.* New York: Avon Books, 1983.

"Brazilian Equity Market Correction Is 'Healthy,' IPO Expert Says." *Forbes,* July 15, 2011. http://www.forbes.com/sites/afontevecchia/2011/07/15/brazilian-equity-market-correction-is-healthy-ipo-expert-says/.

Brenner, Robert. *The Economics of Global Turbulence: The Advanced Capitalist Economies from Long Boom to Long Downturn, 1945–2005.* New York: Verso, 2006.

Bresser Pereira, Luiz Carlos. *Desenvolvimento e crise no Brasil: História, economia e política de Getúlio Vargas a Lula.* São Paulo: Editora 34, 2003.

Bruno, Miguel, Hawa Diawara, Eliane Araújo, Anna Carolina Reis, and Mario Rubéns. "Finance-led growth regime no Brasil: Estatuto teórico, evidências empíricas e consequências macroeconômicas." *Revista de Economia Política* 31, no. 5 (2011): 730-50.

Bryan, Dick, and Michael Rafferty. *Capitalism with Derivatives: A Political Economy of Financial Derivatives, Capital and Class.* New York: Palgrave Macmillan, 2006.

Bryan, Dick, and Michael Rafferty. "Why We Need to Understand Derivatives in Relation to Money: A Reply to Tony Norfield." *Historical Materialism* 20, no. 3 (2012): 97–109.

Buarque, Cristovam. *O que é apartação—o apartheid social no Brasil.* São Paulo: Editora Brasiliense, 1993.

Buffington, Robert M. *Criminal and Citizen in Modern Mexico.* Lincoln: University of Nebraska Press, 2000.

Buso Ferreira, Cassiana. "Representações de intolerância na imprensa escrita: Saques e quebra-quebras em São Paulo (abril de 1993)." Master's thesis, Universidade de São Paulo, 2009.

Bustillo, Inés, and Helvia Velloso. "Bond Markets for Latin American Debt in the 1990s." *CEPAL, Serie Temas de Coyuntura* 12 (2000). http://repositorio.cepal.org/handle/11362/7687.

Caldeira, Teresa P. R. *City of Walls: Crime, Segregation, and Citizenship in São Paulo.* Berkeley: University of California Press, 2001.

Caldeira, Teresa P. R. "The Paradox of Police Violence in Democratic Brazil." *Ethnography* 3 (2002): 235–63.

Cámara Izquierdo, Sergio. "La dinámica global capitalista: Un análisis de largo plazo en México, España y Estados Unidos." *Trayectorias: Revista de Ciencias Sociales de la Universidad Autónoma de Nuevo León* 10, no. 27 (2008): 47–64.

Canetti, Elias. *Crowds and Power.* Translated by Carol Stewart. New York: Continuum, 1978.

Carcanholo, Reinaldo A., and Mauricio de S. Sabadini. "Capital ficticio y ganancias ficticias." *Revista Herramienta* 37 (2008). http://www.herramienta.com.ar/revista-impresa/revista-herramienta-n-37.

Carchedi, Guglielmo. *Behind the Crisis: Marx's Dialectics of Value and Knowledge.* Leiden: Brill, 2011.

Carpentier, Alejo. "On the Marvelous Real in America." In *Magical Realism: Theory, History, Community,* edited by Lois Parkinson Zamora and Wendy Faris, 75–88. Translated by Tanya Huntington and Lois Parkinson Zamora. Durham, NC: Duke University Press, 1995.

Carroll, Amy Sara. "*Muerte sin fin*: Teresa Margolles's Gendered States of Exception." *Drama Review (TDR)* 54, no. 2 (2010): 103–25.

Cava, Bruno. *A multidão foi ao deserto.* São Paulo: Annablume, 2013.

Cava, Bruno, and Giuseppe Cocco, eds. *Amanhã vai ser maior.* São Paulo: Annablume, 2014.

Cavalcanti, Mariana. "Do barraco à casa: Tempo, espaço e valor(es) em uma favela consolidada." *Revista Brasileira de Ciências Sociais* 24, no. 69 (2009): 69–80.

Cavalcanti, Mariana. "Of Shacks, Houses and Fortresses: An Ethnography of Favela Consolidation in Rio de Janeiro." PhD diss., University of Chicago, 2007.

Cavalcanti, Mariana. "The Politics of Concrete and Cocaine in Favela Consolidation." *International Journal of Urban and Regional Research* 32 (2008): 989–1027.

Cavalcanti, Mariana. "Waiting in the Ruins: The Aesthetics and Politics of Favela Urbanization in 'PACification' Rio de Janeiro." In *Infrastructural Lives: Urban Infrastructure in Context*, edited by Stephen Graham and Colin McFarlane, 86–113. New York: Routledge, 2014.

Ceceña, José Luis. *El capital monopolista y la economía mexicana.* Mexico City: Cuadernos americanos, 1963.

Ceceña, José Luis. *El imperio del dolar.* Mexico City: Ediciones "El Caballito," 1972.

Centro de Estudios Espinosa Yglesias. "Deuda Estatal, un problema público nacional." Accessed Mar. 10, 2018. http://www.ceey.org.mx/reporte/deuda-estatal-problema-publico-nacional.

Cevasco, Maria Elisa. *As dez lições sobre os estudos culturais.* São Paulo: Boitempo Editorial, 2003.

Cevasco, Maria Elisa. "The São Paulo Fraction: The Lineaments of a Cultural Formation." *Mediations* 28, no. 1 (Fall 2014): 75–104.

Chakravartty, Paula, and Denise Ferreira da Silva. "Accumulation, Dispossession, and Debt—An Introduction." *American Quarterly* 64, no. 3 (Sept. 2012): 361–85.

Chapman, Debra D. *The Struggle for Mexico: State Corporatism and Popular Opposition.* Jefferson, NC: McFarland, 2012.

Chauí, Marilena. "O inferno urbano e a política do favor, tutela e cooptação." *Blog da Boitempo.* Accessed May 2, 2015. https://blogdaboitempo.com.br/2013/06/28/o-inferno-urbano-e-a-politica-do-favor-tutela-e-cooptacao/.

Chauí, Marilena. Presentation of "10 anos de governos pós neoliberais no Brasil." 2013. https://www.youtube.com/watch?v=FeP4rWe0zdw.

Cheias de charme. Television series, 2012. Globo.

Chen, Chris. "The Limit Point of Capitalist Equality: Notes toward an Abolitionist Antiracism." *Endnotes* 3 (2013). http://endnotes.org.uk/articles/22.

Chesnais, François. *Finance Capital Today: Corporations and Banks in the Lasting Global Slump.* Chicago: Haymarket, 2018.

Chevigny, Paul. *Edge of the Knife: Police Violence in the Americas.* New York: The New Press, 1995.

Chisholm, Andrew M. *Derivatives Demystified: A Step-by-Step Guide to Forwards, Futures, Swaps and Options.* London: Wiley, 2004.

Chitty, Christopher. "Reassessing Foucault: Modern Sexuality and the Transition to Capitalism." *Viewpoint,* Apr. 20, 2017. https://www.viewpointmag.com/2017/04/20/reassessing-foucault-modern-sexuality-and-the-transition-to-capitalism/.

Chitty, Christopher. "Towards a Socialist Art of Government: Michel Foucault's

'The Mesh of Power.'" *Viewpoint*, Sept. 12, 2012. https://www.viewpointmag.com/2012/09/12/towards-a-socialist-art-of-government-michel-foucaults-the-mesh-of-power/.

Choonara, Joseph. "Financial Times." *International Socialism*, 142 (Apr. 2, 2014). http://isj.org.uk/financial-times/#joseph1421.

Chorba, Carrie C. *Mexico, from Mestizo to Multicultural: National Identity and Recent Representations of the Conquest*. Nashville: Vanderbilt University Press, 2007.

Clover, Joshua. "Autumn of the System: Poetry and Finance Capital." *Journal of Narrative Theory* 41, no. 1 (Spring 2011): 34–52.

Clover, Joshua. "Retcon: Value and Temporality in Poetry." *Representations* 126, no. 1 (Spring 2014): 9–30.

Clover, Joshua. *Riot. Strike. Riot: The New Era of Uprisings*. New York: Verso, 2016.

Clover, Joshua. "The Time of Crisis." Oct. 4, 2011. http://occupyeverything.org/2011/the-time-of-crisis/.

Clover, Joshua. "*Value | Theory* | Crisis." *PMLA* 127, no. 1 (2012): 107–14.

Cocco, Giuseppe. *KorpoBraz: Por uma política dos corpos*. Rio de Janeiro: Mauad X, 2014.

Coelho, Christiano A., João M. P. De Mello, and Bruno Funchal. "The Brazilian Payroll Lending Experiment." *Review of Economics and Statistics* 94, no. 4 (2012): 925–34.

Coes, Donald V. *Macroeconomic Crises, Policies, and Growth in Brazil, 1964–90*. Washington, DC: World Bank, 1995.

Cohn, Deborah N. *The Latin American Literary Boom and U.S. Nationalism during the Cold War*. Nashville: Vanderbilt University Press, 2012.

Collier, David, and Ruth Berins Collier. "Who Does What, to Whom, and How: Toward a Comparative Analysis of Latin American Corporatism." In *Authoritarianism and Corporatism in Latin America*, edited by James Malloy, 489–512. Pittsburgh: University of Pittsburgh Press, 1977.

Comaroff, Jean, and John L. Comaroff, eds. *Law and Disorder in the Postcolony*. Chicago: University of Chicago, 2006.

"Communisation and Value-Form Theory." *Endnotes* 2 (Apr. 2010). https://endnotes.org.uk/issues/2/en/endnotes-communisation-and-value-form-theory.

Consejo Nacional de Inclusión Financiera. "Política nacional de inclusión financiera." Accessed June 6, 2017. http://www.gob.mx/cms/uploads/attachment/file/110408/PNIF_ver_1jul2016CONAIF_vfinal.pdf.

Corral, Wilfrido H. "¿Qué queda del sesentayochismo en los nuevos narradores hispanoamericanos?" *Guaraguao* 13, no. 30 (2009): 39–54.

Correa, Eugenia. "Changing Constraints of Monetary Policy: Distortions and Resolutions in Mexico's Financial System." In *Changing Structure of Mexico: Political, Social, and Economic Prospects*, edited by Laura Randall, 159–75. New York: M. E. Sharpe, 2006.

Correa, Eugenia, and Gregorio Vidal. "Financialization and Global Financial Crisis in Latin American Countries." *Journal of Economic Issues* 66, no. 2 (2012): 541–47.

Correa, Eugenia, Gregorio Vidal, and Wesley Marshall. "Financialization in Mexico: Trajectory and Limits." *Journal of Post Keynesian Economics* 35, no. 2 (2012): 255–75.

Costa, Ana Carla A., and João M. P. De Mello. "Judicial Risk and Credit Market Performance: Micro Evidence from Brazilian Payroll Loans." National Bureau of Economic Research Working Paper No. 12252. 2006. http://www.nber.org/papers/w12252.

Costa, Joana Simões de Melo, Ana Luiza Neves de Holanda Barbosa, and Guilherme Hirata. "Efeitos da ampliação dos direitos trabalhistas sobre a formalização, jornada de trabalho e salários das empregadas domésticas." Instituto de Pesquisa Econômica Aplicada Texto para Discussão. Accessed May 2, 2018. http://repositorio.ipea.gov.br/bitstream/11058/7264/1/td_2241.pdf.

Crotty, James. "Owner-Manager Conflict and Financial Theory of Investment Stability: A Critical Assessment of Keynes, Tobin and Minsky." *Journal of Post Keynesian Economics* 12, no. 4 (1990): 519–42.

Cypher, James M., and Raul Delgado Wise. *Mexico's Economic Dilemma: The Developmental Failure of Neoliberalism.* Lanham, MD: Rowman and Littlefield, 2010.

Davis, Mike. *Planet of Slums.* New York: Verso, 2006.

Deleuze, Gilles, and Félix Guattari. *Anti-Oedipus: Capitalism and Schizophrenia.* Translated by Robert Hurley, Mark Seem, and Helen R. Lane. Minneapolis: University of Minnesota Press, 1983.

Del Sarto, Ana, Alicia Ríos, and Abril Trigo, eds. *The Latin American Cultural Studies Reader.* Durham, NC: Duke University Press, 2004.

del Valle, Ivonne. "Mexico's Re-colonization: Unrestrained Violence, Rule of Law and the Creation of a New Order." *Política común* 7 (2015). https://quod.lib.umich.edu/p/pc/12322227.0007.002?view=text;rgn=main.

De Mello, João Manoel P., and Márcio G.P. Garcia. "Bye, Bye Financial Repression, Hello Financial Deepening: The Anatomy of a Financial Boom." *Quarterly Review of Economics and Finance* 52, no. 2 (2012): 135–53.

Denning, Michael. "Wageless Life." *New Left Review* 66 (Nov./Dec. 2010): 79–97.

Díaz-Polanco, Héctor. *La rebelión zapatista y la autonomía.* Mexico City: Siglo XXI, 1998.

Díaz-Polanco, Héctor. "Siete mitos sobre autonomía." In *Ensayos sobre identidad: Visiones desde México.* Santo Domingo: Ediciones Ferilibro, 2010.

Diegues, Carlos, Joaquim Pedro de Andrade, Leon Hirszman, Miguel Borges, and Marcos Farias, dir. *Cinco vezes favela.* 1962. VHS.

Dodd, Randall. "Exotic Derivatives Losses in Emerging Markets: Questions of Suitability, Concerns for Stability." 2009. http://www.financialpolicy.org/kiko.pdf.

Dorantes, Dolores. *Querida fábrica*. Mexico City: Práctica Mortal, 2012.

Dove, Patrick. *The Catastrophe of Modernity: Tragedy and the Nation in Latin American Literature*. Lewisburg, PA: Bucknell University Press, 2004.

Drake, Paul W. "Debt and Democracy in Latin America, 1920s-1980s." In *Debt and Democracy in Latin America*, edited by Barbara Stallings and Robert Kauffman, 39–58. Boulder, CO: Westview Press, 1989.

Duménil, Gérard, and Dominique Levy. *The Crisis of Neoliberalism*. Cambridge, MA: Harvard University Press, 2011.

Dunn, Christopher. *Brutality Garden: Tropicália and the Emergence of a Brazilian Counterculture*. Raleigh: University of North Carolina Press, 2001.

Dunn, Christopher. *Contracultura: Alternative Arts and Social Transformation in Authoritarian Brazil*. Chapel Hill: University of North Carolina Press, 2016.

Durand, Cédric. *Fictitious Capital: How Finance Is Appropriating Our Future*. Translated by David Broder. New York: Verso, 2017.

Dussel Peters, Enrique. *Polarizing Mexico: The Impact of Liberalization Strategy*. Boulder, CO: Lynne Rienner, 2000.

Eisenstadt, Todd A. *Politics, Identity, and Mexico's Indigenous Rights Movements*. Cambridge: Cambridge University Press, 2011.

Elbe, Igno. "Between Marx, Marxism, and Marxisms—Ways of Reading Marx's Theory." *Viewpoint*, Oct. 21, 2013. https://www.viewpointmag.com/2013/10/21/between-marx-marxism-and-marxisms-ways-of-reading-marxs-theory/.

Epstein, Gerald, ed. *Financialization and the World Economy*. London: Edward Elgar, 2005.

Escalante, Amat, dir. *Los bastardos*. Mexico, France, U.S.: Mantarraya Producciones, 2009. DVD.

Escalante, Amat, dir. *Heli*. 2013. Mexico, U.S.: Strand Releasing, June 27, 2017. DVD.

Escobar, Arturo. *Territories of Difference: Place, Movements, Life, Redes*. Durham, NC: Duke University Press, 2008.

Estevez, Dolia. "Remittances Supersede Oil as Mexico's Main Source of Foreign Income." *Forbes*, May 16, 2016. https://www.forbes.com/sites/doliaestevez/2016/05/16/remittances-supersede-oil-as-mexicos-main-source-of-foreign-income/#51983d1c1754.

Estrada, Luis, dir. *El infierno*. Mexico: Bandidos Films, 2010. DVD.

Fallaw, Ben, and Terry Rugeley, eds. *Forced Marches: Soldiers and Military Caciques in Modern Mexico*. Tucson: University of Arizona Press, 2012.

Faria, Vilmar E. "The Current Social Situation in Brazil: Dilemmas and Perspectives." Kellogg Institute, University of Notre Dame, Democracy and Policy Social Series, Working Paper 1 (Spring 1994): 1–18.

Farrell, Greg. *Crash of the Titans: Greed, Hubris, the Fall of Merrill Lynch, and the Near-Collapse of Bank of America.* New York: Crown Business, 2011.

Fausto, Boris, with contributions by Sergio Fausto. *A Concise History of Brazil.* Cambridge: Cambridge University Press, 2014.

Fernández-Kelly, Patricia, and Jon Shefner, eds. *Out of the Shadows: Political Action and the Informal Economy in Latin America.* University Park: Penn State University Press, 2010.

Ferreira, Isabel Cristina. "Crédito consignado e superendividamento." Trabalho de Conclusão de Curso, Faculdade de Direito da Pontifícia Universidade Católica do Rio Grande do Sul. Porto Alegre: PUC, 2008. http://www3.pucrs.br/pucrs/files/uni/poa/direito/graduacao/tcc/tcc2/trabalhos2008_1/isabel_cristina.pdf.

Ferréz. *Capão pecado.* São Paulo: Labortexto Editorial, 2000.

Ferriera Magalhães, Alex. "O direito da favela no contexto pós-programa favela-bairro." PhD diss., Instituto de Pesquisa e Planejamento Urbano e Regional da Universidade Federal do Rio de Janeiro, 2010.

Ffrench-Davis, Ricardo, and Robert Devlin. "Diez años de crisis de la deuda latinoamericana." *Comercio Exterior* (Jan. 1993): 4–20.

Figueroa Sepúlveda, Víctor Manuel. *Industrial Colonialism in Latin America: The Third Stage.* Leiden: Brill, 2013.

Filgueiras, Luiz, and Reinaldo Gonçalves. *A economia política do governo Lula.* Rio de Janeiro: Contraponto, 2007.

Fitzgerald, David. *A Nation of Emigrants: How Mexico Manages Its Migration.* Berkeley: University of California Press, 2008.

Flatley, Jonathan. *Affective Mapping: Melancholia and the Politics of Modernism.* Cambridge, MA: Harvard University Press, 2008.

Flores Curiel, Daniel, and Jorge Valero Gil. "Tamaño del sector informal y su potencial de recaudación en México." Working Paper, Universidad Autónoma de Nuevo León, Facultad de Economía, 2003.

Fornazzari, Alessandro. *Speculative Fictions: Chilean Culture, Economics, and the Neoliberal Transition.* Pittsburgh: University of Pittsburgh Press, 2013.

Foster, John Bellamy, and Fred Magdoff. *The Great Financial Crisis: Causes and Consequences.* New York: Monthly Review Press, 2009.

Foucault, Michel. "The Confession of the Flesh" (1977) interview. In *Power/Knowledge Selected Interviews and Other Writings,* edited by Colin Gordon, 194–228. New York: Pantheon, 1980.

Foucault, Michel. *Discipline and Punish: The Birth of the Prison.* Translated by Alan Sheridan. New York: Vintage Books, 1979.

Foucault, Michel. *History of Sexuality.* Vol. 1: *The Will to Know.* Translated by Robert Hurley. New York: Pantheon, 1978.

Foucault, Michel. *Security, Territory, Population: Lectures at the College de France*

1977–1978. Edited by Michel Senellart. Translated by Graham Burchell. New York: Palgrave Macmillan, 2007.

Foucault, Michel. "The Subject and Power." *Critical Inquiry* 8, no. 4 (1982): 777–95.

Fox, Claire. *The Fence and the River: Culture and Politics at the U.S.-Mexico Border.* Minneapolis: University of Minnesota Press, 1998.

Franco, Jean. *Cruel Modernity.* Durham, NC: Duke University Press, 2013.

Franco, Jean. "Journey to the Land of the Dead: Rulfo's Pedro Páramo." In *Critical Passions: Selected Essays*, edited by Mary Louise Pratt and Kathleen E. Newman, 429–46. Durham, NC: Duke University Press, 1999.

Frieden, Jeffry A. *Debt, Development, and Democracy: Modern Political Economy and Latin America, 1965–1985.* Princeton, NJ: Princeton University Press, 1991.

Fuentes, Carlos. "La cuestión chiapaneca." In *Chiapas para la historia.* Vol. 3, edited by Víctor Díaz Arciniega and Adriana López Téllez, 1640–42. Mexico City: Universidad Autónoma Metropolitana-Azcapotzalco, 1997.

Fumagalli, Andrea, and Sandro Mezzadra, eds. *Crisis in the Global Economy: Financial Markets, Social Struggles, and New Political Scenarios.* Los Angeles: Semiotext(e), 2010.

Gabeira, Fernando. "Morte e vida no caos urbano." *Folha de S. Paulo*, Sept. 4, 1987, A10.

Gagnier, Regenia. "The Global Circulation of Charles Dickens's Novels." *Literature Compass* 10, no. 1 (2013): 82–95.

Gago, Verónica. *La razón neoliberal. Economías barrocas y pragmática popular.* Madrid: Traficantes de Sueños, 2015.

Gaspar, Malu. *Tudo ou nada: Eike Batista e a verdadeira história do grupo X.* Rio de Janeiro: Editora Record, 2014.

Gaspari, Elio, Heloisa Buarque de Hollanda and Zuenir Ventura. *70/80 cultura em trânsito—da repressão à abertura.* Rio de Janeiro: Aeroplano, 2000.

Gaulard, Mylène. "The Brazilian Deindustrialization: Financialization Is Not Guilty." *Revista de Economia Política* 35, no. 2 (Apr.–June 2015): 227–46.

Gigliucci, Paulo. "Crédito consignado a aposentados e pensionistas do INSS." PhD diss., Universidade de São Paulo, 2012. http://www.teses.usp.br/teses/disponiveis/12/12138/tde-29032012-183533/en.php

Gilly, Adolfo. "Nuestra caída en la modernidad," *Nexos*, May 1, 1986. https://www.nexos.com.mx/?p=4620.

Gilmore, Ruth Wilson. *Golden Gulag: Prisons, Surplus, Crisis and Opposition in Globalizing California.* Berkeley: University of California Press, 2007.

Gonçalves, Reinaldo. "Novo nesenvolvimentismo e liberalismo enraizado." Aug. 30, 2012. http://www.bresserpereira.org.br/view.asp?cod=5060.

Gomes de Moura, Iara. "De empregada a 'empreguete': Das lutas simbólicas na televisão brasileira." *Seminário Internacional Fazendo Gênero* 10 (2013). http://www

.fg2013.wwc2017.eventos.dype.com.br/resources/anais/20/1373303820_ARQUIVO_DeempregadaaempregueteartigoFG.pdf.

González Casanova, Pablo, and Héctor Aguilar Camín, eds. *México ante la crisis.* 2 vols. Mexico City: UNAM, 1987.

González Rodríguez, Sergio. *El mal de origen: Ensayo de metapolítica.* Mexico City: Libros Magenta, 2011.

Gootenberg, Paul. "Cocaine's Long March North, 1900-2010." *Latin American Politics and Society* 54, no. 1 (Spring 2012): 159–80.

Gowan, Peter. *The Global Gamble: Washington's Faustian Bid for World Dominance.* New York: Verso, 1999.

Graeber, David. *Debt: The First 5,000 Years.* New York: Melville House, 2011.

Green, Duncan. *Silent Revolution: The Rise and Crisis of Market Economics in Latin America.* New York: Monthly Review Press, 1995.

Griffith-Jones, Stephany. *International Finance and Latin America.* London: Croom Helm, 1984.

Griffith-Jones, Stephany, and Osvaldo Sunkel. *Debt and Development Crises in Latin America: The End of an Illusion.* Oxford: Clarendon Press, 1986.

Grijó, Wesley Pereira. "De voyeur a protagonista: Nova classe média e telenovelas no Brasil." *Estudos em Comunicação* 17 (2014): 191–212.

Grün, Roberto. "A evolução recente do espaço financeiro no Brasil e alguns reflexos na cena política." *DADOS, Revista de Ciências Sociais* 47, no. 1 (2004): 5–47.

Grün, Roberto. "Financeirização de esquerda." *Tempo Social, Revista de Sociologia da USP* 21, no. 2 (2009): 255–97.

Grün, Roberto. "O 'Nó' dos fundos de pensão." *Novos Estudos* 73 (2005): 19–31.

"Grupo Elektra, de Salinas Pliego, manipula el mercado para inflar su acción, revela Bloomberg." *Sin Embargo*, May 12, 2017. http://www.sinembargo.mx/12-05-2017/3215123.

Gugelberger, Georg M. *The Real Thing: Testimonial Discourse and Latin America.* Durham, NC: Duke University Press, 1996.

Guillén Romo, Héctor. *Orígenes de la crisis en México, 1940–1982.* Mexico City: ERA, 1984.

Gutiérrez Aguilar, Raquel. *Horizonte comunitario-popular: Antagonismo y producción de lo común de América Latina.* Puebla: BUAP, 2015.

Guttmann, Robert. "La crisis del patrón dólar." In *Crisis financiera, nuevas manías y viejos pánicos*, edited by A. Girón, P. Rodriguez, and J. Déniz, 183–204. Madrid: Catarata, 2010.

"Há espaço para bancos crescerem na favela." *Brasileiros*, Mar. 3, 2015. http://brasileiros.com.br/2015/03/ha-espaco-para-bancos-crescerem-na-favela/.

Hacking, Ian. *The Emergence of Probability.* 2nd ed. Cambridge: Cambridge University Press, 2006.

Haiven, Max. *Cultures of Financialization: Fictitious Capital in Popular Culture and Everyday Life*. New York: Palgrave, 2014.

Hale, Charles. *Más Que un Indio: Racial Ambivalence and the Paradox of Neoliberal Multiculturalism in Guatemala*. Santa Fe, NM: School of American Research Press, 2006.

Hallward, Peter. *Absolutely Postcolonial: Writing between the Singular and the Specific*. Manchester: Manchester University Press, 2001.

Hanchard, Michael George. *Orpheus and Power: The Movimento Negro of Rio de Janeiro and Sao Paulo, Brazil, 1945-1988*. Princeton, NJ: Princeton University Press, 1994.

Harding, Sandra. *Whose Science? Whose Knowedge? Thinking from Women's Lives*. Ithaca, NY: Cornell University Press, 1991.

Harman, Chris. *Zombie Capitalism: Global Crisis and the Relevance of Marx*. Chicago: Haymarket Books, 2009.

Harnecker, Marta. *Los conceptos elementales del materialismo histórico*. Mexico City: Siglo XXI, 1968.

Hart, Stephen M. *A Companion to Latin American Literature*. Cambridge: Cambridge University Press, 2007.

Harvey, David. *A Brief History of Neoliberalism*. Oxford: Oxford University Press, 2005.

Harvey, David. *The Enigma of Capital and the Crises of Capitalism*. London: Profile Books, 2010.

Harvey, David. *Limits to Capital*. New York: Verso, 2007.

Haslip-Viera, Gabriel. *Crime and Punishment in Late Colonial Mexico City, 1692–1810*. Albuquerque: University of New Mexico Press, 1999.

Hein, Eckhard, and Till van Treeck. "'Financialisation' in Post-Keynesian Models of Distribution and Growth—a Systematic Review." Macroeconomic Policy Institute (IMK) at Hans Boeckler Foundation, Düsseldorf, Oct. 2008. http://www.boeckler.de/pdf/p_imk_wp_10_2008.pdf.

Heinrich, Michael. *An Introduction to the Three Volumes of Karl Marx's Capital*. New York: Monthly Review Press, 2012.

Heise, Tatiana Signorelli. *Remaking Brazil: Contested National Identities in Contemporary Brazilian Cinema*. Cardiff: University of Wales Press, 2012.

Herlinghaus, Hermann. *Violence without Guilt: Ethical Narratives from the Global South*. London: Palgrave, 2009.

Hermanson, Jeff, and Enrique de la Garza Toledo. "El corporativismo y las nuevas luchas en las maquilas de México: El papel de las redes internacionales de apoyo." In *Sindicatos y nuevos movimientos sociales en América Latina*, edited by Enrique de la Garza Toledo, 181–213. Buenos Aires: CLASCO, 2005.

Hernandez, Daniel. "The War on Crime, the War on Youth?" *Intersections: A blog by*

Daniel Hernandez, Aug. 22, 2008. http://danielhernandez.typepad.com/daniel_hernandez/2008/08/the-war-on-crime-the-war-on-youth.html.

"The Holding Pattern." *Endnotes* 3 (2013). https://endnotes.org.uk/issues/3/en/endnotes-the-holding-pattern.

Hong, Grace Kyungwon. "Existentially Surplus: Women of Color Feminism and the New Crises of Capitalism." *GLQ: A Journal of Gay and Lesbian Studies* 18, no. 1 (2012): 87–106.

Hope, Alejandro. "*Plus Ça Change*: Structural Continuities in Mexican Counternarcotics Policy." Brookings, July 2016. https://www.brookings.edu/wp-content/uploads/2016/07/Hope-Mexico-final.pdf.

Ilyina, Anna. "The Role of Derivatives in Emerging Market Crises." In *Emerging Local Securities and Derivatives Markets: Recent Developments*, edited by Ramana Ramaswamy, Jorge Roldos, Donald J. Mathieson, and Anna Ilyina, 69–91. Washington, DC: International Monetary Fund, 2004.

INEGI (Instituto Nacional de Estadística y Geografía). "Encuesta Nacional de Ocupación y Empleo (ENOE)." 2014. http://www.beta.inegi.org.mx/contenidos/proyectos/enchogares/regulares/enoe/tabulados/15ymas/informalidad_tasas_15ymas_xls.zip.

Instituto GEOC. "41,16% dos brasileiros sentiram no bolso a recessão econômica em 2014." Press release, 2014.

International Labor Organization. "Statistical Update on Employment in the Informal Economy." June 2012. http://laborsta.ilo.org/applv8/data/INFORMAL_ECONOMY/2012–06-Statistical%20update%20-%20v2.pdf.

International Monetary Fund. *Global Financial Stability Report*. Oct. 2017. https://www.imf.org/en/Publications/GFSR/Issues/2017/09/27/global-financial-stability-report-october-2017.

Iskander, Natasha. *Creative State: Forty Years of Migration and Development Policy in Morocco and Mexico*. Ithaca, NY: Cornell University Press, 2010.

Jaguaribe, Beatriz. "Beyond Reality: Notes on the Representations of the Self in *Santo Forte* and *Estamira*." *Journal of Latin American Cultural Studies: Travesia* 19, no. 3 (2010): 261–77.

Jaguaribe, Beatriz. *Rio de Janeiro: Urban Life through the Eyes of the City*. New York: Routledge, 2014.

Jameson, Fredric. "The Brick and the Balloon." *New Left Review* 228 (1998): 25–46.

Jameson, Fredric. "Culture and Finance Capital." *Critical Inquiry* 24, no. 1 (Autumn 1997): 246–65.

Jameson, Frederic. *Postmodernism or, The Cultural Logic of Late Capitalism*. Durham, NC: Duke University Press, 1991.

Jappe, Anselm. "Sohn-Rethel and the Origin of 'Real Abstraction': A Critique of Production or a Critique of Circulation?" *Historical Materialism* 21, no. 1 (2013): 3–14.

Jardim, Maria Chaves. "A construção social do mercado de trabalho no setor de construção civil nas obras do Programa de Aceleração do Crescimento (PAC): Consensos e conflitos." *Sociedade e Estado* 30, no. 1 (2015): 165–87.

Jardim, Maria Chaves. *Entre a solidariedade e o risco: Sindicatos e fundos de pensão em tempos de Governo Lula.* São Carlos: Tese de doutorado, UFSCar, 2007. http://www.bdtd.ufscar.br/htdocs/tedeSimplificado/tde_busca/processaArquivo.php?codArquivo=1756.

Joseph, Tiffany. "How Does Racial Democracy Exist in Brazil?" *Ethnic and Racial Studies* 36, no. 10 (2013): 1524–43.

Kaltenbrunner, Annina, and Juan Pablo Painceira. "Subordinated Financial Integration and Financialisation in Emerging Capitalist Economies: The Brazilian Experience." *New Political Economy* 23, no. 3 (2017). doi: 10.1080/13563467.2017.1349089.

Karatani, Kojin. *Transcritique: On Kant and Marx.* Translated by Sabu Kohso. Cambridge, MA: MIT Press, 2003.

Kay, Cristóbal. *Latin American Theories of Development and Underdevelopment.* London: Routledge, 1993.

Keefe, Patrick Radden. "Cocaine Incorporated." *New York Times*, June 15, 2012. http://www.nytimes.com/2012/06/17/magazine/how-a-mexican-drug-cartel-makes-its-billions.html.

Kilanski, Kristine, and Javier Auyero. "Introduction." In *Violence at the Urban Margins*, edited by Javier Auyero, Philippe Bourgois and Nancy Scheper-Hughes, 1–20. New York: Oxford University Press, 2015.

Kilmer, Beau. "Debunking the Mythical Numbers about Marijuana Production in Mexico and the United States." In *Rethinking the "War on Drugs" through the US-Mexico Prism*, edited by Ernesto Zedillo and Haynie Wheeler, 168–75. New Haven, CT: Yale Center for the Study of Globalization, 2012.

Kliman, Andrew. *The Failure of Capitalist Production: Underlying Causes of the Great Recession.* Ann Arbor, MI: Pluto Press, 2011.

Kliman, Andrew, and Shanon D. Williams. "Why 'Financialisation' Hasn't Depressed US Productive Investment." *Cambridge Journal of Economics* 39, no. 1 (2014): 67–92.

Koonings, Kees, and Dirk Kruijt, eds. *Armed Actors: Organised Violence and State Failure in Latin America.* New York: Zed Books, 2004.

Kornbluh, Anna. *Realizing Capital: Financial and Psychic Economies in Victorian Form.* New York: Fordham University Press, 2014.

Krippner, Greta. *Capitalizing on Crisis: The Political Origins of the Rise of Finance.* Cambridge, MA: Harvard University Press, 2012.

Kulíck, Don. *Travesti: Sex, Gender and Culture among Brazilian Transgendered Prostitutes.* Chicago: University of Chicago Press, 1998.

Kurz, Robert. *O colapso da modernização: Da derrocada do socialismo de caserna à crise da economia mundial.* Rio de Janeiro: Paz e Terra, 1993.

La Berge, Leigh Claire. “The Rules of Abstraction: Methods and Discourses of Finance,” *Radical History Review* 118 (Winter 2014): 93–112.

La Berge, Leigh Claire. *Scandals and Abstraction: Financial Fiction of the Long 1980s.* New York: Oxford University Press, 2015.

Laclau, Ernesto, and Chantel Mouffe. *Hegemony and Socialist Strategy: Towards a Radical Democratic Politics.* London: Verso, 1984.

Laera, Alejandra. *Ficciones del dinero: Argentina, 1890–2001.* Buenos Aires: Fondo de Cultura Económica, 2014.

Lamas, Marta. “Necropolítica y rehabilitación.” *Proceso,* July 1, 2015.

Langley, Paul. *The Everyday Life of Global Finance: Saving and Borrowing in Anglo-America.* Oxford: Oxford University Press, 2008.

Lapavitsas, Costas. *Profiting without Producing: How Finance Exploits Us All.* New York: Verso, 2013.

Larkins, Erika Robb. *The Spectacular Favela: Violence in Modern Brazil.* Oakland: University of California Press, 2015.

Lattanzi Shutika, Debra. *Beyond the Borderlands: Migration and Belonging in the United States and Mexico.* Berkeley: University of California Press, 2011.

Laval, Christian, Luca Paltrinieri and Ferhat Taylan, eds. *Marx et Foucault: Lectures, Usages, Confrontations.* Paris: La Découverte, 2015.

Lavinas, Lena. *The Takeover of Social Policy by Financialization: The Brazilian Paradox.* New York: Palgrave, 2017.

Lazzarato, Maurizio. *The Making of Indebted Man: An Essay on the Neoliberal Condition.* Translated by Joshua David Jordan. Los Angeles: Semiotext(e), 2012.

Lehnen, Leila. *Citizenship and Crisis in Contemporary Brazilian Literature.* New York: Palgrave Macmillan, 2013.

Leitão, Míriam. “A questão do X.” *O Globo,* Apr. 20, 2013. http://blogs.oglobo.globo.com/miriam-leitao/post/a-questao-do-x-494017.html.

Leiva, Fernando Ignacio. *Latin American Neostructuralism: The Contradictions of Post-Neoliberal Development.* Minneapolis: University of Minneapolis Press, 2008.

Leys, Ruth. “The Turn to Affect: A Critique.” *Critical Inquiry* 37, no. 3 (Spring 2011): 434–72.

Lins, Paulo. *Cidade de Deus.* São Paulo: Companhia das Letras, 1997.

Lins, Paulo. *City of God.* Translated by Alison Entrekin. New York: Black Cat, 2006.

LiPuma, Edward, and Benjamin Lee. *Financial Derivatives and the Globalization of Risk.* Durham, NC: Duke University Press, 2004.

Lissakers, Karin. *Banks, Borrowers, and the Establishment: A Revisionist Account of the International Debt Crisis.* New York: Basic Books, 1991.

Lomnitz, Claudio. *Death and the Idea of Mexico.* New York: Zone Books, 2005.

Lomnitz, Claudio. “Time and Dependency in Latin America Today.” *South Atlantic Quarterly* 111, no. 2 (2012): 347–57.

Lomnitz, Claudio. "Times of Crisis: Historicity, Sacrifice, and the Spectacle of Debacle in Mexico City." *Public Culture* 15, no. 1 (2003): 127–48.

Love, Heather. *Feeling Backward: Loss and the Politics of Queer History.* Cambridge, MA: Harvard University Press, 2007.

Lukács, Georg. *History and Class Consciousness: Studies in Marxist Dialectics.* Translated by Rodney Livingstone. Cambridge, MA: MIT Press, 1971.

Lukács, Georg. *Theory of the Novel: A Historico-Philosophical Essay on the Forms of Great Epic Literature.* Translated by Anna Bostock. Cambridge, MA: MIT Press, 1971.

Lund, Joshua. *The Mestizo State: Reading Race in Modern Mexico.* Minneapolis: University of Minnesota Press, 2012.

Machado da Silva, Luiz Antonio. "A política na favela." *Cadernos Brasileiros* 9, no. 41 (1967): 35–47.

Maito, Esteban Ezequiel. "La transitoriedad histórica del capital: La tendencia descendente de la tasa de ganancia desde el siglo XIX." *Razón y Revolución* 26 (2013): 129–59.

Maldonado Alvarado, Benjamín. *Autonomía y comunalidad india: Enfoques y propuestas desde Oaxaca.* Oaxaca: CONACULTA, 2002.

Marazzi, Christian. *The Violence of Financial Capitalism.* Translated by Kristina Lebedeva. Los Angeles: Semiotext(e), 2011.

Marichal, Carlos. *A Century of Debt Crisis in Latin America: From Independence to the Great Depression, 1820–1930.* Princeton, NJ: Princeton University Press, 1989.

Mariña, Abelardo, and Fred Moseley. "The Rate of Profit in the Postwar Mexican Economy, 1950–1993." In *The Political Economy Reader*, edited by R. Baiman et al., 184–92. Armonk, NY: M. E. Sharpe, 1999.

Marini, Ruy Mauro. "Brazilian Subimperialism." *Monthly Review* 23, no. 9 (1972): 14–24.

Marini, Ruy Mauro. *Dialéctica de la dependencia.* In *América Latina, dependencia y globalización. Fundamentos conceptuales Ruy Mauro Marini.* Edited by Carlos Eduardo Martins. Bogotá: Siglo del Hombre and CLACSO, 2008.

Marois, Thomas. *States, Banks and Crisis: Emerging Finance Capitalism in Mexico and Turkey.* London: Elgar, 2012.

Marquetti, Adalmir, Eduardo Maldonado Filho, and Vladimir Lautert. "The Profit Rate in Brazil, 1953–2003." *Review of Radical Political Economics* 42, no. 4 (2010): 485–504.

Martin, Randy. *Financialization of Daily Life.* Philadelphia: Temple University Press, 2002.

Martin, Randy. *Knowledge LTD: Toward a Social Logic of the Derivative.* Philadelphia: Temple University Press, 2015.

Martínez, María Elena. *Genealogical Fictions: Limpieza de Sangre, Religion, and Gender in Colonial Mexico.* Stanford, CA: Stanford University Press, 2008.

Marx, Karl. *Capital*. Vol. 1. Translated by B. Fowkes. London: Penguin, 1991.

Marx, Karl. *Capital*. Vol. 3. Translated by David Fernbach. New York: Penguin, 1991.

Marx, Karl. *Grundrisse: Foundations of the Critique of Political Economy*. Translated by Martin Nicolaus. New York: Vintage, 1973.

Mateo Tomé, Juan Pablo. "Medidas de la rentabilidad del capital en México, 1970–2003." *Análisis Económico* 23, no. 53 (2008): 143–72.

Mathieson, Donald J., Jorge E. Roldos, Ramana Ramaswamy, and Anna llyina. "Emerging Local Securities and Derivatives Markets." Accessed Nov. 1, 2015. International Monetary Fund, https://www.imf.org/external/pubs/ft/wefs/2004/derivmkts.pdf.

Mattick, Paul. *Business as Usual: The Economic Crisis and the Failure of Capitalism*. London: Reaktion Books, 2011.

Mauro, Rosana, and Eneus Trindade. "Telenovela e discurso como mudança social na análise da personagem Maria da Penha em *Cheias de charme*." *Em questão* 18, no. 2 (2012): 169–82.

Mbembe, Achille. *Critique of Black Reason*. Translated by Laurent Dubois. Durham, NC: Duke University Press, 2017.

Mbembe, Achille. "Necropolitics." Translated by Libby Meintjes. *Public Culture* 15, no. 1 (2003): 11–40.

McCann, Bryan. *Hard Times in the Marvellous City: From Dictatorship to Democracy in the Favelas of Rio de Janeiro*. Durham, NC: Duke University Press, 2014.

McClanahan, Annie. *Dead Pledges: Debt, Crisis, and Twenty-First Century Culture*. Palo Alto, CA: Stanford University Press, 2017.

McClanahan, Annie. "Investing in the Future: Finance Capital's Philosophy of History." *Journal of Cultural Economy* 6, no. 1 (2012): 78–93.

McClanahan, Annie. "Salto Mortale: Narrative, Speculation, and the Chance of the Future." PhD diss., University of California–Berkeley, 2010.

McNally, David. *Global Slump: The Economics and Politics of Crises and Resistance*. Oakland, CA: PM Press, 2010.

Medialdea, Bibiana. "Brazil: An Economy Caught in a Financial Trap (1993–2003)." *Revista de Economia Política* 33, no. 3 (2013): 427–45.

Medina, Cuahtémoc, ed. *¿De qué otra cosa podríamos hablar? / What Else Could We Talk About?* Barcelona: RM, 2009.

Medina, Cuahtémoc, ed. *Estética y violencia: Necropolítica, militarización y vidas lloradas*. Mexico City: MAUC, 2012.

Medina, Cuahtémoc. "SEMEFO: The Morgue." In *The Mexico City Reader*, edited by Rubén Gallo and translated by Lorna Scott Fox and Rubén Gallo, 309–26. Madison: University of Wisconsin Press, 2004.

Melamed, Jodi. *Represent and Destroy: Rationalizing Violence in the New Racial Capitalism*. Minneapolis: University of Minnesota Press, 2011.

Melber, Henning, ed. *The Rise of Africa's Middle Class: Myths, Realities and Critical Engagements.* London: Zed Books, 2016.

Mendes, Alexandre F. "Between Shocks and Finance: Pacification and the Integration of the Favela into the City in Rio de Janeiro." *South Atlantic Quarterly* 113, no. 4 (2014): 866–73.

Mendoza Hernández, Antonio. "Financiarización y ganancias de corporaciones en México." *Ola Financiera* 3, no. 5 (2010): http://www.journals.unam.mx/index.php/ROF/article/view/23068.

México Unido Contra la Delincuencia. Accessed Nov 5, 2015. http://www.mucd.org.mx/.

Mezzadra, Sandro, and Brett Nielson. "Fronteras de inclusión diferencial: Subjetividad y luchas en el umbral de los excesos de justicia." *Papeles del CEIC* (Sept. 2014): 1–31.

Miller, Marilyn Grace. *Rise and Fall of the Cosmic Race: The Cult of Mestizaje in Latin America.* Austin: University of Texas Press, 2004.

Miller, Nicola. *In the Shadow of the State.* New York: Verso, 1999.

"Misery and Debt." *Endnotes* 2 (2010). https://endnotes.org.uk/issues/2/en/endnotes-misery-and-debt.

Mitropoulos, Angela. *Contract and Contagion: From Biopolitics to Oikonomia.* Brooklyn, NY: Minor Compositions, 2012.

Moisés, José Álvaro, et al. *Cidade, povo e poder.* Rio de Janeiro: CEDEC and Paz e Terra, 1981.

Moisés, José Álvaro, et al. *Contradições urbanas e movimentos sociais.* Rio de Janeiro: CEDEC and Paz e Terra, 1977.

Molloy, Ivan. *Rolling Back Revolution: The Emergence of Low Intensity Conflict.* London: Pluto Press, 2001.

Molloy, Molly. "Colombia . . . Comparison w/ Mexican 'Drug War' Deaths." *Frontera List*, Aug. 25, 2016. https://fronteralist.org/2016/08/25/colombia-comparison-w-mexican-drug-war-deaths/.

Moloeznik, Marcos Pablo. "Organized Crime, the Militarization of Public Security, and the Debate on the 'New' Police Model in Mexico." *Trends in Organized Crime* 16, no. 2 (2013): 177–94.

Moloeznik, Marcos Pablo, and María Eugenia Suárez de Garay. "El proceso de militarización de la seguridad pública en México 2006–2012." *Frontera Norte* 24, no. 48 (2012): 121–44.

Monsiváis, Carlos. *Los rituales del caos.* Mexico City: Ediciones Era, 1995.

Monteagudo, Clarissa. "Sete anos depois, criança símbolo do PAC tem morte suspeita." *EXTRA*, July 24, 2015. https://extra.globo.com/noticias/rio/sete-anos-depois-crianca-simbolo-do-pac-tem-morte-suspeita-16931792.html.

Montemayor, Carlos. "Chiapas, otra vez." In *Chiapas para la historia*, vol. 3, edited by

Víctor Díaz Arciniega and Adriana López Téllez, 1634. Mexico City: Universidad Autónoma Metropolitana-Azcapotzalco, 1997.

Mora, Mariana. *Kuxlejal Politics: Indigenous Autonomy, Race, and Decolonizing Research in Zapatista Communities.* Austin: University of Texas Press, 2017.

Morais, Lecio, and Alfredo Saad-Filho. "Lula and the Continuity of Neoliberalism in Brazil: Strategic Choice, Economic Imperative or Political Schizophrenia?" *Historical Materialism* 13, no. 1 (2005): 3–32.

Morais, Lecio, and Alfredo Saad-Filho. "Neo-developmentalism and the Challenges of Economic Policy-Making under Dilma Rousseff." *Critical Sociology* 38, no. 6 (2012): 789–98.

Moreira, Ivana. "BMG é o pioneiro no crédito consignado." *Valor Econômico*, July 5, 2005, A4.

Moreira Alves, Maria Helena. *State and Opposition in Military Brazil.* Austin: University of Texas Press, 1988.

Moreno-Brid, Juan Carlos, and Jaime Ros. *Development and Growth in the Mexican Economy: A Historical Perspective.* Oxford: Oxford University Press, 2009.

Morera Camacho, Carlos. *El capital financiero en México y la globalización: Límites y contradicciones.* Mexico City: Ediciones Era, 1998.

Morgenson, Gretchen, and Joshua Rosner. *Reckless Endangerment: How Outsized Ambition, Greed, and Corruption Created the Worst Financial Crisis of Our Time.* New York: St. Martin's Griffin, 2012.

Müller, Lúcia. "Negotiating Debts and Gifts: Financialization Policies and the Economic Experiences of Low-Income Social Groups in Brazil." *Vibrant* 11, no. 1 (2014): 191–221.

Nealon, Christopher. "Value | *Theory* | *Crisis*." *PMLA* 127, no. 1 (2012): 101–6.

"Negros dias do abril: Saques apavoram São Paulo." *Veja*, Apr. 13, 1983, 26–34.

Nemser, Daniel. *Infrastructures of Race. Concentration and Biopolitics in Colonial Mexico.* Austin: University of Texas Press, 2017.

Neri, Marcelo Côrtes. *A nova classe média: O lado brilhante dos pobres.* Rio de Janeiro: Fundação Getulio Vargas, 2010.

Ngai, Sianne. "Visceral Abstractions." *GLQ: A Journal of Gay and Lesbian Studies* 21, no. 1 (2015): 33–63.

Norfield, Tony. "Derivatives and Capitalist Markets: The Speculative Heart of Capital." *Historical Materialism* 20, no. 1 (2012): 103–32.

Novaes, André Reyes. "Favelas and the Divided City: Mapping Silences and Calculations in Rio de Janeiro's Journalistic Cartography." *Social and Cultural Geography* 15, no. 2 (2014): 201–25.

Nun, José. *Marginalidad y exclusión social.* Mexico City: Fondo de Cultura Económica, 2001.

Observatorio de favelas. *O que é a favela, afinal?* 2009. http://observatoriodefavelas.org.br/wp-content/uploads/2013/09/o-que-%C3%A9-favela-afinal.pdf.

Oliveira, Francisco de. "The Duckbilled Platypus." *New Left Review* 24 (2003): 40–57.

Oliveira, Francisco de. "Lula in the Labyrinth." *New Left Review* 42 (2006): 5–22.

Oliveira, Nelson de, ed. *Cenas da favela: As melhores histórias da periferia brasileira.* São Paulo: Geração Editorial, 2007.

Oliveira, Pamela. "Dilma é a única a lamentar a morte de Christiano: 'Meus sentimentos aos familiares e à comunidade.'" *EXTRA*, July 24, 2015. http://extra.globo.com/noticias/rio/dilma-a-unica-lamentar-morte-de-christiano-meus-sentimentos-aos-familiares-a-comunidade-16931821.html.

Oliveri, Ernest J. *Latin American Debt and the Politics of International Finance.* Westport, CT: Praeger, 1992.

Orloff, Ann, and Kimberly Morgan, eds. *The Many Hands of the State: Theorizing Political Authority and Social Control.* Cambridge: Cambridge University Press, 2017.

Osorno, Diego Enrique. *La guerra de los Zetas: Viaje por la frontera de la necropolítica.* Mexico City: Grijalbo, 2012.

Overmyer-Velázquez, Rebecca. *Folkloric Poverty: Neoliberal Multiculturalism in Mexico.* University Park: Penn State University Press, 2010.

Padilha, José, dir. *Tropa de elite.* 2007. Brazil: Cinedigm. 2010. DVD.

Padilla, Tanalís. *Rural Resistance in the Land of Zapata: The Jaramillista Movement and the Myth of the Pax Priísta, 1940–1962.* Durham, NC: Duke University Press, 2008.

Painceira, Juan Pablo. "Developing Countries in the Era of Financialisation: From Deficit-Accumulation to Reserve-Accumulation." In *Financialisation in Crisis*, edited by Costas Lapavitsas, 185–215. Leiden: Brill, 2012.

Paley, Dawn. *Drug War Capitalism.* Oakland, CA: AK Press, 2015.

Paley, Dawn. "La guerra en México: Contrainsurgencia ampliada versus lo popular." *El Apantle* 2 (2016): 177–98.

Palley, Thomas I. *Financialization: What It Is and Why It Matters.* Levy Economics Institute. Working Paper no. 525. 2007. http://www.levyinstitute.org/pubs/wp_525.pdf.

Palma, José Gabriel. "How the Full Opening of the Capital Account to Highly Liquid Financial Markets Led Latin America to Two and a Half Cycles of 'Mania, Panic and Crash.'" 2013. http://www.econ.cam.ac.uk/research/repec/cam/pdf/cwpe1201.pdf.

Palma, José Gabriel. "How to Create a Financial Crisis by Trying to Avoid One: The Brazilian 1999-Financial Collapse as 'Macho-Monetarianism' Can't Handle 'Bubble Thy Neighbour' Levels of Inflows." Cambridge Working Papers in Economics 1301. N.d. http://www.econ.cam.ac.uk/research-files/repec/cam/pdf/cwpe1301.pdf.

Palou, Pedro Ángel, Eloy Urroz, Ignacio Padilla, Ricardo Chávez Castañeda, and

Jorge Volpi. *Crack Manifesto.* Translated by Celia Bortolin and Scott Miller. http://www.dalkeyarchive.com/crack-manifesto/.

Palou, Pedro Ángel, Eloy Urroz, Ignacio Padilla, Ricardo Chávez Castañeda, and Jorge Volpi. "Manifiesto Crack." *Descritura*, Aug. 5, 1997, 32–43.

Pansters, Wil, ed. *Violence, Coercion and State-Making in Twentieth-Century Mexico: The Other Half of the Centaur.* Stanford, CA: Stanford University Press, 2012.

Parra-Bernal, Guillermo. "Brazil Partially Approves Banks' Plan to Set Up Credit Bureau." Reuters, Nov. 9, 2016. https://www.reuters.com/article/us-banks-brazil-credit-bureau-idUSKBN1342Z3.

Paschel, Tianna S. *Becoming Black Political Subjects: Movements and Ethno-Racial Rights in Colombia and Brazil.* Princeton, NJ: Princeton University Press, 2016.

Paula, Luiz Fernando de. *Financial Liberalization and Economic Performance: Brazil at the Crossroads.* New York: Routledge, 2011.

Paulani, Leda Maria. "A experiência brasileira entre 2003 e 2014: Neodesenvolvimentismo?" *Cadernos do Desenvolvimento* 12, no. 20 (2017): 135–55.

Paulani, Leda Maria. "A hegemonia neoliberal." Talk from Aug. 27, 2010. http://www.centrocelsofurtado.org.br/arquivos/image/201109261233410.LivroCAIXA_C_0_35.pdf.

Paulani, Leda Maria. "A inserção da economia brasileira no cenário mundial: Uma reflexão sobre a situação atual à luz da história." *Boletim de Economia e Política Internacional* 10 (Apr. 2012): 89–102.

Paulani, Leda Maria. *Brasil Delivery.* São Paulo: Boitempo Editorial, 2008.

Payer, Cheryl. *The Debt Trap.* London: Penguin Books, Harmondsworth, 1974.

Paz, Octavio. *The Labyrinth of Solitude and Other Writings.* Translated by Lysander Kemp, Yara Milos, and Rachel Phillips Belash. New York: Grove Press, 1985.

Pellegrini Calderón, Alessandra. *Beyond Indigeneity: Coca Growing and the Emergence of a New Middle Class in Bolivia.* Tucson: University of Arizona Press, 2016.

Pellizzoni, Luigi. *Ontological Politics in a Disposable World: The New Mastery of Nature.* New York: Ashgate, 2015.

Pelúcio, Larissa. *Abjeção e desejo: Uma etnografia travesti sobre o modelo preventivo de aids.* São Paulo: Annablume Editora, 2009.

Pelúcio, Larissa. "Sexualidade, gênero e masculinidade no mundo dos t-lovers: A construção da identidade de um grupo de homens que se relacionam com travestis." Talk from the Twelfth Congresso Brasileiro de Sociologia, 2005. http://www.clam.org.br/uploads/conteudo/tloversconstrucaodeindentidaderecente.pdf.

Pera, Cristóbal. "¿Nación? ¿Qué nación? La idea de América Latina en Volpi y Bolaño." *Revista de Estudios Hispánicos* 46, no. 1 (2012): 99–113.

Pereira, Anthony W. Review of *The Unpast: Elite Violence and Social Control in Brazil, 1954–2000. Luso-Brazilian Review* 43, no. 2 (2006): 169–70.

Perezcano, Rigoberto. *Norteado*, 2009. Mexico, Spain: Venevision International, 2011. DVD.

Perlman, Janice. *Favela: Four Decades of Living on the Edge in Rio de Janeiro.* New York: Oxford University Press, 2010.

PEW Research Center. "A Demographic Portrait of Mexican-Origin Hispanics in the United States." May 1, 2013. http://www.pewhispanic.org/2013/05/01/a-demographic-portrait-of-mexican-origin-hispanics-in-the-united-states/

Pinheiro, Paulo Sérgio. *Escritos indignados: Polícia, prisões e política no estado autoritário (no 20 aniversário do regime de Exceção, 1964–1984).* São Paulo: Brasiliense, 1984.

Pochmann, Marcio. *O mito da grande classe média: Capitalismo e estructura social.* São Paulo: Biotempo, 2014.

Pollin, Robert. "The Resurrection of the Rentier." *New Left Review* 46 (July/Aug. 2007): 140–53.

Poovey, Mary. *Genres of the Credit Economy: Mediating Value in Eighteenth- and Nineteenth-Century Britain.* Chicago: University of Chicago Press, 2008.

Portantiero, Juan Carlos. *Los usos de Gramsci.* Mexico City: Folios, 1981.

Posner, Richard A. *Catastrophe: Risk and Response.* New York: Oxford University Press, 2004.

Postone, Moishe. *Time, Labor and Social Domination: A Reinterpretation of Marx's Critical Theory.* Cambridge: Cambridge University Press, 1996.

Power, Timothy J., and Mahrukh Doctor. "Another Century of Corporatism? Continuity and Change in Brazilian Corporatist Structures." In *Authoritarianism and Corporatism in Latin America, Revisited,* edited by Howard J. Wiarda, 218–41. Gainesville: University Press of Florida, 2004.

Prahalad, C. K. *The Fortune at the Bottom of the Pyramid: Eradicating Poverty through Profits.* Philadelphia: Wharton School Publishing, 2004.

Prebisch, Raúl. *The Economic Development of Latin America and Its Principal Problems.* UN document no. E/CN.12/89/Rev.1. Lake Success, NY: United Nations, 1950.

Queirós, Adirley, dir. *A cidade é uma só?* 2013.

Quemada-Díez, Diego. *La jaula de oro.* 2013. Mexico, Spain: Cazador Solitario Films/Kino Lorber, 2016. DVD.

Quijano, Aníbal. *Notas sobre el concepto de marginalidad social.* Santiago: CEPAL, 1968.

Rastello, Luca. *I Am the Market: How to Smuggle Cocaine by the Ton, in 5 Easy Lessons.* New York: Faber and Faber, 2011.

Rath, Thomas. *Myths of Demilitarization in Postrevolutionary Mexico, 1920–1960.* Chapel Hill: University of North Carolina Press, 2013.

Reiter, Bernd, and Gladys L. Mitchell, eds. *Brazil's New Racial Politics.* Boulder, CO: Lynne Rienner, 2010.

Rendón Monzón, Juan José. *La comunalidad: Modo de vida en pueblos indios.* Mexico City: CONACULTA, 2003.

Resende, Beatriz. *Contemporâneos: Expressões da literatura brasileira contemporânea no século XXI.* Rio de Janeiro: Casa da Palavra, 2008.

Ribeiro, Luiz Cesar de Queiroz. "Cidade desigual ou cidade partida? Tendências da metrópole do Rio de Janeiro." In *Futuro das metrópoles*, edited by Luiz César de Queiroz Ribeiro. Rio de Janeiro: Letra Capital Editora, 2015.

Ribeiro, Luiz Cesar de Queiroz, and Edward E. Telles. "Rio de Janeiro: Emerging Dualization in a Historically Unequal City." In *Globalizing Cities*, edited by Peter Marcuse and Ronald van Kempem, 78–94. London: Basil Blackwell, 2000.

Ricardo López, A., and Barbara Weinstein, eds. *The Making of the Middle Class: Toward a Transnational History.* Durham, NC: Duke University Press, 2012.

Richard, Nelly, ed. *En torno a los Estudios Culturales.* Santiago: Editorial ARCIS-CLACSO, 2010.

Roberts, Michael. *The Great Recession: Profit Cycles, Economic Crisis: A Marxist View.* 2009. Accessed Nov 15, 2015. https://archive.org/details/TheGreatRecession.ProfitCyclesEconomicCrisisAMarxistView.

Roberts, Michael. *The Long Depression: Marxism and the Global Crisis of Capitalism.* Chicago: Haymarket Books, 2016.

Roberts, Michael. "Revisting a World Rate of Profit." Paper presented at the 2015 Conference of the Association of Heterodox Economists, Southampton Solent University, July 2015. https://thenextrecession.files.wordpress.com/2017/09/revisiting-a-world-rate-of-profit-june-2015.pdf.

Roddick, Jackie. *Dance of the Millions: Latin America and the Debt Crisis.* New York: Monthly Review Press, 1988.

Rodríguez, Ileana, ed. *The Latin American Subaltern Studies Reader.* Durham, NC: Duke University Press, 2001.

Rodríguez, Ileana. *Liberalism at Its Limits: Crime and Terror in the Latin American Cultural Text.* Pittsburgh: University of Pittsburgh Press, 2009.

Rodriguez Mendoza, Miguel. "Debt, Trade and Development in Latin America." In *The Debt Crisis in Latin America,* edited by Institute of Latin American Studies, 67–80. Stockholm: ILAS, 1986.

Rodríguez Nieto, Sandra. "Pensiones de trabajadores son usadas para financiar negocios de Higa y del cuñado de Salinas." May 15, 2017. http://www.sinembargo.mx/15-05-2017/3209309.

Rohter, Larry. *Brazil on the Rise: The Story of a Country Transformed.* New York: Palgrave Macmillan, 2012.

Rose, R. S. *The Unpast: Elite Violence and Social Control in Brazil, 1954–2000.* Athens, OH: Center for International Studies Ohio University, 2005.

Roy, Ananya, and Nezar AlSayyad, eds. *Informality: Transnational Perspectives from the Middle East, Latin America, and South Asia.* Lanham, MD: Lexington Books, 2004.

Rubin, Isaak Illich. *Essays on Marx's Theory of Value.* Detroit: Black and Red, 1972.

Saad-Filho, Alfredo. "The Political Economy of Neoliberalism in Latin America." In *Neoliberalism: A Critical Reader*, edited by Alfredo Saad-Filho and Deborah Johnston, 222–30. London: Pluto Press, 2005.

Sabet, Daniel M. *Police Reform in Mexico: Informal Politics and the Challenge of Institutional Change.* Palo Alto, CA: Stanford University Press, 2012.

Sader, Emir. "The Weakest Link: Neoliberalism in Latin America." *New Left Review* 52 (2008): 5–31.

Saldívar, Emiko. "'It's Not Race, It's Culture': Untangling Racial Politics in Mexico." *Latin American and Caribbean Ethnic Studies* 9 (2014): 89–108.

Sales-Sarrapy, Carlos, Fernando Solis-Soberon, and Alejandro Villagomez-Amezcua. *Pension System Reform: The Mexican Case.* National Bureau of Economic Research. Working Paper No. 5780. Sept. 1996. http://www.nber.org/papers/w5780.

Salla, Fernando. "Os impasses da democracia brasileira: O balanço de uma década de políticas para as prisões no Brasil." *Lusotopie* 10 (2003): 419–35.

Salomon, Marta. "Procuradoria investigará se Lula beneficiou o BMG." *Folha de S. Paulo*, May 1, 2006. http://www1.folha.uol.com.br/fsp/brasil/fc0105200602.htm.

Sánchez Prado, Ignacio M. *Naciones intelectuales: Las fundaciones de la modernidad literaria mexicana (1917–1959).* West Lafayette, IN: Purdue University Press, 2009.

Sánchez Prado, Ignacio M. *Strategic Occidentalism: On Mexican Fiction, the Neoliberal Book Market, and the Question of World Literature.* Evanston, IL: Northwestern University Press, 2018.

Sánchez Vázquez, Adolfo. "La filosofía de la praxis como nueva práctica de la filosofía." *Cuadernos Políticos* 12 (Apr.–June 1977): 64–68.

Sandoval Manzano, José G. "Valor nuevo producido y rentabilidad: México, 1950–2015." *Ciencia Económica* 5, no. 9 (July–Dec. 2017): 3–18.

Sanfelici, Daniel. "Financeirização e a produção do espaço urbano no Brasil: Uma contribuição ao debate." *EURE: Revista Latinoamericana de Estudios Urbano Regionales* 39, no. 118 (2013): 27–46.

Santos, Lidia. "El Cosmopolitismo de Mercado." *Revista de Crítica Literaria Latinoamericana* 35, no. 69 (2009): 153–65.

Sartre, Jean-Paul. *Search for a Method.* Translated by Hazel E. Barnes. New York: Alfred A. Knopf, 1967.

Schøllhammer, Karl Erik. *Ficção brasileira contemporânea.* Rio de Janeiro: Civilização Brasileira, 2009.

Schwarz, Mauricio-José. *Crónica del desconcierto.* Mexico City: Editorial Planeta, 1995.

Schwarz, Roberto. "An Audacious Book." *Mediations* 27, no. 1–2 (Fall/Spring 2013–2014): 401–6.

Schwarz, Roberto. "City of God." *New Left Review* 12 (Nov.–Dec. 2001): 103–12.

Serasa Experien (blog). "Inadimplência atinge 60 milhões." Apr. 13, 2016. http://

noticias.serasaexperian.com.br/blog/2016/04/13/inadimplencia-atinge-60-milhoes-de-brasileiros-e-bate-recorde-80-dos-devedores-ganham-ate-dois-salarios-minimos/.

Serasa Experien (blog). "Mapa da Inadimplência no Brasil." Accessed July 19, 2015. http://www.serasaexperian.com.br/estudo-inadimplencia/.

Serasa Experien (blog). "Um em cada três moradores da comunidade de Paraisópolis, em São Paulo, está inadimplente." Accessed Jan. 6, 2015. http://www.serasaconsumidor.com.br/um-em-cada-tres-moradores-da-comunidade-de-paraisopolis-em-sao-paulo-esta-inadimplente-revela-estudo-inedito-da-serasa/.

"Setembro quente no Rio de Janeiro." *Veja*, Sept. 7, 1983, 38–43.

Shonkwiler, Alison. *The Financial Imaginary: Economic Mystification and the Limits of Realist Fiction*. Minneapolis: University of Minnesota Press, 2017.

Silva, Denise Ferreira da. "The End of Brazil: An Analysis of the Debate on Racial Equity on the Edges of Global Market Capitalism." *Columbia University National Black Law Journal* 1, no. 1 (2010): 1–18.

Silva, Denise Ferreira da. "No-bodies: Law, Raciality and Violence." *Griffith Law Review* 18, no. 2 (Aug. 2009): 212–36.

Silva, Denise Ferreira da. *Toward a Global Idea of Race*. Minneapolis: Minnesota University Press, 2007.

Silva, Hélio. *Travesti: A invenção do feminino*. Rio de Janeiro: Relume Dumará, 1993.

Silva, Joseli Maria, and Marcio Jose Ornat. "Transfeminism and Decolonial Thought: The Contribution of Brazilian Travestis." *Transgender Studies Quarterly* 3, no. 1–2 (2016): 220–27.

Singer, André. "Brasil, junho de 2013, classes e ideologias cruzadas." *Novos Estudos-CEBRAP* 97 (2013): 23–40.

Singer, André. "Rebellion in Brazil: Social and Political Complexion of the June Events." *New Left Review* 85 (2014): 15–37.

Skidmore, Thomas. *The Politics of Military Rule in Brazil 1964–1985*. Oxford: Oxford University Press, 1990.

Smith, Christen A. *Afro-Paradise: Blackness, Violence, and Performance in Brazil*. Champaign: University of Illinois Press, 2016.

Smith, John. *Imperialism in the Twenty-First Century: Globalization, Super-Exploitation, and Capitalism's Final Crisis*. New York: Monthly Review Press, 2016.

Soares, Luiz Eduardo, Andre Batista, and Rodrigo Pimentel. *Elite da Tropa*. Rio de Janeiro: Objectiva, 2006.

Soederberg, Susanne. *Debtfare States and the Poverty Industry: Money, Discipline, and the Surplus Population*. RIPE Series in Global Political Economy. New York: Routledge, 2014.

Soederberg, Susanne. *The Politics of the New International Financial Architecture: Reimposing Neoliberal Domination in the Global South*. London: Zed Books, 2004.

Sohn-Rethel, Alfred. *Intellectual and Manual Labor: A Critique of Epistemology.* Translated by Martin Sohn-Rethel. Trenton, NJ: Humanities Press, 1983.

Sotelo Valencia, Adrián. *Sub-Imperialism Revisited: Dependency Theory in the Thought of Ruy Mauro Marini.* Leiden: Brill, 2017.

Soto Esquivel, Roberto. *Especulación e innovación financiera: Mercados de derivados y consecuencias macroeconómicas en México.* Mexico City: Miguel Ángel Porrúa, 2010.

Souza, Jessé. *Os Batalhadores.* Belo Horizonte: Editora UFMG, 2012.

Souza e Silva, Jailson de. "Adeus 'Cidade Partida.'" 2013. http://observatoriodefavelas.org.br/wp-content/uploads/2013/06/Adeus-Cidade-Partida_Por-Jailson-de-Souza-e-Silva.pdf.

Souza e Silva, Jailson de. "Carta para Zuenir Ventura." In *O novo carioca*, edited by Jailson de Souza e Silva, Jorge Luiz Barbosa, and Marcus Vinícius Faustini, 19–22. Rio de Janeiro: Mórula Editorial, 2012.

Spinetto, Juan Pablo, and Jonathan Levin. "Brazil Fire Sale from Petrobras to Vale Seen Driving IPO Revival." Bloomberg, July 7, 2015. http://www.bloomberg.com/news/articles/2015–07–08/brazil-fire-sale-from-petrobras-to-vale-seen-driving-ipo-revival.

St. Louis Federal Reserve. "Effective Federal Funds Rate." https://fred.stlouisfed.org/series/FEDFUNDS.

Stockhammer, Englebert. "Financialisation and the Slowdown of Accumulation." *Cambridge Journal of Economics* 28, no. 5 (2004): 719–41.

Stoler, Ann Laura. *Duress: Imperial Durabilities in Our Times.* Durham, NC: Duke University Press, 2016.

Strathausen, Carsten. "A Critique of Neo-Left Ontology." *Postmodern Culture* 16, no. 3 (2006). http://pmc.iath.virginia.edu/issue.506/16.3strathausen.html.

Strozier, Robert M. *Foucault, Subjectivity, and Identity: Historical Constructions of Subject.* Detroit: University of Wayne State Press, 2002.

Sue, Christina A. *Land of the Cosmic Race: Race Mixture, Racism, and Blackness in Mexico.* Oxford: Oxford University Press, 2013.

Sunkel, Osvaldo. *Development from Within: Towards a Neostructuralist Approach for Latin America.* Boulder, CO: Lynne Rienner, 1993.

Sussekind, Flora. *Tal brasil, qual romance.* Rio de Janeiro: Achiamé, 1984.

Svampa, Maristella. *Debates latinoamericanos: Indianismo, desarrollo, dependencia, populismo.* Buenos Aires: Edhasa, 2016.

Svampa, Maristella, and Enrique Viale. *Maldesarrollo: La Argentina del extractivismo y el despojo.* Buenos Aires: Katz, 2014.

Taleb, Nassim Nicholas. *Fooled by Randomness: The Hidden Role of Chance in the Markets and in Life.* New York: Texere, 2001.

Tarica, Estelle. *The Inner Life of Mestizo Nationalism.* Minneapolis: University of Minnesota Press, 2008.

Tavares, Maria da Conceição. *Da substituição de importações ao capitalismo financiero.* Rio de Janeiro: Zahar Editores, 1972.

Tavares, Maria da Conceição, and J. L. Fiori. *Poder e dinheiro, uma economia política da globalização.* Petrópolis: Editora Vozes, 1997.

Telles, Edward. *Pigmentocracies: Ethnicity, Race and Color in Latin America.* Raleigh: University of North Carolina Press, 2014.

Telles, Edward. *Race in Another America: The Significance of Skin Color in Brazil.* Princeton, NJ: Princeton University Press, 2004.

Telles, Vera. "Entrevista: Vera Telles." *Revista Humanidades em Diálogo.* Dec. 2014. http://www.veratelles.net/wp-content/uploads/2016/07/Entrevista-Humanidades_2014.pdf.

Tett, Gillian. *Fool's Gold: The Inside Story of J.P. Morgan and How Wall St. Greed Corrupted Its Bold Dream and Created a Financial Catastrophe.* New York: Simon and Schuster, 2010.

Toscano, Alberto. "The Open Secret of Real Abstraction." *Rethinking Marxism: A Journal of Economics, Culture and Society* 20, no. 2 (2008): 273–87.

Toscano, Alberto. "The Uses of the Useless: Political Philosophies of Unemployment." Accessed Nov 5, 2015. http://cartographiesoftheabsolute.wordpress.com/2012/11/27/the-uses-of-the-useless-political-philosophies-of-unemployment/.

"Três resenhas do livro *O colapso da modernização,* de Robert Kurz." *Novos Estudos* 36 (July 1993): 42–57.

Trigo, Abril. *Crisis y transfiguración de los estudios culturales latinoamericanos.* Santiago: Editorial Cuarto Propio, 2012.

Tsang, Eileen. *The New Middle Class in China Consumption, Politics and the Market Economy.* New York: Palgrave, 2014.

"Um duro aviso para o governo." *Veja,* July 8, 1987, 18–27.

United Nations. *2008 World Drug Report.* 2008. https://www.unodc.org/documents/wdr/WDR_2008/WDR_2008_eng_web.pdf.

Valencia, Sayak. *Capitalismo gore.* Barcelona: Melusina, 2010.

Valenzuela Arce, José Manuel. *Los estudios culturales en México.* Mexico City: Fondo de Cultura Económica, 2003.

Valladares, Lícia do Prado. *A invenção da favela: Do mito de origem a favela.com.* Rio de Janeiro: Editora FGV, 2005.

Valladares, Lícia do Prado. "Social Science Representations of Favelas in Rio de Janeiro: A Historical Perspective." 2000. http://lanic.utexas.edu/project/etext/llilas/vrp/valladares.pdf.

van der Zwan, Natascha. "Making Sense of Financialization." *Socio-Economic Review* 12, no. 1 (2014): 99–129.

Vargas, João H. Costa. *Never Meant to Survive: Genocide and Utopias in Black Diaspora Communities.* Lanham, MD: Rowman and Littlefield, 2010.

Vekemans, Roger. *Marginaliad, promoción popular y neo-Marxismo*. Bogotá: CEDIAL, 1976.

Ventura, Zuenir. *Cidade partida*. São Paulo: Companhia das Letras, 1994.

Vidal Luna, Francisco, and Herbert S. Klein. *The Economic and Social History of Brazil since 1889*. Cambridge: Cambridge University Press, 2014.

Vilches, Elvira. *New World Gold: Cultural Anxiety and Monetary Disorder in Early Modern Spain*. Chicago: University of Chicago Press, 2010.

Virno, Paolo. *A Grammar of the Multitude*. Translated by Isabella Bertoletti, James Cascaito, and Andrea Casson. New York: Semiotext(e), 2004.

Volpi, Jorge. "Cuando nací el boom estaba allí." Interview with Ernesto Carlín. *Tanque de Casma* (blog), 2006. http://tanquedecasma.blogspot.com/2006/07/cuando-nac-el-boom-estaba-all.html.

Volpi, Jorge. *En busca de Klingsor*. Mexico City: Penguin Random House, 2016.

Volpi, Jorge. *In Search of Klingsor*. Translated by Kristina Cordero. London: Fourth Estate, 2002.

Volpi, Jorge. *El insomnio de Bolivar*. Mexico City: Grijalbo, 2010.

Volpi, Jorge. *Memorial del engaño*. Madrid: Alfaguara, 2014.

Wacquant, Loïc. *Punishing the Poor: The Neoliberal Government of Social Insecurity*. Durham, NC: Duke University Press, 2009.

Wainwright, Tom. *Narconomics: How to Run a Drug Cartel*. New York: Public Affairs, 2016.

Walsh, Catherine, ed. *Estudios culturales latinoamericanos: Retos desde y sobre la región andina*. Quito: Universidad Andina Simón Bolívar/Abya-Yala, 2003.

Watts, Johnathan. "Brazil's *Bolsa Familia* Scheme Marks a Decade of Pioneering Poverty Relief." *Guardian*, Dec. 17, 2013. http://www.theguardian.com/global-development/2013/dec/17/brazil-bolsa-familia-decade-anniversary-poverty-relief.

Welch, John. *Capital Markets in the Development Process: The Case of Brazil*. London: Macmillan, 1993.

Wennerlind, Carl. *Casualties of Credit: The English Financial Revolution: 1620–1720*. Cambridge, MA: Harvard University Press, 2011.

Whitfield, Esther. *Cuban Currency: The Dollar and "Special Period" Fiction*. Minneapolis: University of Minnesota Press, 2008.

Wiarda, Howard J. ed. *Authoritarianism and Corporatism in Latin America—Revisited*. Gainesville: University Press of Florida, 2004.

Williams, Gareth. *The Mexican Exception: Sovereignty, Police, and Democracy*. New York: Palgrave MacMillan, 2011.

Williams, Gareth. *The Other Side of the Popular: Neoliberalism and Subalternity in Latin America*. Durham, NC: Duke University Press, 2002.

Williams, Raymond. *The Long Revolution*. New York: Columbia University Press, 1961.

Williams, Raymond. *Marxism and Literature.* New York: Oxford University Press, 1977.

Winant, Howard. *The World Is a Ghetto: Race and Democracy since World War II.* New York: Basic Books, 2001.

Wingrove, Elizabeth. "Ontology: A Useful Category of Analysis." *Hedgehog Review* (Summer 2005): 86–92.

Wright, Harry K. *Foreign Enterprise in Mexico.* Chapel Hill: University of North Carolina Press, 1971.

Wright, Melissa. "Necropolitics, Narcopolitics, and Femicide: Gendered Violence on the Mexican-U.S. Border." *Signs* 36, no. 3 (2011): 707–31.

Wyly, Elvin, C. S. Ponder, Pierson Nettling, Bosco Ho, Sophie Ellen Fung, Zachary Liebowitz, and Dan Hammel. "New Racial Meanings of Housing in America." *American Quarterly* 64, no. 3 (2012): 571–604.

Yaccoub, Hilaine. "A chamada 'nova classe média': Cultura material, inclusão e distinção social." *Horizontes Antropológicos* 17, no. 36 (2011): 197–231.

Yépez, Heriberto. *Empire of Neomemory.* Translated by Brian Whitener, Jen Hofer, and Christian Nagler. Oakland, CA: ChainLinks, 2013.

Yépez, Heriberto. *El imperio de la neomemoria*. Oaxaca de Juárez, Oaxaca: Almadía, 2007.

Zaloom, Caitlyn. *Out of the Pits: Traders and Technology from Chicago to London.* Chicago: University of Chicago Press, 2006.

Zaluar, Alba. *Condomínio do diabo.* Rio de Janeiro: Editora UFRJ, 1994.

Zaluar, Alba, and Marcos Alvito, eds. *Um século de favela.* 5th ed. Rio de Janeiro: FGV, 2006.

Zavala, Oswaldo. *Los cárteles no existen: Narcotráfico y cultura en México*. Barcelona: Malpaso, 2018.

Zaverucha, Jorge. *FHC, forças armadas e polícia: Entre o autoritarismo e a democracia, 1999–2002.* Rio de Janeiro: Editora Record, 2005.

Zerilli, Linda M. G. "The Turn to Affect and the Problem of Judgment." *New Literary History,* 46 (2015): 261–86.

Zibechi, Raúl. *The New Brazil: Regional Imperialism and the New Democracy.* Oakland, CA: AK Press, 2014.

Žižek, Slavoj. *The Sublime Object of Ideology.* New York: Verso Books, 1989.

INDEX